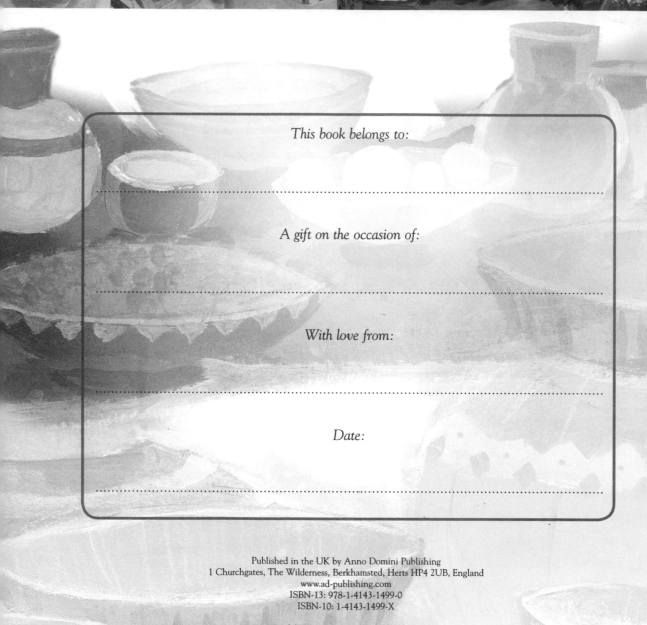

This book belongs to:

....

A gift on the occasion of:

....

With love from:

....

Date:

....

Published in the UK by Anno Domini Publishing
1 Churchgates, The Wilderness, Berkhamsted, Herts HP4 2UB, England
www.ad-publishing.com
ISBN-13: 978-1-4143-1499-0
ISBN-10: 1-4143-1499-X

First Tyndale House Publishers, Inc. edition 2007
Visit Tyndale's exciting Web site at www.tyndale.com
TYNDALE and Tyndale's quill logo are registered trademarks of Tyndale House Publishers, Inc.
The One Year is a registered trademark of Tyndale House Publishers, Inc.
Tyndale Kids logo is a trademark of Tyndale House Publishers, Inc.

Publishing Director Annette Reynolds
Consulting Editor Jenny Hyatt
Editor Nicola Bull
Art Director Gerald Rogers
Pre-production Krystyna Kowalska Hewitt
Production John Laister

Printed and bound in Singapore

The ONE YEAR

children's BIBLE

Rhona Davies
illustrated by Marcin Piwowarski

Tyndale House Publishers, Inc.
Carol Stream, Illinois

CONTENTS

JANUARY 1 — IN THE BEGINNING

In the beginning there was nothing. It was dark and empty and shapeless.

"Let there be light!" God said. As soon as he said the words, light came into existence. God saw that the light was good. God divided the light, so that there was day and there was night.

God made the sky and separated it from the waters below.

God brought the waters together into seas and created dry land.

"Let the land produce plants and trees full of seeds and fruits," God said. Then all varieties of green and leafy plants filled the land, from tall redwood trees to trees bearing olives and oranges, acorns and chestnuts. God saw that all he had made was good.

"Let there be lights in the sky for the night and the day," God said. "Let them mark times and seasons, days, months, and years." So the golden sun became the light that shone in the day and the silvery moon the light that beamed in the night sky. God also filled the darkness with stars, and he saw that all he had made was good.

"Let the waters be filled with living creatures and the skies with every kind of winged bird. Let them multiply and increase in number." Then every kind of fish and sea creature swam and splashed in the seas, and the air above became filled with color and shape and sound. There were dolphins and sea horses, eagles, owls, robins and wrens, buzzing bees, and beautiful butterflies.

"Let there be all sorts of creatures to move on the land," God said. So there were sheep and goats, elephants and giraffes, lions, tigers, and graceful gazelles.

God looked at everything that he had made and saw that it was good.

Then God made man and woman. He put them in charge of his creation, to care for it and gather food from it. God loved the people he had made, and he saw that everything he had made was very good. Then God rested.

GENESIS 1:1–2:3

In the beginning God created the heavens and the earth.
Genesis 1:1

JANUARY 2 — THE PERFECT WORLD

God gave Adam and Eve a beautiful garden to live in. It was full of plants and trees with fruit they could eat. The garden was watered by a river that ran through it, and Adam and Eve tended the garden and worked in it.

Adam and Eve were good company for each other. They shared the work, and they lived happily together. Adam gave names to all the creatures that God had made.

God told them that they could eat anything that grew in the garden except the fruit of one tree in the middle of the garden, the tree of the knowledge of good and evil.

GENESIS 2:4-25

The LORD God said, "It is not good for the man to be alone. I will make a helper who is just right for him."
Genesis 2:18

JANUARY 3—GOOD AND EVIL

One of the creatures in the garden was a snake.

He came to Eve and tempted her.

"Did God really tell you not to eat from any of the trees in the garden?" he asked.

"God told us we can eat from every tree except the tree in the middle of the garden," said Eve. "If we eat from that tree, we will die."

"You will not die," said the snake. "God does not want you to eat from that tree because if you do, you will know good and evil just as God does."

Eve looked at the tree. She saw how lovely its fruit looked and thought about what the snake had said. She took some of the fruit and ate it. Then she gave it to Adam, and he ate some too.

As soon as they had eaten, Adam and Eve knew what they had done. They realized why God had told them not to eat the fruit. Now they had disobeyed God and it was too late to make things right. They felt guilty and ashamed,

GENESIS 3:1-8

The woman . . .
saw that the tree
was beautiful
and its fruit
looked delicious,
and she wanted
the wisdom it
would give her.
So she took some
of the fruit and
ate it. Then she
gave some to her
husband . . . and
he ate it, too.
Genesis 3:6

and when they heard God coming in the garden, they found trees to hide among so he would not see them.

JANUARY 4—ADAM AND EVE ARE SENT AWAY

God called out to Adam. "Where are you?"

"I was afraid, so I hid," replied Adam.

"Have you eaten from the tree of the knowledge of good and evil?" God asked.

"It wasn't me," said Adam. "The woman gave me the fruit, and I ate it."

"What have you done?" God asked Eve.

"It wasn't my fault," said Eve. "The snake tricked me, and I ate the fruit."

God was very sad. He turned to the snake and told him that he would crawl on his belly from that time on. He turned to Eve and told her that she would have pain as she gave birth to her children. He told Adam that thorns and thistles would choke the plants he grew.

Then God banished Adam and Eve from the garden he had given them. They had chosen to disobey him. They now knew the difference between what was right and what was wrong. They would know suffering and death; they could not be God's friends in the same way anymore.

January 5 — Cain and Abel

After a time Eve gave birth to a son. They called him Cain. Then Eve had a second child, a son named Abel.

Both boys grew up to be farmers. They knew how much they depended on God to give them sun and rain for the harvests and to help their animals give birth to healthy lambs and baby goats. Cain planted seeds and grew crops while Abel kept the sheep and goats.

One day Cain brought some of his crops as a gift to God, to thank him for the harvest. Abel also brought a gift of the first of his newborn lambs.

God saw not only the gifts that were brought but also the two brothers. He knew that Abel had brought his gift out of faith, because he loved God and knew that all good things come from him. God also knew that Cain had brought his gift because he thought he had to, not because he cared about God. God was pleased with Abel, but he was disappointed with Cain. And Cain knew it.

Cain was jealous.

"Why are you angry, Cain?" asked God. "Do what is right and you will be accepted. But beware of your bad temper. You are not in control of it, and it may destroy you."

Cain knew that God was right. But he wouldn't listen. He could think of nothing except having revenge on his brother.

Cain asked Abel to go out into the field with him. He planned to wait for the right moment—and kill him there.

Later God asked Cain where his brother was.

"How should I know?" lied Cain. "Is it my job to look after him?"

"I warned you about your anger," said God. "Now your brother's death is on your own heart. You will know what it is to feel guilty for doing wrong."

GENESIS 3:9-24

After sending them out, the LORD God stationed mighty cherubim to the east of the Garden of Eden. And he placed a flaming sword that flashed back and forth to guard the way to the tree of life.
Genesis 3:24

GENESIS 4:1—5:4

It was by faith that Abel brought a more acceptable offering to God than Cain did. Abel's offering gave evidence that he was a righteous man, and God showed his approval of his gifts.
Hebrews 11:4

But God was good to Adam and Eve. He gave them another son, Seth, because Cain had killed his brother, and then other sons and daughters.

JANUARY 6 — NOAH'S ARK

Many years passed, and the land became full of people. But few remembered who God was. They did as they pleased. They took what they wanted from others. They spoiled the world that God had made and thought only of themselves. God knew that the world had become an evil place, full of greed, hatred, and violence. He decided to wash it clean and start all over again.

There was one man who remembered God. His name was Noah. Noah had a wife and three sons: Shem, Ham, and Japheth.

"Noah!" God said one day. "I am going to end all the evil there is in the world. I want you to build an ark—a huge boat that will float on the floodwaters that I will send to wash the earth clean. I will tell you exactly how to build it so that you and your family and two of every kind of creature will be safe inside the ark."

God told Noah how to build the ark. He told him how long it was to be, how many decks it should have, and where to put the door. God told Noah to coat the ark with tar to keep water out, and to fill it with food supplies.

Noah set about building the ark. He began to make the huge boat miles

GENESIS 6

"Bring a pair of every kind of animal—a male and a female—into the boat with you to keep them alive during the flood."
Genesis 6:19

from any sea. It took him many years of his life, and the people around him watched and thought he was crazy.

January 7—The Great Flood

The ark was ready.

God told Noah to collect two of every kind of living creature—seven pairs of every kind of bird, and seven pairs of every animal that would be used for sacrifice. The animals came to Noah as if they too knew what God had planned, and Noah took them all on board the ark. Then God shut the door.

Outside the rain began to fall. The rain fell steadily until the streams and rivers were full and burst their banks. The rain fell until underground springs broke through the earth. The rain fell until no dry land could be seen anywhere.

Everything that had lived on the earth was destroyed by the flood. But the ark that God had told Noah to build floated on the waters. God kept Noah, his family, and all the animals safe inside the ark.

GENESIS 7

The rain continued to fall for forty days and forty nights.
Genesis 7:12

January 8—The Rainbow

Inside the ark, Noah, his wife, his three sons, and their wives worked to care for the animals. Days passed. Weeks passed. And still the rain fell.

Then one day it stopped. The ark floated gently.

Slowly, very slowly, the waters began to go down. The ark rested on the Ararat mountains. More weeks passed, and the tops of the mountains became visible.

Then Noah took hold of a raven and set it free in the air. The bird stretched its wings and flew, but there was nowhere for it to land. It flew back and forth until there was food for it to find on the earth.

Noah waited a little longer, and then he sent out a dove to see if the land was dry yet. But water still covered the ground. The dove returned to the ark.

After seven days, Noah sent out the dove again. This time the bird returned with an olive leaf. Noah knew that the waters were going down.

Another seven days passed, and Noah sent out the dove for the third time.

When the bird did not return, Noah knew that it had found somewhere to rest. But Noah waited until God told him it was time to leave the ark.

Then they came out—Noah, his family, and all the creatures that had been kept safe.

GENESIS 8:1–9:17

"When I see the rainbow in the clouds, I will remember the eternal covenant between God and every living creature on earth."
Genesis 9:16

Noah watched as all the animals went to find their homes on the earth. Then he built an altar and sacrificed some of the birds he had brought for that purpose. Noah thanked God for keeping them all safe.

"I will never destroy all the earth with water again," promised God. "I have put a rainbow in the sky as a sign of my promise."

JANUARY 9—THE TOWER OF BABEL

Noah's sons had children of their own. Their families went on to have families too, and soon people spread out again across the land.

One of Ham's descendants was Nimrod. He was a mighty hunter and built the city of Nineveh.

At that time everyone spoke the same language. They started to build not with stones but with bricks baked in the hot sun. First they built cities; then one group of people decided to build a tower. The tower reached high into the sky so that everyone would know how great they were.

God saw the people as they were building the tower. He saw that once more they thought they were great and powerful and did not need him. God saw that they were proud and soon would be just like the people who had lived before the flood.

So God caused their language to be confused; now they couldn't understand each other.

The tower was abandoned, and the people began to make new groups of people who each shared the same language.

God then scattered them further over all the earth.

GENESIS 10:1–11:9

That is why the city was called Babel, because that is where the LORD confused the people with different languages.
Genesis 11:9

JANUARY 10—TERAH'S JOURNEY

One of Shem's descendants was called Terah, who had three sons: Abram, Nahor, and Haran. Terah did not worship God, but like the people around him, he worshipped a moon god.

Haran, Terah's son, had a son named Lot, but then Haran died.

Nahor married Milcah and gave Terah grandchildren.

Abram married Sarai, but though they wanted a family very much, they did not have any children.

They all lived in the wealthy city of Ur of the Chaldeans, until one day Terah decided to move.

He left behind Nahor and his family but took Abram and Sarai and his grandson Lot. They planned to travel to the land of Canaan, but on the way

GENESIS 11:26-32

Terah took his son Abram, his daughter-in-law Sarai (his son Abram's wife), and his grandson Lot (his son Haran's child) and moved away from Ur of the Chaldeans. He was headed for the land of Canaan.
Genesis 11:31

they stopped and made their home in a place called Haran. Terah never left there. He died many years later, having never reached Canaan.

JANUARY 11 — THE PROMISED LAND

GENESIS 12:1-9

The LORD had said to Abram, "Leave your native country, your relatives, and your father's family, and go to the land that I will show you."
Genesis 12:1

God had chosen Abram even before his father moved to Haran. God had spoken to Abram while he still lived in Ur. God wanted to take him to Canaan, the land where God would set his people apart from other nations, and make them a people who loved him and knew how to live the way he intended all people to live.

"You must leave here," God had said to Abram. "I will show you where you must go. I am going to make your family into a great nation."

Now Terah was dead, and Abram did as God had told him. He packed up his possessions, prepared his servants, and took with him his wife, Sarai, and his nephew Lot.

They traveled together through the land, pitching their tents and moving on until they reached Canaan. Then God spoke to Abram again.

"This is the land I promise to give to you and your children," he said.

Abram built an altar there and thanked God. He believed God's promise, even though there were other people already living in Canaan.

JANUARY 12 — LOT'S CHOICE

GENESIS 13

Abram moved his camp to Hebron and settled near the oak grove belonging to Mamre. There he built another altar to the LORD.
Genesis 13:18

As time passed it became clear that Abram and Lot needed to choose different parts of the land in which to make their home. They each had many sheep, goats, oxen, and camels. They each had many tents and servants.

Both men had become wealthy in possessions. The land did not have enough water for them all to enjoy, and the servants started to argue.

"Let's not argue," said Abram to Lot. "We have this whole land to live in. Choose where you want to live, and I will take my family somewhere else."

Lot looked around him. He saw that the plain before him was green and alive. There was plenty of water. It would be a good place to live.

"I am happy to live in the Jordan valley," Lot said. So the men parted. Lot left Abram and pitched his tents close to the city of Sodom.

Abram lived instead in the land of Canaan.

"I have not forgotten my promise," said God to Abram when Lot had gone. "This land is yours. You will have so many descendants that no one will be able to count them. They will be as many as the grains of dust that fly in the wind. Now go and explore the land that I have given you."

So Abram moved his tents near the great trees of Mamre at Hebron. He built an altar there and thanked God for all he had given him.

January 13 — God's Promise

Abram was living in the land God had given him. He had enough to eat and drink and took pleasure in his daily life . . . but there was something missing. God had promised him descendants. He and Sarai were no longer young—and they still had no child.

God knew what Abram wanted.

"Don't be afraid, Abram," said God. "I will protect you. I will be everything you need."

Genesis 15

Abram trusted God. He told God all the fears in his heart.

"Oh, Lord," said Abram, "how can you reward me and make my descendants great, when Sarai and I have no children? My servant, Eliezer, will inherit everything I have."

"No, he won't," said God. "You will have a son who comes from your own body, a child who is yours in every way." Then God said, "Look up into the night sky. Count the stars! That's how many descendants you will have!"

Abram looked, and he believed what God had told him.

At sunset, Abram fell into a deep sleep. He dreamed, and as he dreamed, God gave him a vision of what the future would hold.

Abram believed the LORD, and the LORD counted him as righteous because of his faith.
Genesis 15:6

"You will have descendants, but they will be strangers in a foreign land. They will live as slaves and be treated badly for 400 years. But I will punish the nation who enslaves them, and I will make sure that your descendants leave that country with great riches. Then they will return here to this land, and it will all belong to them. And you, Abram, will live to a good old age and die peacefully. This is my promise to you."

January 14—Sarai's Servant

Abram and Sarai lived for 10 years in Canaan. Sarai knew what God had promised, but she still had no children.

So Sarai decided to follow an ancient custom that would give Abram a child. She brought to Abram her Egyptian servant, Hagar.

"Take my servant, and let her be your wife too. Then perhaps she will bear us a son."

Abram did as Sarai asked and took Hagar as his wife. Before long Hagar was pregnant. But as soon as she knew that she was expecting Abram's child, she did not want Sarai to treat her as a servant anymore. She began to dislike Sarai because Sarai could not have children.

"This is your fault!" Sarai complained unfairly to her husband. "Hagar dislikes me. Now what should I do?"

"Hagar is your servant," replied Abram. "Do what you think best."

So Sarai started to treat Hagar badly. Hagar became so unhappy that she ran away.

Hagar stopped by a spring in the desert and rested and drank some water there. Then an angel appeared and questioned her about where she had come from and where she was going.

"You must return to Sarai!" the angel commanded her, when she admitted she had run away. "God has seen how sad you are, but your son will be special. You will call him Ishmael, and he will have many descendants."

Hagar was amazed. "Now I know that God sees everything!" she said and went back to Sarai. Some time later, Ishmael was born.

Genesis 16

Hagar gave Abram a son, and Abram named him Ishmael.
Genesis 16:15

JANUARY 15—ABRAHAM WELCOMES STRANGERS

Ishmael grew up to be strong, and he was a blessing to Abram. But when he was 13 years old, God spoke again to Abram.

"I have not forgotten my promise," he said. "I will make you great. And as a sign that you belong to me, all the men in your family and all the male servants who are part of your larger family must be circumcised. You will also have new names and be called Abraham and Sarah. And by this time next year, Sarah will have a son called Isaac."

Then Abraham and all the men among them were circumcised, just as God had said.

Some time later, when Abraham was resting outside his tent in the heat of the day, he noticed three strangers approaching. As was the custom, he went to them and made them welcome.

"Come and rest!" Abraham said to them. "Let me bring you water to wash your feet and some food to eat."

GENESIS 17:1–18:15

"Is anything too hard for the LORD? I will return about this time next year, and Sarah will have a son."
Genesis 18:14

The men accepted Abraham's invitation, and he chose the best calf to be prepared and cooked for the visitors. They sat and ate while he stood apart under the trees.

"Where is your wife, Sarah?" they asked.

Immediately Abraham knew that he was in God's presence.

"She is there, inside the tent," Abraham replied.

"By this time next year, Sarah will have a son."

Sarah was listening at the entrance to the tent. She looked at her wrinkled skin and bent fingers, then laughed to herself.

As if I could have a baby at my age! she thought.

But God knew what she was thinking.

"Is anything too hard for God?" asked one of Abraham's visitors. "You will have a son when I come again."

JANUARY 16—ABRAHAM PRAYS FOR SODOM

The men prepared to leave Abraham and move on toward the cities of Sodom and Gomorrah.

"The people living in those cities have returned to evil ways," God told Abraham. "It is widely known that the evil they do is so terrible that they cannot be allowed to live. I will visit them to see if what I hear is true. If it is, the city must be destroyed."

Abraham looked down toward Sodom and thought about the people who lived in the city. His nephew Lot and Lot's family still lived there.

"What if you find 50 good men?" Abraham asked God. "Surely you won't destroy the city then."

"No," replied God. "If I find 50 good men, it will be saved."

"What if you find 45 good men?" asked Abraham.

"Then I won't destroy the city," replied God.

"What about 40?" Abraham pleaded.

"I won't destroy the city," said God.

Abraham took a deep breath. "Don't be angry with me," he said. "But what if you find 30 good men?"

"I will spare the city," promised God.

Once more Abraham spoke. "And for 20?"

God promised to spare the people of Sodom if he found 20 good men.

"What if you find just 10 good men in the whole city?" asked Abraham.

"For the sake of 10 good men, I will not destroy it," said God finally.

GENESIS 18:16-33

"Suppose you find fifty righteous people living there in the city—will you still sweep it away and not spare it for their sakes?"
Genesis 18:24

JANUARY 17 — RESCUE BY ANGELS

Lot was sitting in the gateway to the city of Sodom when the two men, angels sent by God, arrived. He stood up to greet them and offered them a place to stay as Abraham had done earlier in the day.

"We will stay the night in the city square," they answered.

But Lot was concerned for their safety.

"Please! Come and stay in my house," he insisted.

The angels finally agreed, and Lot prepared a meal for them in his home.

Outside the house, a crowd was gathering. Men of all ages began to block the way out. Fists thumped on the door. Voices were heard, growing louder, demanding that Lot send the men out.

"We know you have two men staying with you," they shouted. "Hand them over!"

Eventually Lot went outside and tried to calm the crowd.

"These men are my guests," he said. "They are under my protection, and I cannot let you hurt them!"

But the crowd was fierce and violent.

"You're not one of us," they shouted to Lot. "It doesn't matter to us if you die first!"

Genesis 19:1-29

Lot's wife looked back as she was following behind him, and she turned into a pillar of salt.
Genesis 19:26

The two angels pulled Lot inside the door, then struck the men outside with blindness so that Lot and his family could escape.

While the angry crowd stumbled around outside in confusion, the angels warned Lot to leave immediately.

"Go quickly!" the angels said. "Take your wife and children and any other family you have with you now! We are here to bring judgment against the evil in this city. It will be destroyed by morning!"

Lot went to try to warn the two men who were promised in marriage to his daughters, but they thought he was joking.

So the angels led Lot, his wife, and his daughters to the edge of the city.

"Now run for your lives!" ordered the angels. "Don't stop until you reach the mountains. And don't look back!"

But Lot feared that they could not cover the distance fast enough. He begged that they should go only as far as the small town of Zoar, and the angels agreed that Zoar would not be destroyed.

The sun had risen by the time they reached Zoar.

Then God sent down burning rain until Sodom and Gomorrah were destroyed. But Lot's wife forgot the angels' warning. She looked back to see what had happened, and she was turned into a pillar of salt.

When Abraham awoke that morning, he looked down the plain. All he could see was dense smoke. So Abraham knew that there were fewer than 10 good people left in the city of Sodom.

JANUARY 18 — SARAH HAS A SON

"Who would believe that Abraham and I would have a son in our old age?" asked Sarah, as she nursed Isaac.

God had fulfilled his promise. Sarah had become pregnant and given birth to a baby boy. She was happy at last.

But as Isaac grew and became a little boy, Ishmael, Hagar's son, teased him. Sarah did not like it. Before long Sarah had convinced herself that Ishmael would steal her son's inheritance.

"I want you to make Hagar and her son leave," she said. "It will not be good for Isaac if they stay here with us."

GENESIS 21:1-21

Abraham named their son Isaac.
Genesis 21:3

But Ishmael was also Abraham's son. Abraham could not drive him away.

Then God spoke to Abraham. "Do what Sarah asks, Abraham. I will let no harm come to Hagar or her son. But it is through Isaac that you will be blessed and your family will grow."

So Abraham gave Hagar food and water, and she and Ishmael went off into the desert.

After a while they ran out of water, and Hagar thought that they would die. She sat Ishmael in the shade of some bushes and walked far enough away that she wouldn't see him suffer.

But God heard Ishmael weeping. An angel spoke to Hagar.

"Don't be frightened," he said. "God knows your problems. Take Ishmael and keep going. I have promised that he will live to see his descendants."

Then Hagar saw that there was a well from which she could draw water. She filled her water pouch and gave him a drink.

God looked after Ishmael as he grew up. He became a skilled archer and married an Egyptian woman.

JANUARY 19—GOD TESTS ABRAHAM

When Isaac was much older, Abraham heard God speak to him.

"Abraham!" God said. "Take Isaac with you to a mountain in Moriah. I want you to give your precious son to me as a sacrifice."

GENESIS 22:1-19

"I will certainly bless you. I will multiply your descendants beyond number, like the stars in the sky and the sand on the seashore. Your descendants will conquer the cities of their enemies."
Genesis 22:17

Abraham was stunned. His heart pounded. But God had always been faithful to him. He had kept his promises. How could he deny him now?

Abraham cut wood for a fire and took Isaac and some servants with him on the three-day walk into the mountains. He made the last part of the journey with Isaac alone.

"Father," asked Isaac, after they had walked a while in silence. "We have brought wood for the sacrifice, but where is the lamb?"

"God will provide a lamb," said Abraham sadly.

Abraham laid the wood on the stones for the altar. Then he tied his son's hands and placed him on the wood. Just as Abraham lifted the knife to sacrifice his much-loved son, he heard God's voice from heaven.

"Stop!" God said. "You have shown me how much you love me. I will bless you, and you will have as many descendants as there are stars in the sky!"

Then Abraham saw a ram caught in a bush. God had provided the sacrifice. His son Isaac was safe.

JANUARY 20—WATER FOR TEN CAMELS

Sarah died, and Abraham grew older. He became anxious for his son to have a wife. He wanted to see his grandchildren before he died.

So Abraham asked his servant to go on a journey to find the right young woman.

"Find a wife for Isaac," said Abraham. "I want him to marry a woman from our own people."

So the servant took 10 camels and expensive gifts and traveled back across the desert to the village where Abraham's brother lived.

The servant reached the well as the sun was setting. He made his camels kneel down as the women were coming from their homes to draw water. Then the servant prayed.

Genesis 24:1-21

"This is my request. I will ask one of them, 'Please give me a drink from your jug.' If she says, 'Yes, have a drink, and I will water your camels, too!'—let her be the one you have selected as Isaac's wife. This is how I will know that you have shown unfailing love to my master."
Genesis 24:14

"Lord, God of Abraham," he prayed, "be kind to us today so that we can find the wife you have chosen for Isaac. May she be the first girl who offers to draw water for me and all these camels."

Before he had finished praying, Abraham's great-niece Rebekah came to draw water. Abraham's servant went to her and asked for a drink. Rebekah not only gave him water, but she also offered to water his 10 camels. The servant watched as she went back to the well and filled her water jar again and again and again.

She will be a good wife for Isaac, the servant thought.

JANUARY 21 — A WIFE FOR ISAAC

Abraham's servant asked Rebekah who she was and whether he could stay with her family that night.

When Rebekah told him, he was sure that God had led him there and that this was his choice of a wife for Isaac.

Rebekah accepted the servant's gifts of a golden nose ring and two bracelets and rushed home to tell her family about the man by the well. Her brother Laban came to greet him and invited him back to their home.

Servants came to feed the camels, and a meal was prepared for him. But Abraham's servant would not eat until he had explained why he was there. He told them about Abraham's wish to find a wife for his son Isaac from his people. He told them about his prayer and the way that God had answered that prayer by sending Rebekah.

Then everyone in the family was happy. They knew that this must be what God wanted and would not prevent it from happening. The servant brought them the gifts he had with him, and they asked Rebekah if she was happy to go back with him.

The next day the two of them left together on the journey back to Abraham.

Isaac saw them as they drew near and went out to meet them. When he heard the story, he was happy. He married Rebekah, and he loved her.

JANUARY 22 — ESAU AND JACOB

Isaac was 40 years old when he married Rebekah, and he wanted very much to give grandchildren to his father, Abraham. But years went by and no children came.

Isaac prayed that God would bless them with a family just as his father had before him. God answered, and Rebekah found that she was expecting twins. God told Rebekah that the two children would each establish a separate people—and that the older child would serve the younger one.

Two baby boys were born within minutes of each other. The first was covered in red hair; he was named Esau. The second was born holding on to his brother's heel; he was named Jacob.

The two boys were very different, and soon it became clear that Esau was his father's favorite. Esau grew up to be a skilled hunter and liked the outdoor life. Rebekah loved the younger brother more. He was a quiet young man and did not like to go far from home.

One day Esau came home from hunting, hungry and tired. Jacob was cooking a thick lentil stew. The smell of it made Esau desperately hungry.

GENESIS 24:22-67

[Rebekah] became his wife. He loved her deeply, and she was a special comfort to him after the death of his mother.
Genesis 24:67

GENESIS 25:19-34

Jacob gave Esau some bread and lentil stew. Esau ate the meal, then got up and left. He showed contempt for his rights as the firstborn.
Genesis 25:34

"Mmm . . . let me have some of that! It smells delicious!" he said.

Jacob seized his chance.

"Give me your birthright, and I will," he said.

"I will die if I don't eat now!" said Esau. "You're welcome to my inheritance!"

Then Esau ate the stew with some bread until he was full, and then he left Jacob. His birthright as the older son meant nothing to him.

JANUARY 23—ISAAC'S BLESSING

Isaac began to lose his sight as he grew older. He became frail and old and realized he might not have long to live.

One day he called for his older son, Esau.

"Go and hunt some wild game and make my favorite meal for me," he said. "Then I will bless you."

Esau took his bow and arrow and went from the tents to hunt. It was years since he had given his birthright away in exchange for a bowl of lentil stew—and he had forgotten about it.

Rebekah had not forgotten. She overheard her husband's conversation. She wanted Jacob to receive Isaac's special blessing.

"Go and kill two goats and give them to me," she ordered Jacob. "I will cook for your father, and he will bless you instead of your brother."

Jacob was uncertain. His father was almost blind, but he was not stupid.

"But Esau's skin is hairy," he said. "Father may not be able to see me, but

GENESIS 27:1–28:5

Isaac said, "Now, my son, bring me the wild game. Let me eat it, and then I will give you my blessing."
Genesis 27:25

I don't smell like Esau. And when he touches me, he will know I'm not my brother."

Rebekah had already thought of that. She dressed Jacob in Esau's clothes and tied goatskin to his arms and neck. She prepared the food just as Isaac liked it and sent Jacob in to receive the blessing.

"How could you have found this food so quickly, my son?" Isaac asked.

"God blessed me and gave me success," Jacob lied.

Isaac touched his son and smelled his clothes.

"Are you really Esau?" he asked again. "Your voice does not sound right, yet you feel and smell like Esau."

"I am," Jacob replied.

So Isaac blessed his younger son instead of Esau, the older one.

When Esau returned and found out he had been tricked, both he and his father were angry. But it was too late. The blessing had been given. So Esau held a grudge against his brother and planned to wait until his father's death so that he could kill Jacob.

Rebekah did not intend to let this happen. She suggested to Isaac that Jacob go to her brother, Laban, to find a wife from among her own people, just as he had done when he married her.

So Isaac sent Jacob to Laban, where Rebekah knew he would be safe.

JANUARY 24—JACOB'S DREAM

GENESIS 28:10-22

As [Jacob] slept, he dreamed of a stairway that reached from the earth up to heaven. And he saw the angels of God going up and down the stairway.
Genesis 28:12

Jacob set out toward Haran, where his uncle Laban lived.

When it was night, Jacob lay down to sleep, with a stone as a pillow. He dreamed of a long flight of stairs, stretching from the earth at the bottom into heaven itself. In his dream Jacob saw angels moving up and down the staircase. At the very top, Jacob saw God.

"I am the God of your father, Isaac, and your grandfather, Abraham," said God. "I promise I will give you and your descendants the land you are lying on. I will watch over you now, and I will never leave you."

When Jacob awoke, he knew that he had seen God, and he was afraid. He took the stone he had used as a pillow and stood it up like a pillar to mark the special place where he had met with God.

"If you look after me as you have promised, I will obey you and follow you always," said Jacob.

Then he continued his journey until he reached the place where his uncle lived with his family.

JANUARY 25 — JACOB FALLS IN LOVE

Jacob saw some shepherds and their sheep waiting by a large well. He approached them and asked where they were from.

"We are from Haran," they replied.

Jacob was delighted. That was where his uncle lived.

GENESIS 29:1-30

"Do you know Laban?" he asked hopefully.

"Yes," they replied. "That's Laban's daughter Rachel over there."

Jacob looked up. He saw a shepherdess leading her flock of sheep toward the well. Jacob went to meet Rachel and watered her sheep from the well. Then he kissed her and told her that he was her cousin. She was so pleased, she ran to tell her father.

Jacob worked seven years to pay for Rachel. But his love for her was so strong that it seemed to him but a few days.
Genesis 29:20

Laban hurried to meet his nephew and greeted him like a father would. He took Jacob home and made him welcome as part of the family.

After Jacob had stayed a month, Laban asked Jacob how he should be paid for working for his uncle. "Name your price," he said.

Jacob thought carefully. He had only been with Laban a short time, but he had fallen in love with Laban's younger daughter, Rachel.

"I will work for you for seven years if you let me marry Rachel," said Jacob.

Laban agreed. Jacob worked hard, knowing that the time would come when he could have Rachel as his wife.

At the end of the seven years, Laban organized a big feast to celebrate his daughter's marriage. But Laban intended to trick Jacob. The custom was that the older daughter should marry first. So when the wedding took place, Leah was dressed in her bridal clothes and covered with a veil. Instead of marrying Rachel, Jacob married Leah, Laban's older daughter.

When Jacob found out, it was too late.

"Why did you trick me?" asked Jacob angrily. He wanted Rachel, not Leah.

"It is our custom," replied Laban. "But I will let you marry Rachel now and have both daughters if you agree to work for me for another seven years."

Jacob agreed. He loved Rachel very much.

JANUARY 26—JACOB RUNS AWAY

God saw that Jacob did not love Leah, so he gave her children to love. She had six sons—Reuben, Simeon, Levi, Judah, Issachar, and Zebulun—and a daughter named Dinah.

Rachel had no children, so she asked Jacob to give her children by taking her servant as his wife. So Dan and Naphtali were born.

Leah gave Jacob her servant also, so Gad and Asher were born.

Finally Rachel had a son of her own. She and Jacob were delighted. They called him Joseph, and he became Jacob's favorite.

Jacob had now been with Laban for 20 years. God told Jacob it was time for him to return to his father's home.

"Don't go!" begged Laban. "God has blessed me because you are here."

"Very well," said Jacob. "But if I stay, let me have any spotted or speckled sheep or goat from your herd, so I can build up my own."

Laban agreed, but secretly he took every spotted or speckled goat away so that Jacob would have to stay longer.

Jacob set about increasing the number of sheep and goats that he could

GENESIS 29:31–31:21

Jacob began to notice a change in Laban's attitude toward him.
Genesis 31:2

call his own, and because God blessed all he did, soon Jacob owned all the strongest animals—and they were speckled and spotted.

Laban no longer felt happy to have Jacob as part of his family. Jacob felt unwelcome. The two men had started to trick each other. They could not trust each other. It was time to separate.

Secretly, Jacob prepared his wives and children for the long journey. He did not tell Laban they were going.

January 27 — Jacob Wrestles with an Angel

Jacob left with Laban's daughters and grandchildren, and his healthy sheep and goats. He was now a man of great wealth. God had kept his promise to Jacob.

Genesis 32:22-32

But Jacob had left home in the first place because he had done a terrible thing to his twin brother. He knew it was time to return and say he was sorry.

Jacob sent his wives ahead on camels. He was alone, sitting by the Jabbok River. Then all at once a man appeared who started to wrestle with Jacob. They struggled all night long, each one trying to overpower the other. The man touched Jacob's hip and twisted it so Jacob was in terrible pain, but still he would not give in.

"Your name will no longer be Jacob," the man told him. *"From now on you will be called Israel, because you have fought with God and with men and have won."*

Genesis 32:28

Then the sky began to change color as dawn broke.

"Let me go now," said the man. "The sun is rising."

"No!" said Jacob. "I will not let you go until you bless me."

The man asked, "What is your name?"

"Jacob!" came the reply.

"From now on you will also be known as Israel," said the man, "for you have struggled with God and have not been defeated."

Jacob limped away. He knew that this had been some sort of test. He had been wrestling with an angel sent by God. God had plans for him.

JANUARY 28 — FRIENDS AND BROTHERS

Jacob was frightened. He had already sent messengers ahead with gifts for his twin brother: sheep, goats, donkeys, and camels.

Jacob had prayed to God. "You told me to go back home," said Jacob. "You promised to protect me!"

GENESIS 33; 35:1-15

Now Esau was coming to meet him, bringing 400 men with him. Jacob was certain that Esau wanted to kill him.

Jacob named the place Bethel (which means "house of God"), because God had spoken to him there.
Genesis 35:15

Jacob divided his family and herds into small groups. He hoped that if Esau attacked one, the rest would escape.

Then Jacob went on ahead to meet his brother. Jacob bowed down to the ground. But Esau had not come to fight. He threw his arms around Jacob and

hugged him. Both men started to cry. Esau had forgiven Jacob. He was no longer angry. Neither was jealous of the other.

Jacob introduced Esau to his wives and children, and they were friends and brothers once more.

Then Jacob made his way to Bethel, where he settled with his family. He made an altar to thank God for keeping him safe and giving him so much. God gave Jacob the name Israel and promised that his descendants, the Israelites, would number as many as the grains of sand in the desert.

January 29 — Rachel Dies

Jacob moved his tents toward Bethlehem. Rachel, the wife he loved the best, was expecting her second child any day.

While they were on the journey, Rachel began to give birth, and she had another son. Rachel was weak and lived only long enough to know that her husband named him Benjamin.

Rachel was buried near Bethlehem. Jacob then returned to the land of Mamre near Hebron, where Abraham and Isaac had made their home.

Not long after, Isaac also died, having lived to a great age, and his twin sons buried him.

Genesis 35:16-29

Rachel died and was buried on the way to Ephrath (that is, Bethlehem).
Genesis 35:19

January 30 — Jacob's Special Son

Jacob now had 12 sons, but he loved Joseph more than his other children, and Joseph knew it.

By the time he was 17, Joseph was helping his brothers to look after his father's flocks. But Joseph watched his brothers and listened to them, and then he told his father the bad things they said and did.

Israel gave Joseph a very special long-sleeved coat. When Joseph's brothers saw it, they knew that he was loved much more than they were. They hated him.

One night Joseph had a dream. His dream was so strange that he told his brothers the next day.

"Listen to this!" he said. "Last night I dreamed that we were all tying together bundles of grain when my bundle stood up straight, and your bundles bowed down before mine!"

This made his brothers even angrier than when their father had given him a beautiful coat!

"So do you plan to rule over us now?" they said.

Then Joseph dreamed again. This time he told his father, too.

"I had another strange dream!" he said. "I dreamed that the sun, the moon, and 11 stars all bowed down before me!"

Israel told Joseph not to boast in this way.

"Do you really think your mother and I as well as your brothers will bow down before you?" he asked.

His brothers hated Joseph even more. But his father wondered what it all meant.

GENESIS 37:1-11

Jacob loved Joseph more than any of his other children because Joseph had been born to him in his old age. So one day Jacob had a special gift made for Joseph— a beautiful robe.
Genesis 37:3

JANUARY 31—SOLD TO BE A SLAVE

Joseph's brothers had taken the sheep to graze. His father sent Joseph to find out how they were.

Joseph walked many miles across the desert until he found them not far from the ancient city of Dothan. But his brothers saw him coming, dressed in the fine coat his father had given him.

"Here comes that dreamer," they muttered to each other. By the time Joseph had come close to them, they decided to kill him.

Reuben didn't like his younger brother, but he didn't want to be part of a plan to murder him.

"Let's not kill him," Reuben said. "Put him here in this empty well."

So as soon as Joseph reached them, the brothers tore off his coat and forced him down into the well. They were eating a meal when they saw some Midianite traders, loaded up with spices, on their way to Egypt. It was not long before Judah suggested a plan to sell their brother.

So Joseph was pulled out of the well, sold for 20 pieces of silver, and taken to Egypt to be sold as a slave. His brothers then killed a goat and dipped Joseph's fine coat in the blood. They returned to their father and said they had found the coat.

GENESIS 37:12-36

When the Ishmaelites, who were Midianite traders, came by, Joseph's brothers pulled him out of the cistern and sold him to them for twenty pieces of silver. And the traders took him to Egypt.
Genesis 37:28

Jacob believed that his much-loved son had been attacked by a wild animal and was dead. He was overcome with grief.

FEBRUARY 1 — PRISON DREAMS

Joseph was taken to Egypt and sold to Potiphar, the captain of the guard.

But Joseph worked hard, and God blessed Potiphar's home because of him. Soon Potiphar trusted him with everything he owned—and Joseph became his chief servant.

Joseph had grown into a strong, good-looking young man. Potiphar's wife saw this and wanted him for herself. But Joseph was a good servant and kept away from her. This made her so angry that she claimed he had attacked her. Potiphar was furious and threw Joseph into prison.

Once more Joseph worked hard, even though things were difficult for him. God did not abandon him. He blessed Joseph again so that soon he was put in charge of the other prisoners.

GENESIS 39–40

*The LORD was
with [Joseph] and
caused everything
he did to succeed.*
Genesis 39:23

After a while, Joseph was put in charge of Pharaoh's cupbearer and baker. When they each had a strange dream, Joseph told them that God could help them understand the meanings of the dreams. This meant bad news for the baker—he was killed by Pharaoh soon afterward. But there was good news for the cupbearer, who was released, as Joseph told him his dream had predicted.

But the cupbearer did not speak up for Joseph when he was free again. He forgot all about him.

FEBRUARY 2 — PHARAOH'S STRANGE DREAMS

Two long years went by. Joseph remained in prison.

Then Pharaoh had strange and disturbing dreams. No one could explain them to him, but he believed they must mean something important.

The cupbearer then remembered Joseph.

"There is a man in your prison who can help," he said, and he told Pharaoh what had happened when he and the baker had also had strange dreams.

Pharaoh sent for him and told Joseph what he had dreamed.

"In the first dream, seven thin cows ate up seven fat, healthy cows," said Pharaoh. "In the second dream, seven thin, straggly ears of corn swallowed up seven healthy ears of corn."

"Both dreams have the same meaning," said Joseph. "God is warning you that there will be seven years of good harvest followed by seven years with no food. If you store the grain wisely, you and your people will survive."

Pharaoh knew immediately who should help him store the grain and look after the good harvests. He put Joseph in charge of the whole land of Egypt. He put a ring on Joseph's finger and a gold chain around his neck. Pharaoh had him ride in a chariot while dressed in fine robes, and wherever Joseph went, people bowed down to him.

Joseph was 30 years old when his dreams began to come true.

FEBRUARY 3 — FAMINE IN CANAAN

Over the next seven years there was plenty of food. Joseph made sure that all the extra grain was stored carefully. Then as year after year passed, the harvests failed in Egypt and in all the lands around it.

GENESIS 41:1-46

Joseph responded, "Both of Pharaoh's dreams mean the same thing. God is telling Pharaoh in advance what he is about to do."
Genesis 41:25

Joseph opened the storehouses and sold the grain to the Egyptians. Everyone had what was needed to get through the seven years of famine.

Back in Canaan, Jacob heard that there was grain in Egypt. He heard that others were going to buy food there and sent 10 of his sons to buy some. Jacob kept only his youngest son, Benjamin, at home with him.

When the brothers arrived, they went to the Egyptian governor and bowed down before him. Many years had passed since they had sold their brother into slavery. They did not expect to see him there; they did not expect to see him dressed as a ruler with power to save their lives. None of the brothers recognized Joseph as the man before them.

Joseph, however, knew that the men on their knees were his father's sons. He did not speak to them in the language of the Israelites but used an interpreter so they would not know he understood them.

GENESIS 41:47–42:17

Joseph gathered all the crops grown in Egypt and stored the grain from the surrounding fields in the cities.
Genesis 41:48

"Are you spies?" Joseph asked them.

"No, sir," they replied. "We are brothers from Canaan. Our youngest brother is at home with our father. We are hungry and have come to buy food."

"I don't believe you!" Joseph said. "You must prove this by bringing your brother here to me."

Then Joseph had them put in prison to think about what he had said.

February 4—Simeon Is Taken Hostage

After three days, Joseph released his brothers from prison.

"Return home," he said, "but as proof that you are not spies, you must leave one brother here and return with your father's youngest son."

The brothers turned away and discussed the matter.

"This is all our own fault!" they said to each other. "Joseph pleaded with us for his life, but we wouldn't listen. We did a terrible wrong, and now we are being punished!"

Joseph understood all they said and wept for the past wasted years.

Then Joseph had Simeon taken from them and bound up. He sold grain to his brothers and sent them home but secretly had all their silver coins replaced in their sacks.

That night the brothers opened their grain sacks to feed their donkeys and found that the money they had paid for the grain had been returned. They were frightened.

What could have happened? What would happen to them now?

When the brothers returned to their father, Jacob, they told him everything. They explained that they must return with Benjamin, or Simeon would die.

Jacob shook his head.

"Once I had 12 sons," he said. "Joseph was lost many years ago; now I have lost Simeon. Benjamin is the only son left to me from his mother, Rachel. I cannot let him go. If anything happens to him, I will surely die of sorrow."

So Benjamin did not go. The family lived through the famine by eating the grain they had brought back from Egypt until there was no more left.

GENESIS 42:18–43:1

Jacob exclaimed, "You are robbing me of my children! Joseph is gone! Simeon is gone! And now you want to take Benjamin, too. Everything is going against me!"
Genesis 42:36

FEBRUARY 5 — JACOB LETS BENJAMIN GO

"You must go back to Egypt for more grain," Jacob said to his sons, "or we will all die of hunger!"

Judah would not return without Benjamin.

"We were warned what would happen," he told his father. "You will lose all your sons if you will not take this risk. Either we go with Benjamin or we die here of starvation."

So Jacob made sure that his sons packed not only silver to pay for more grain but also enough to replace the silver they had brought back from Egypt. Then he packed honey, spices, pistachio nuts, and almonds as gifts for the Egyptian governor.

Then, very sadly, Jacob let his youngest son go with them to Egypt.

GENESIS 43:2-15

The men packed Jacob's gifts and double the money and headed off with Benjamin. They finally arrived in Egypt and presented themselves to Joseph.
Genesis 43:15

FEBRUARY 6 — JOSEPH'S FEAST

When the brothers arrived, they went to the governor with Benjamin. They quickly explained to the manager of Joseph's household that they had found their silver in their grain sacks and had brought it back.

GENESIS 43:16-34

Joseph hurried from the room because he was overcome with emotion for his brother. He went into his private room, where he broke down and wept.
Genesis 43:30

"Don't be afraid," the man told them. "Your God is taking care of you. I was paid for the grain you bought. God made sure that you had silver to return to your country."

Then Simeon was returned to them safely, and all the brothers were invited to a feast at Joseph's house. They gave him their gifts, but they still did not realize that the great man in front of them was their lost brother, Joseph.

Joseph asked about their father, and then when he saw his younger brother, Benjamin, he wept privately for joy. When the brothers sat down to the feast, Joseph made sure that Benjamin had more to eat and drink than anyone else. The brothers could not understand their good fortune.

FEBRUARY 7 — THE SILVER CUP

When the time came for the men to return to their father, Joseph arranged for them to be given as much grain as they could carry. As before, he made sure that their silver was also put back in their sacks. Finally, he asked his servant to put his own silver cup in Benjamin's sack.

As the brothers left the city, Joseph ordered his men to catch up with them and accuse them of stealing the silver cup.

The brothers were shocked. They denied that any one of them could be guilty of stealing from the man who had treated them so well. They were so sure that they said that if anyone was found to have stolen the cup, that brother would die, and all the others would become slaves in Egypt.

GENESIS 44

The palace manager searched the brothers' sacks, from the oldest to the youngest. And the cup was found in Benjamin's sack!
Genesis 44:12

Their bags were searched, beginning with the oldest brother. When the silver cup was found in Benjamin's sack, the brothers tore their clothes in disbelief.

They returned to Joseph, and Judah put himself at Joseph's mercy.

"Please don't harm Benjamin!" Judah pleaded. "We will all become your slaves rather than that!"

"There is no need," Joseph said. "You may all go back to your father. I will make only Benjamin my slave."

Then Judah asked to speak to Joseph alone. He explained that his father would die of grief if anything happened to Benjamin. He begged to be allowed to take Benjamin's place for the sake of his aging father.

FEBRUARY 8—JACOB'S LOST SON

Joseph ordered his servants to leave him alone with his brothers. Then he wept so loudly that all his household heard him.

"I am your brother Joseph," he told them. "You sold me into slavery and you wished me harm, but God meant only that good should come of it. There will be famine for another five years. But God made sure I was here in Egypt and helped me to become known to Pharaoh so that your lives could be saved.

"Now you must return to your father and mine. Tell him that I am governor of all Egypt and that it is safe for him to come here. You will live in the land of Goshen with your families and sheep and goats and all that you own, and you will have plenty to eat during the famine."

Joseph's brothers wept for joy. God had blessed them in ways they could not have imagined.

As Joseph sent his brothers home to Jacob in fine clothes and with more

GENESIS 45:1–46:27

"Please, come closer," [Joseph] said to them. So they came closer. And he said again, "I am Joseph, your brother, whom you sold into slavery in Egypt."
Genesis 45:4

food—and with carts to collect all they wanted to bring with them—his parting words were, "Don't argue with each other on the way!"

When Jacob heard all that had happened, he could hardly believe it. His son Joseph was still alive! He agreed to leave the land of Canaan and took all his children and grandchildren with him to live in Egypt.

FEBRUARY 9—JACOB DIES IN EGYPT

Joseph went in his chariot to meet his father in the land of Goshen. There was much weeping as the two men threw their arms around each other.

Jacob and his family then settled in Goshen and made it their home. God blessed them and soon they had property there, and many grandchildren and great-grandchildren were born to Jacob. He lived in Egypt for 17 years, and when he knew it was time for him to die, he made Joseph promise that he would be buried in the land of his ancestors, not in Egypt.

Joseph had married and had two sons of his own: Manasseh and Ephraim. Joseph brought the boys to see his father as he lay dying.

"I never thought I would see you again, my son," he said to Joseph. "Now I am able to see not just you but also your sons. God will be with you all. He will

take you back to the land he promised to give to my grandfather, Abraham; to my father, Isaac; and to me; and he will bless you."

Jacob blessed each one of his sons, and then he died. Joseph wept over his father, and then he had him embalmed in the way of the Egyptians. He asked permission from Pharaoh, and then he took his father's body back to Canaan to bury him.

GENESIS 46:28–50:14

Jacob's sons did as he had commanded them. They carried his body to the land of Canaan and buried him in the cave in the field of Machpelah, near Mamre. This is the cave that Abraham had bought as a permanent burial site from Ephron the Hittite.
Genesis 50:12-13

FEBRUARY 10—SLAVES IN EGYPT

Joseph lived to see his own great-great-grandchildren. Before his death, he told his brothers that God would one day take them back to the Promised Land. Then Joseph died and was embalmed, and he was buried in a coffin in Egypt.

Years passed, and there were many descendants of Joseph living in Egypt. A time came when the new Pharaoh looked at all the Israelites who lived in the land and he was afraid.

"There are too many Israelites," he said. "Soon they will join with our enemies and overcome us. We must make them slaves and force them to build us new cities."

So the Egyptians were cruel to the Israelites. They made them work hard for them and treated them badly. But still the Israelites seemed to grow in number, and God blessed them.

Then Pharaoh ordered the midwives to kill all the baby boys born to Israelite women. But the midwives would not obey Pharaoh; they told him that the women were strong and gave birth before they arrived to help. So God blessed the Egyptian midwives. But Pharaoh had another plan. He gave an order that all baby boys must be thrown into the Nile River and be drowned.

EXODUS 1

The more the Egyptians oppressed them, the more the Israelites multiplied and spread, and the more alarmed the Egyptians became.
Exodus 1:12

FEBRUARY 11—MIRIAM AND THE PRINCESS

One day an Israelite woman gave birth to a son. She hid him until he was three months old. She could not let the Egyptians take her baby away.

Then when he was too big to hide any longer, she put the baby in a basket.

She coated it with tar to make it waterproof and told her daughter, Miriam, to hide it in the reeds along the bank of the Nile River.

When Pharaoh's daughter came to bathe in the river, she heard the sound of a baby crying and felt sorry for him.

"Should I find someone to nurse him for you?" asked Miriam, who was watching nearby.

"Yes," said the princess. "I will keep this baby and call him Moses."

Miriam went to fetch her mother.

"Look after this baby until he is old enough to live with me," said the princess. Miriam's mother took her little son away to care for him.

EXODUS 2:1-10

When she could no longer hide him, she got a basket made of papyrus reeds and waterproofed it with tar and pitch. She put the baby in the basket and laid it among the reeds along the bank of the Nile River.
Exodus 2:3

FEBRUARY 12 — MOSES KILLS A SLAVE DRIVER

Moses grew up strong and healthy. He lived with the Egyptians, but he saw how badly his own people were treated.

One day, Moses stood and watched the Israelites working under the hot sun. He saw the marks on their bodies where they had been beaten. He saw the sweat dripping from their foreheads. Then he saw an Egyptian beating one of his own people.

Moses had seen enough.

Looking around to make sure no one was watching him, Moses grabbed the Egyptian and killed him. Then he buried the man's body in the sand.

The next day, Moses saw two Israelites fighting.

"Why are you hurting each other?" he asked them.

"What does it matter to you?" one of the men replied. "Are you going to kill me as you killed that Egyptian?"

Moses was frightened. He realized someone had seen the killing. Soon the news would reach Pharaoh. Moses prepared to leave before Pharaoh issued orders for his death. He ran away to Midian.

EXODUS 2:11-15

The man replied, "Who appointed you to be our prince and judge? Are you going to kill me as you killed that Egyptian yesterday?" Then Moses was afraid, thinking, "Everyone knows what I did."
Exodus 2:14

FEBRUARY 13 — THE ANGEL IN THE BURNING BUSH

Moses made his home in Midian. He married Zipporah, one of seven daughters born to Jethro, the priest, and had a son named Gershom.

Moses was in the desert in Horeb, looking after his father-in-law's sheep one day, when he saw something strange. A bush was on fire, but the flames did not burn it up. Moses went over to take a closer look.

"Moses! Moses!" called a voice from the flames.

"Yes, here I am," he replied.

"Take off your shoes!" ordered the angel of the Lord from the burning bush. "You are on holy ground."

Moses was so afraid, he hid his face.

"I am the God of Abraham, the God of Isaac, and the God of Jacob. I have seen how my people, the Israelites, are suffering as slaves in Egypt. I want them to be free to live in the land I have promised them. I want you to go to Pharaoh and bring my people out of Egypt."

EXODUS 2:16–3:12

There the angel of the LORD appeared to [Moses] in a blazing fire from the middle of a bush. Moses stared in amazement. Though the bush was engulfed in flames, it didn't burn up.
Exodus 3:2

Moses was amazed.

"But I can't go to Pharaoh," said Moses. "Why would he listen to me?"

"I will be with you," replied God.

FEBRUARY 14 — MOSES IS AFRAID

Moses was afraid. He did not want to be the Israelites' leader.

"The people will not believe me," argued Moses. "What should I say?"

"Tell them that the God of Abraham, the God of Isaac, and the God of Jacob sent you to bring them out of their slavery in Egypt.

"Take your staff and throw it on the ground," ordered God.

Moses threw it. The staff hit the ground and turned into a snake. Moses ran from the snake.

"Now pick it up by its tail," said God.

As Moses picked it up, it changed back into a staff.

"Put your hand inside your cloak," said God.

EXODUS 3:13–4:18

God replied to Moses, "I AM WHO I AM. Say this to the people of Israel: I AM has sent me to you."
Exodus 3:14

Moses did as God asked. When he took his hand out from under his cloak, it was white with a skin disease. Quickly he put it back, and when he removed it, his hand was whole and healthy again.

"Show them these things," said God, "and they will know that I have sent you. If they still doubt, then take some water from the Nile River. As you pour it onto the ground, it will turn to blood."

Moses had one last protest.

"I do not speak well," he said. "I have always found it difficult to speak to people. Please send someone else."

"I made you, and I know all about you," God said. "I can help you with all you have to do. But your brother, Aaron, can go with you. He will speak for you. Take your staff. You will need it to prove that I have sent you."

So Moses went back to his father-in-law and started making arrangements to return to Egypt.

FEBRUARY 15 — BRICKS WITHOUT STRAW

God sent Aaron to meet Moses, and Moses explained all that God had told him to do. Then they went to the people and told them that God had heard their cries for help. They performed the signs that God had given them—and the people believed that God had sent Moses to help them.

Then together, Moses and Aaron went to see Pharaoh.

"We have come with a message from the Lord, the God of Israel: 'Let my people go so that they can worship me,'" they said.

"I don't know your God," said Pharaoh, "and I don't want to let the Israelites go. They are slaves, and I need them to work. I will not let them go!"

When Moses and Aaron had gone, Pharaoh gave new orders to his slave drivers.

"Let the Israelites gather their own straw to make bricks. But they must work even harder so that they produce just as many bricks as before!"

The Israelites cried out to Pharaoh, "How can we make the same number of bricks without straw?"

"You are lazy," said Pharaoh. "Get back to work!"

Some of the Israelites then went and complained to Moses and Aaron. "This is your fault!" they said. "You have made Pharaoh hate us even more!"

Then Moses spoke to God.

"Why have you allowed me to cause such trouble?" he asked.

"They are my people," promised God. "I will rescue them."

EXODUS 4:27–6:5

After this presentation to Israel's leaders, Moses and Aaron went and spoke to Pharaoh. They told him, "This is what the LORD, the God of Israel, says: Let my people go so they may hold a festival in my honor in the wilderness."

Exodus 5:1

FEBRUARY 16—PLAGUES IN EGYPT

EXODUS 7–10

"When I raise my powerful hand and bring out the Israelites, the Egyptians will know that I am the LORD."
Exodus 7:5

Moses and Aaron went to see Pharaoh again.

"The Lord, the God of Israel says, 'Let my people go, so that they can worship me,'" they said.

Just as before, Pharaoh refused to let the Israelites go.

God spoke to Moses. "Tell Aaron to stretch out his staff," he said.

Aaron stretched out his staff, and the water in Egypt turned to blood. All the fish in the Nile died; the smell was terrible throughout the land.

Moses and Aaron went to see Pharaoh again.

"The Lord, the God of Israel says, 'Let my people go, so that they can worship me,'" they said. "If you refuse, God will send a plague of frogs."

Just as before, Pharaoh refused to let the Israelites go.

Aaron stretched out his staff, and Egypt was covered in frogs. Then Pharaoh agreed to let the people go, as long as God took away the frogs.

Moses asked God and the frogs all died. But then Pharaoh changed his mind. He refused to let the Israelites go.

Seven more times Moses asked Pharaoh to let the Israelites go. When Pharaoh refused, God sent plagues of gnats, flies, and locusts. Every Egyptian animal died, and the people were covered in sores. Violent hailstorms battered the land, and all of Egypt was plunged into darkness.

After each plague Pharaoh agreed to let the Israelites go, but as soon as God took away the plague, Pharaoh changed his mind.

FEBRUARY 17 — THE FINAL PLAGUE

"I will give Pharaoh one more warning," said God to Moses. "If he still refuses to listen, every Egyptian, including Pharaoh, will want you to leave."

Then God told Moses that this time the firstborn son of every living creature in Egypt would die—including Pharaoh's own son. But God would protect his people and keep them safe. He gave Moses special instructions to follow.

Moses warned Pharaoh, but Pharaoh would not listen. He did not want the Israelites to leave Egypt.

That night all the Israelite families coated their door frames with blood from a lamb, so that the angel of death would pass over them. They ate a special meal of roast lamb with flat bread and herbs. They had their cloaks wrapped around them, their sandals on their feet, and a staff in their hands.

"This night must never be forgotten," Moses told the people. "We must tell our children and our grandchildren everything that happens tonight."

That night, after midnight, every firstborn Egyptian son died. The cries of the Egyptians could be heard throughout the land.

EXODUS 11:1–12:30

All the firstborn sons will die in every family in Egypt, from the oldest son of Pharaoh, who sits on his throne, to the oldest son of his lowliest servant girl who grinds the flour. Even the firstborn of all the livestock will die.
Exodus 11:5

FEBRUARY 18 — PHARAOH LETS THE PEOPLE GO

Pharaoh called Moses and Aaron and told them to go. "Take your cattle and sheep and leave this land!" he shouted.

The Egyptians gave the Israelites gold and silver—all they asked for.

Then Moses told the people that God would lead them to Canaan.

Exodus 12:31-42;
13:17-18

*The people of Israel
had lived in Egypt
for 430 years.*
Exodus 12:40

By day God appeared as a pillar of cloud to lead the people, and by night
he was a pillar of fire. God did not take them by the road that crossed the land
of the Philistines but by the desert road toward the Red Sea.

February 19—Crossing the Red Sea

It was not long before Pharaoh began to regret that he had let his workforce of
slaves leave Egypt. He decided to chase them and bring them back.

Pharaoh took 600 of his best chariots and every other chariot he could find
in Egypt. He took horses, horsemen, and troops on foot. The Israelites soon
saw that the Egyptians were coming after them, and they were terrified.

"Were there no graves in Egypt?" they demanded of Moses. "Have you
brought us here into the desert to die?"

But Moses was not afraid. He knew that God would save his people.

The pillar of cloud moved behind the people so it stood between them and
the Egyptians and brought confusion to Pharaoh's men.

Then Moses stretched out his hand over the Red Sea, and God sent a wind
to blow back the waters during the night so that all the Israelites could pass
over safely to the other side on dry land.

The Egyptians started to follow, but Moses stretched out his hand

Exodus 14:5-31

*The people of Israel
walked through the
middle of the sea
on dry ground, with
walls of water on
each side!*
Exodus 14:22

again, now from the safety of the far bank. And God sent back the water to cover Pharaoh and his army and their chariots in the Red Sea. None of the Egyptians survived, but all God's people were safe.

FEBRUARY 20—GOD IS GREAT

When Moses and the Israelites saw what had happened to the Egyptians, they wanted to tell God how great and wonderful he was. He had saved them from years of suffering! So Moses led the Israelites in a song of praise.

Our God is great and mighty!
He threw horses and riders into the sea.
Our God is strong and mighty!
He came to rescue us all.
He came for us as he promised.
He loves us and leads us.

EXODUS 15:1-21

Miriam the prophet,
Aaron's sister, took
a tambourine and
led all the women
as they played
their tambourines
and danced.
Exodus 15:20

Then Miriam, Moses' sister, took her tambourine and began to play and dance. She wanted to thank God for all that he had done. The other Israelite women saw what she did, and they followed her, dancing and playing tambourines.

"Sing to the Lord God," sang Miriam. "He is the greatest!"

FEBRUARY 21—WANDERING IN THE DESERT

Moses led the Israelites into the desert beyond the sea. They walked in the heat of the sun for three days but found no water. When they did find water, it tasted bitter and they could not drink it.

The people grumbled and complained to Moses. Moses spoke to God. "Throw that piece of wood into the water," said God.

Moses obeyed God, and the water became sweet to drink.

The people rested and then traveled on through the desert. But soon they were complaining again.

EXODUS 15:22–16:36

*Moses led the
people of Israel
away from the
Red Sea, and they
moved out into
the desert of Shur.
They traveled in
this desert for
three days without
finding any water.*
Exodus 15:22

"If only we had died in our beds in Egypt!" the people said to Moses. "At least we didn't go hungry there."

God heard the grumblings of his people. "In the mornings I will make bread fall from the sky like rain. In the evenings I will provide quail for my people to eat. The people are to collect just enough for their daily needs, and on the day before the Sabbath day, they are to collect twice as much so that the Sabbath can be a day of rest."

Everything happened just as God had said. They called the bread that God gave them *manna*. It looked like a thin layer of frost on the ground, and it tasted like wafers made from honey. God continued to provide bread for the people every day that they wandered in the desert.

FEBRUARY 22 — WATER FROM THE ROCK

EXODUS 17:1-7

*There was no water
there for the people
to drink. So once
more the people
complained against
Moses. "Give us
water to drink!"
they demanded.
"Quiet!" Moses
replied. "Why are
you complaining
against me? And
why are you testing
the LORD?"*
Exodus 17:1-2

The Israelites continued to wander through the desert, moving camp as God led them on.

Soon they were grumbling again. They could find no water to drink.

"We must have water!" they complained to Moses.

So Moses called to God to help him. He was sure the people were angry enough to kill him if he couldn't find water for them.

God answered Moses. He told Moses to take with him some of the people and go to the rock at Horeb, where he should hit it with his staff. God said that if he did this, water would pour from the rock and the people would have good water to drink.

Moses did as God instructed, and water poured from the rock in front of the people, just as God had said.

Exodus 17:8-16

FEBRUARY 23 — THE BATTLE WITH THE AMALEKITES

When the Israelites reached Rephidim, they were attacked by the Amalekites, the tribal people who lived in that part of the desert. It was clear that they wanted to fight. Moses had no choice but to defend the Israelites.

Moses told Joshua to choose men to make up an army.

The next day Moses; his brother, Aaron; and Hur went up the hill overlooking the desert valley where the battle would take place. Moses held out his staff over the fighting men and watched the battle. For as long as he held up his staff, Joshua's men were the stronger side. But when Moses tired and lowered his staff, the Amalekites seemed to take control of the battle.

So Hur and Aaron found a large stone for Moses to sit on. Then they stood on either side of him and supported his arms so Moses could hold up the staff until sunset, when the Amalekites were defeated.

Then Moses made an altar to thank God for protecting them against the enemy. He called it "the LORD is my banner" because he had lifted his staff high in the air.

As long as Moses held up the staff in his hand, the Israelites had the advantage. But whenever he dropped his hand, the Amalekites gained the advantage.
Exodus 17:11

FEBRUARY 24 — GOD SPEAKS FROM THE MOUNTAIN

After two months in the desert, the Israelites camped at the foot of Mount Sinai.

Moses climbed the mountain, and God told him what to tell the people.

"You have seen how I saved you from the Egyptians and brought you safely across the Red Sea. Now I will make a promise to you: You will be my special people if you will obey me and keep your side of the agreement."

Moses told the people what God had said, and they promised to obey.

God told Moses that he would come down and speak to him on the mountain when they heard the sound of a ram's horn. The people were to prepare themselves and keep their distance until then.

Three days later, thunder and lightning struck, and there was a thick cloud

Exodus 19

All of Mount Sinai was covered with smoke because the LORD had descended on it in the form of fire. The smoke billowed into the sky like smoke from a brick kiln, and the whole mountain shook violently.
Exodus 19:18

over the mountain. At the sound of a trumpet blast, Moses led the people to the foot of the mountain. There was fire and smoke, the ground shook, and the trumpet sounded over and over again so that the Israelites trembled.

Then God came to the mountaintop, and Moses went up to meet him.

FEBRUARY 25 — THE TEN COMMANDMENTS

God gave Moses the laws for his people to obey. He carved them onto two stone tablets with his own hand.

EXODUS 20:1-17; 31:18

God gave the people all these instructions: "I am the LORD your God, who rescued you from the land of Egypt, the place of your slavery. You must not have any other god but me."
Exodus 20:1-3

"I am the Lord your God, who brought you out of Egypt, where you were slaves. Do not worship any god but me.

"Do not make idols that look like anything in the sky or on the earth or in the ocean. Don't bow down and worship idols.

"Do not misuse my name. I am the Lord your God.

"Remember that the Sabbath day belongs to me. You have six days when you can do your work, but the seventh day of each week belongs to me, your God. No one is to work on that day.

"Respect your father and your mother, and you will live a long time in the land I am giving you.

"Do not murder.

"Be faithful in marriage.

"Do not steal.

"Do not tell lies about others.

"Do not want anything that belongs to someone else. Don't want anyone's house, wife or husband, slaves, oxen, donkeys, or anything else."

FEBRUARY 26—A SPECIAL PLACE FOR GOD

God didn't just give Moses commandments so the Isrealites would know how best to live lives that pleased him. He also told Moses how he wanted the people to worship him.

God told Moses that they were to build a special tent, a Tabernacle. It should have linen curtains made from blue, purple, and scarlet yarn. The altar should be made of acacia wood, and all the bowls and shovels and meat forks should be made of bronze.

There should be a golden lamp stand with six branches, the cup of each one shaped like almond flowers. The table should be decorated with gold.

God also gave instructions about what the priests should wear. As well as fine linen garments, they should wear a breastplate decorated with 12 beautiful stones—ruby, topaz, beryl, turquoise, sapphire, emerald, jacinth, agate, amethyst, chrysolite, onyx, and jasper—each one to represent one of the 12 tribes of Israel.

"I have chosen Bezalel and Oholiab to do the work," God said to Moses. "I have filled Bezalel with my Spirit so that he will be able to work with many different materials. I will help all the craftsmen to use their gifts."

When God had finished talking to Moses, he gave him the two stone tablets, and Moses took them down the mountain.

EXODUS 25–31

I will live among the people of Israel and be their God, and they will know that I am the LORD their God. I am the one who brought them out of the land of Egypt so that I could live among them. I am the LORD their God.

Exodus 29:45-46

FEBRUARY 27—THE GOLDEN CALF

Moses stayed on the mountain talking with God for 40 days and 40 nights.

At first the people waited, wondering what news Moses would bring from God. Day after day passed. But the longer the people waited, the more tired and restless they became.

"Where has Moses gone?" they asked Aaron eventually. "Anything could

EXODUS 32:1-8

When the people saw how long it was taking Moses to come back down the mountain, they gathered around Aaron. "Come on," they said, "make us some gods who can lead us. We don't know what happened to this fellow Moses, who brought us here from the land of Egypt."
Exodus 32:1

have happened to him in all this time. We cannot wait any longer. Make us gods that we can see and touch!"

Aaron immediately had an idea. The Egyptians had worshipped many golden statues while they had been Pharaoh's slaves. Aaron told the people to give him all their gold jewelry. Then he melted it down and made it into the shape of one of the Egyptian gods. It was a golden calf.

The people were delighted. They thanked the golden calf for leading them out of Egypt. But Aaron realized that this was against God's law. He built an altar and announced that the following day would be a festival to the Lord.

Meanwhile, God had seen the making of the golden calf.

"Go back to the people," God told Moses. "Already they have forgotten that I brought them out of Egypt. They have made an idol to worship."

FEBRUARY 28 — MOSES BREAKS THE STONE TABLETS

Moses hurried down the mountain, carrying the two stone tablets on which God's Ten Commandments were written.

Joshua was waiting for him. Together they heard the noise the people were making.

"The people are shouting! Perhaps they are being attacked!"

"This is not the sound of battle!" Moses replied. "This is the sound of singing and dancing. The people are having a party."

EXODUS 32:15-35

When they came near the camp, Moses saw the calf and the dancing, and he burned with anger. He threw the stone tablets to the ground, smashing them at the foot of the mountain.
Exodus 32:19

Moses went closer and saw the golden calf and the way the people were dancing around it. God's laws had been broken. Moses threw the stone tablets down at the bottom of the mountain—now they were also broken.

Then Moses destroyed the golden calf. He was furious with his brother, Aaron.

"How could you let this happen?" he asked Aaron angrily.

"The people wanted this," said Aaron. "I gave them what they asked for."

"God will punish those who have broken his commandments!" said Moses. Then he turned to the people.

"Who is on the Lord's side?" he asked them. "Anyone who still loves God, come here to me."

Many of the people came to Moses; many more did not.

"God will bless those people who stand firm and worship only him. But he will punish those who do not. I will speak to God and ask for his mercy."

But a plague swept through the people, and many died because they had worshipped the golden calf.

MARCH 1—MOSES ASKS FOR GOD'S MERCY

God was very angry with the Israelites.

"I made a promise to Abraham, Isaac, and Jacob that I cannot break," said God. "I promised that their descendants would live in a land that I would give them. Leave this place, take the people, and go to the Promised Land. But because they have disobeyed me, I will not go with you."

When the people heard what God had said, they were sorry. They wanted God to stay with them.

Moses would sometimes pitch a special tent away from the main camp. Joshua, his assistant, would stand outside the tent. When Moses needed to ask God something, he would go inside, and a pillar of cloud would cover the tent entrance. Then God would speak to Moses as a special friend.

The Israelites would stand at the entrances to their own tents and watch. They would worship God until Moses returned to the camp.

Now Moses spoke to God on behalf of all the people.

"If you are pleased with me, Lord, and will hear me, please teach me your ways. Help me to serve you better. You have called us your own people. But if you will not go with us, how are we different from any other group of people? We need you. Please don't send us to the Promised Land alone."

EXODUS 33:1-16

The LORD replied, "I will personally go with you, Moses, and I will give you rest—everything will be fine for you."
Exodus 33:14

MARCH 2—THE SPACE IN THE ROCK

EXODUS 33:17–34:30

"As my glorious presence passes by, I will hide you in the crevice of the rock and cover you with my hand until I have passed by."
Exodus 33:22

God saw that Moses wanted to obey him and save his people.

"I will do what you ask," God said. "I love my people. I love you and I know you."

"Now let me know you better," said Moses bravely. "Let me see your glory."

"No one can see my face and live," said God. "But there is a place where you can stand on the mountain and I will pass by you. You must stand in the hollow of the rock, and I will cover you with my hand to protect you. But you cannot see my face."

God told Moses to come alone to the mountain the following morning with two new stone tablets.

Moses stood in the hollow of the rock on Mount Sinai. God came and passed in front of him as he had promised.

Then God spoke. "I am the Lord. I am faithful and kind. I love the people I have made, and I long to forgive their disobedience."

Moses fell on the ground and worshipped God.

"I will make a covenant with you, a special promise," said God. "I will lead you to the land I promised to give Abraham and his descendants. But if you disobey my laws, I will punish you."

God wrote the commandments on the two new stone tablets and gave Moses other laws to help the people obey him. Then Moses came down from the mountain.

When the people saw Moses, they were afraid to go near him—his face shone because he had been in God's presence.

MARCH 3—THE CLOUD OF GOD'S PRESENCE

Moses told the people about the special tent they needed to make for God.

"We need to make an Ark (a special wooden chest), a table, an altar, and a lamp stand, and there will be special clothes for the priests to wear. If you are willing, give God anything you have that can be used."

EXODUS 35–40

The cloud covered the Tabernacle, and the glory of the LORD filled the Tabernacle.
Exodus 40:34

The people brought their gold, silver, bronze, and precious jewels. The women spun linen and made cloth out of goat's hair. They brought the best spices and the purest olive oil. They worked for six days of the week and rested on the seventh, as God had commanded.

When the people had finished making everything for the tent of meeting, Moses was pleased with them. The stone tablets were placed inside the Ark, and this was put in the Most Holy Place, separated by a curtain.

Aaron and his sons prepared to be God's priests. They washed themselves and dressed in the special clothes God had designed for them.

Moses set a courtyard around the tent of meeting, made with more curtains. Then a cloud covered the tent, and God's presence filled it. His presence was so great that Moses could not enter.

God's presence remained with the Israelites, just as he had promised. When the cloud lifted, it was time to move on, with God leading the way.

MARCH 4—MIRIAM AND AARON COMPLAIN

For some time the Israelites traveled through the desert. Whenever the cloud rested, they set up camp. When the cloud lifted, they moved on toward the land God had promised them.

Numbers 12

*Moses was very
humble—more
humble than
any other person
on earth.*
Numbers 12:3

But soon they felt their journey was too hard. They started to complain about their troubles, and they complained about the food. They began to wish they were back in Egypt, where they had meat whenever they wanted it and sweet melons and cucumbers. They blamed Moses for everything.

Even Miriam and Aaron complained. They gossiped about Moses' wife and spoke against their brother.

"Why is Moses so special?" they asked. "Can't God speak through us, too?"

God heard what they said.

"Listen carefully to what I have to say," said God. "I have spoken to Moses face-to-face, and he is faithful to me. Who are you to challenge him?"

When the cloud of God's presence lifted, Miriam saw that her skin was covered in a skin disease called leprosy.

"Forgive us, Lord!" cried Aaron. "Please don't let Miriam suffer like this!"

Moses also cried out to God for Miriam to be healed.

"She must stay outside the camp for seven days," said God. "Then she can return."

The people waited. They did not continue their journey until Miriam had returned to the camp.

MARCH 5 — SPIES IN THE LAND

As the Israelites approached Canaan, God told Moses to send one man from each of the 12 tribes to explore the Promised Land.

Moses sent out the men with detailed instructions to find out what kind of people lived there. They were to see how the cities were protected and how fruitful the land was.

At the end of 40 days, the men returned. Two of them carried between them a pole with a heavy branch bearing a single cluster of juicy grapes. They also brought figs and pomegranates.

Moses gathered the people, and they listened to the spies' report.

"The land is good and fruitful," said the spies. "It would be a wonderful place to live. Just look at this fruit!"

But it was not all good news.

"We saw strong, powerful people as big as giants, living in walled cities,"

warned 10 of the spies. "They are too strong for us to fight. We are too weak to try to take over this land."

Then the Israelites were upset. They cried. They complained.

"Let's choose another leader," they said, "and go back to Egypt."

Moses and Aaron got down on their knees in front of all the Israelites. Joshua and Caleb, the other two spies, joined them.

"God has promised to give us this wonderful land. He will help us."

The Israelites would not believe them. They planned to stone them to death. Then God's presence appeared at the tent of meeting.

"How long will you refuse to trust me?" asked God. "Those who have doubted me will wander in the desert for 40 years. Only their children will enter Canaan. Of everyone here today, Caleb and Joshua alone will live in the Promised Land."

NUMBERS 13.1–14:35

The LORD now said to Moses, "Send out men to explore the land of Canaan, the land I am giving to the Israelites. Send one leader from each of the twelve ancestral tribes."

Numbers 13:1-2

MARCH 6—FORTY YEARS IN THE DESERT

When the Israelites heard what God had said, they were sorry.

"We will do what God wanted," they said. "We will go and fight the people who live in the land so that we can make our home in Canaan."

NUMBERS 14:39-45

*"Do not go up into
the land now. You
will only be crushed
by your enemies
because the LORD
is not with you."*
Numbers 14:42

"It's too late now!" cried Moses. "You cannot enter the land safely without God's help. He made a promise, and you refused to believe him. If you go into the land, you will be defeated. God will not go with you."

Moses would not move from the camp. He stayed with the Ark of God's Covenant.

But the Israelites did not listen to him. They went into the hill country, where they were attacked by both the Canaanites and the Amalekites, and they were defeated.

Then the Israelites moved back from the borders of Canaan and made their way toward the desert. For 40 years they wandered there, eating the manna that God provided for their daily needs.

MARCH 7 — MOSES STRIKES THE ROCK

Life in the desert was hard. By the time the Israelites had been there for 40 years, many of those who had lived in Egypt had died. Their descendants arrived at Kadesh, and Miriam died and was buried there. But the people were faced with no water again. A new generation of Israelites began to doubt God's care for them.

"Why did you bring us here?" they moaned to Moses and Aaron. "This is a terrible place. We are thirsty, and there is no water here."

Aaron and Moses left the people and went to the tent of meeting.

NUMBERS 20:1-13

*Moses raised his
hand and struck
the rock twice with
the staff, and water
gushed out. So the
entire community
and their livestock
drank their fill.*
Numbers 20:11

"Take your staff," God said to Moses, "and gather the people so that they will see what I can do. But this time just speak to the rock, and it will pour out water."

Moses took his staff and gathered the people to watch him. But Moses was angry. He had heard the moaning of their parents, and they were no better. Instead of obeying God, Moses held his staff in the air and then hit the rock with it twice.

Immediately, water poured out from the rock, and the people had plenty for their needs.

But God was not pleased with Moses and Aaron. "You did not do what I said. Now you will not be able to lead my people into the Promised Land."

MARCH 8 — THE DEATH OF AARON

As the Israelites approached the land of Edom, they sent messengers to ask if they could go through that country.

"You cannot pass this way," warned the Edomites. "We will come with swords if you try!"

The Israelites asked again—but the Edomites came with a large army and turned God's people back from their borders.

So the people came instead to Mount Hor. Here God told Moses to call Aaron to go to the top of the mountain with his son Eleazar.

"It is time for Aaron to pass on his priestly duties to his son before he dies," said God. So Moses took Aaron's special clothes and dressed Aaron's son in them.

Soon afterward, Aaron died. He was mourned by the Israelites for 30 days.

NUMBERS 20:14-29

When the people realized that Aaron had died, all Israel mourned for him thirty days.
Numbers 20:29

MARCH 9 — THE SNAKE ON A POLE

Again the people traveled around Edom to go to the Red Sea because they could not go through the Edomites' land.

They began to complain once more. First it was the lack of water; then they complained to one another about the bread that God provided for them.

NUMBERS 21:4-9

Moses made a snake out of bronze and attached it to a pole. Then anyone who was bitten by a snake could look at the bronze snake and be healed!
Numbers 21:9

God heard their grumblings and sent poisonous snakes to slither through the camp and bite them.

The Israelites realized that God was angry with them.

"We have sinned," they cried to Moses. "We shouldn't have complained. God has saved us from our enemies. Ask God to take the snakes away."

So Moses prayed.

"Make a bronze snake and put it on a pole," said God. "Anyone who has been bitten should look at the snake on the pole, and they will not die."

Moses did as God told him. Those who looked at the snake lived.

MARCH 10—TWO VICTORIES IN BATTLE

When the Israelites came to Moab, they asked Sihon, king of the Amorites, if they could pass through peacefully. Sihon had already fought for the land and taken it from the Moabites. Sihon would not let them pass through.

Sihon then brought his whole army together and marched into the desert to defend his land. But the Israelites fought back bravely. They began to take Sihon's land and the cities and settlements around it. When they had defeated Sihon, the Israelites settled in the land.

Moses then led the people toward Bashan, near the top of the Sea of

Galilee. King Og and his army marched toward them from Bashan. He did not want the Israelites in his land.

"Don't be afraid of him," God said to Moses. "This victory will also be yours."

So Moses and the people fought King Og until he and his army were also defeated.

Then the Israelites took the land and camped along the Jordan in the plains of Moab. The walls of the city of Jericho were on the other side of the river.

NUMBERS 21:21–22:1

After Moses sent men to explore the Jazer area, they captured all the towns in the region and drove out the Amorites who lived there.
Numbers 21:32

MARCH 11 — BALAAM'S DONKEY

Balak, king of Moab, saw what had happened to King Sihon and to King Og. He saw the large number of Israelites, and he was frightened for his own land and people.

"Send a message to Balaam, the sorcerer," he ordered. "Tell him to come and curse the Israelites, so that I can defeat them. Promise to give him as much money as he wants."

But God spoke to Balaam and warned him not to listen to Balak's messengers. "You must not curse these people. They are my people, and I have blessed them."

Balaam heard God's warning but decided to go to Balak anyway. He saddled his donkey and set off the next morning.

God was angry with Balaam. He sent an angel with a drawn sword to stand in his path. Balaam did not see the angel, but his donkey did. It veered off the road and into the field. Balaam beat the donkey.

Balaam rode on until the angel appeared again in a path between two vineyards. The donkey squeezed against a wall and crushed Balaam's foot. So Balaam beat his donkey once more.

Then the angel blocked Balaam's path in a place where there was nowhere to turn. The donkey lay down, and Balaam beat it again. Then God gave the donkey the gift of speech.

"Why did you beat me?" the donkey asked Balaam. "Would I have stopped if there hadn't been a good reason?"

NUMBERS 22:2-35

The LORD gave the donkey the ability to speak. "What have I done to you that deserves your beating me three times?" it asked Balaam.
Numbers 22:28

Suddenly Balaam was able to see the angel in front of him.

"Why did you beat your donkey?" asked the angel. "It has saved your life! Now listen to what God wants you to do. You can go to Balak, but you must tell him only the words that God gives you to speak."

MARCH 12—BALAAM'S BLESSING

Balaam went to King Balak and asked him to build seven altars. He told him to prepare seven bulls and seven rams and sacrifice them on the altars.

NUMBERS 23–24

Then Balaam went to a barren hilltop to listen to God's message. God told him what to say. Then Balaam brought the message to Balak. "You brought me here to curse Jacob's descendants, the sons of Israel. But how can I curse those whom God has blessed? Everywhere around me I see these people who are not like all the other peoples. They are a good people, and I hope I may die as they do."

The LORD gave Balaam a message for King Balak. Then he said, "Go back to Balak and give him my message."
Numbers 23:5

Balak was very angry.

"I have brought you here to curse my enemies, not bless them!" he said.

"I can only say the words God gives me to say," replied Balaam.

Again Balak prepared seven altars, and again God gave Balaam the words to say.

"God does not lie. God keeps his promises. God brought his people out of Egypt, and he will be with them and bless them," said Balaam.

A third time Balak prepared seven altars, and a third time Balaam delivered God's blessing on his people.

"God saved his people from slavery in Egypt, and he will bless them with a land full of good things. God will make them strong against all their enemies, and no one will be able to stand against them."

Balak was furious! He sent Balaam away with no money for his trouble.

But Balaam left him with a warning: "No amount of money would prevent me from giving you the words that God gave me. But God has warned me that there will come a time in the future when one will come from Israel who is so strong that he will defeat your people."

MARCH 13—A HOLY NATION

After many years in the desert, the Israelites were camped on the border of the Promised Land. It was time for Moses to remind them of all that God had done since their ancestors had left Egypt.

Moses warned them to live in a way that pleased God, following the Ten Commandments. He told them that God wanted them to be a special people who cared about others, who were generous and kind.

"When you enter Canaan," Moses told them, "you must help those among you who are poor. Share what you have, and if you lend or borrow money, after seven years the debt will be canceled. No one among you should be treated unfairly. Be generous to one another, and God will bless you.

"You will be a great nation, and your enemies will be defeated," Moses continued. "You will have abundant harvests and plenty of water, and you will be blessed with many children. Other countries will watch and see that God has blessed you. But God will make you a special and holy nation only if you love him and obey his commandments. He has set before you life or death. Choose life, and live for a long time in the land he will give you."

DEUTERONOMY 29–30

"Today I have given you the choice between life and death, between blessings and curses. Now I call on heaven and earth to witness the choice you make. Oh, that you would choose life, so that you and your descendants might live!"
Deuteronomy 30:19

MARCH 14 — GOD CHOOSES JOSHUA

Moses was now an old man. He had served God well and led his people through many years in the desert. His brother, Aaron, and his sister, Miriam, had died long before.

DEUTERONOMY
31:1-23; 34

*"Do not be afraid
or discouraged,
for the LORD will
personally go ahead
of you. He will be
with you; he will
neither fail you nor
abandon you."*
Deuteronomy 31:8

So Moses spoke to the people one last time. "I am 120 years old, and I cannot lead you anymore. God has told me that I will not cross the Jordan River into the Promised Land. God himself will go with you, and he will give you all that he has promised. Be strong and brave. God will go with you, and you will never be alone."

Then Moses called Joshua to him and laid his hands on him in front of all the people. "Be strong and full of courage. God has chosen you to lead his people into the Promised Land. You must take them there and divide the land between them."

Moses blessed the people, and then he climbed Mount Nebo. God showed Moses all the land that he would give to the Israelites.

"This is the land I promised to give to the descendants of Abraham, Isaac, and Jacob," God said.

Moses looked at the land and was content to die. He died in Moab and was buried there.

The Israelites mourned his death. They knew that Moses had spoken to God face-to-face. He had done wonderful things, and he had spoken God's words to his people.

Then God's Spirit came to Joshua. He was wise and obedient, and the Israelites listened to him.

MARCH 15 — RAHAB AND THE SPIES

Joshua prepared to enter Canaan by sending spies into the city of Jericho on the other side of the Jordan River.

The spies went secretly to a house built into the city walls and talked to Rahab, the woman who lived there. But the king of Jericho was told that there were spies in Rahab's house, so he sent a message for her to hand them over.

Rahab hid the spies under the bundles of plants drying on her roof. Then she sent a message to the king saying that the spies had left earlier by the city gate.

JOSHUA 2:1-21

"Now swear to me by the LORD that you will be kind to me and my family since I have helped you."
Joshua 2:12

Rahab watched as the king's men went in pursuit of the spies. When it was safe, she went to the men who were hiding and made a bargain with them.

"All my people know that your God dried up the waters of the Red Sea and saved you from the Egyptians," she said. "We know that he is with you now and will give you the city of Jericho. We are afraid because God is on your side. Promise me that you will help me and save my family when you come to capture the city."

The spies agreed. They told her to hang a scarlet cord from her window in the city wall and to have her whole family there in the room when the Israelites came into the city. Then the spies went out through the window and down the city walls, escaping to hide in the hills.

JOSHUA 2:23–5:1

The priests who were carrying the Ark of the LORD's Covenant stood on dry ground in the middle of the riverbed as the people passed by. They waited there until the whole nation of Israel had crossed the Jordan on dry ground.
Joshua 3:17

MARCH 16 — CROSSING THE JORDAN RIVER

The spies brought Joshua news that the people of Jericho feared for their lives. God had gone before them to take the city.

Now Joshua had to cross the Jordan River with all the people.

"Today, everyone will know that I am with you, just as I was with Moses," said God. He told Joshua how he would lead the people across the river.

At Joshua's command, the priests carried the Ark (the special wooden chest) into the river, and the people followed. Immediately, the waters that ran downstream stopped flowing. The priests stayed in the middle of the river, and the Israelites—men, women, and children—crossed on dry land.

"Choose one man from each of the 12 tribes," God said to Joshua. "Tell them to take one stone each from the middle of the riverbed and to place it near where you camp tonight. Then your children and grandchildren will know what I have done for you."

When all the people had crossed the river, the priests carrying the Ark of the Covenant walked to the other side too. Only then did the waters flow again.

No one wanted to fight against the Israelites after this. Everyone in Canaan heard what God had done for them.

MARCH 17 — VICTORY IN JERICHO

JOSHUA 5:13–6:25

When the people heard the sound of the rams' horns, they shouted as loud as they could. Suddenly, the walls of Jericho collapsed, and the Israelites charged straight into the town and captured it.
Joshua 6:20

Joshua camped with the people outside Jericho. They celebrated the Passover and waited until God told them what to do next.

Then a man with a sword in his hand appeared in Joshua's path. Joshua knew the man had been sent by God, and he fell to his knees.

"I am the commander of God's army," said the man. "This is what you must do. Seven priests must lead you in a march around the city walls. The priests must walk in front of the Ark, each carrying a trumpet, for six days. On the seventh day, they must march around the city walls seven times, blowing their trumpets. On the long trumpet blast, signal to the people to shout. Then the city walls will collapse."

The gates of the city of Jericho stood before Joshua and his army, firmly closed against them.

For six days they marched as God had told them. On the seventh day, at the sound of the long trumpet blast, the people shouted, and the walls of Jericho crumbled and fell down.

Then the Israelites marched into the city. God had given them the victory. They found Rahab and her family and kept them safe, as they had promised.

MARCH 18—STOLEN SILVER AND GOLD

"Don't take anything for yourselves when we march into the city!" Joshua warned his troops as they entered Jericho. "Everything belongs to God."

But Achan found a beautiful robe, some silver, and a bar of gold, and he hid them secretly under his tent.

Joshua then sent 3,000 soldiers into Ai to take the city. Spies had been sent in and reported that it could be defeated without the whole army in place. But the Israelites were defeated at Ai, and 36 soldiers were killed.

Joshua prayed to God.

"Why have you let us be defeated, Lord? We trusted you to help us."

JOSHUA 7

*Israel violated the
instructions about
the things set apart
for the LORD. A
man named Achan
had stolen some
of these dedicated
things, so the LORD
was very angry
with the Israelites.
Achan was the son
of Carmi . . . of the
tribe of Judah.*
Joshua 7:1

"Someone has disobeyed me," God replied. "He stole from Jericho and kept riches for himself. Then he lied about it."

Joshua gathered the people. When Achan stood accused in front of him, Joshua challenged him.

"Tell me what you have done," he said. "Men died because of this. Hide nothing from me."

Achan admitted that he had cheated and lied, and Joshua sent his men to find the stolen items. Then Achan was put to death for his disobedience.

MARCH 19—VICTORY AT AI

God told Joshua that the time was right to attack the city of Ai.

"Don't be discouraged," said God. "This time you will win the battle."

Joshua chose his army.

JOSHUA 8:1-29

*The LORD said
to Joshua, "Do
not be afraid or
discouraged."*
Joshua 8:1

"Half of you must go by night and hide on the far side of the city," he said. "In the morning, the rest of us will attack the city gates. The king of Ai will chase us, and we will lead his army away from the city. Then we can take Ai while it is not defended."

Joshua and his army advanced. The king and his troops ran out to fight the Israelites as they had done before. Then they chased them as far as the desert.

God told Joshua to give the rest of the army a signal—and when he did

they came from behind and burned the city to the ground. When the Israelites saw the smoke, they turned back to fight the soldiers of Ai, who were now surrounded.

Joshua's men drove them into the desert. God had given them the victory.

MARCH 20 — THE PEACE TREATY

As Joshua took the Israelites further into Canaan, all the kings around grew afraid.

The people of Gibeon decided not to fight. They preferred to make a deal with Israel. So they dressed in old clothes and loaded their donkeys with cracked wineskins and stale bread to trick the Israelites.

"We have come from far away," they lied. "We want to make a peace treaty with you."

Joshua and his leaders did not ask God what they should do. They made a peace treaty with the Gibeonites. When they realized that these men were their enemies and lived in Canaan, they were angry.

"We will not break our promise," said Joshua, "but you must now work for us, cutting wood and carrying water for us."

"Your God is a great God," the Gibeonites told Joshua. "We know that he has promised to give you this land and destroy everyone else who lives here. We wanted peace. We will work for you rather than die."

JOSHUA 9

When the people of Gibeon heard what Joshua had done to Jericho and Ai, they resorted to deception to save themselves.
Joshua 9:3-4

MARCH 21 — THE SUN STANDS STILL

King Adoni-zedek from Jerusalem heard about the pact the Gibeonites had made with Joshua.

He feared what Joshua could do with their help, so he joined forces with four other kings in Canaan.

"Come with me and let's attack Gibeon!" he said.

Once the attack had begun, the Gibeonites sent for help.

"Joshua! Come and rescue us! The Amorite kings want us dead!" the messenger reported. "We are your servants. Help us!"

JOSHUA 10:1-15

There has never been a day like this one before or since, when the LORD answered such a prayer. Surely the LORD fought for Israel that day!
Joshua 10:14

God spoke to Joshua. "Don't be afraid. I will help you defeat the Amorites."

So Joshua marched toward Gibeon and took the Amorites by surprise. As the enemy armies fled, God sent huge hailstones from the sky, which fell on the enemy soldiers and killed them.

Then in the middle of the day, Joshua prayed.

"Don't let the sun go down till we have the victory!" he said.

And God answered him. The sun did not set until the battle was won.

MARCH 22—THE BATTLE FOR CANAAN

JOSHUA 11–12

As the LORD had commanded his servant Moses, so Moses commanded Joshua. And Joshua did as he was told, carefully obeying all the commands that the LORD had given to Moses.
Joshua 11:15

As Joshua led the Israelites northward, King Jabin of Hazor watched his progress.

"Come and fight these Israelites with me!" he said to his allies. They gathered a huge army, with horses and chariots, and set out to confront the Israelites.

When Joshua saw his enemies approaching, it seemed that they numbered more than the grains of sand on a beach.

"Don't be afraid," God said to Joshua. "By this time tomorrow you will have defeated them."

Joshua trusted God and made a surprise attack at the water near Merom. By crippling the horses and burning the chariots, Joshua was able to defeat his enemies.

Joshua led the Israelites in victory over 31 kings. Canaan was theirs at last. Now the Israelites could enjoy the land that God had promised them.

MARCH 23 — THE TWELVE TRIBES OF ISRAEL

The Israelites had the land of Canaan before them. Joshua's last task was to divide the land between all the tribes of Israel.

Jacob had had 12 sons. The sons of Levi were priests and did not take a share of the land. The land that should have been Joseph's was divided between his two sons. So the land was divided into 12 parts.

At last, the people could stop wandering and receive their inheritance, their new home.

"Don't forget all that God has done for you," said Joshua. "Remember to love him and keep his laws, and he will never forget his promises to you. You will live safely in the land as long as you don't marry the people on your borders or worship their gods. The Lord is our God. He has made an agreement with us as he did with Abraham, Isaac, and Jacob."

JOSHUA 13–19

"Be sure to give this land to Israel as a special possession, just as I have commanded you."
Joshua 13:6

MARCH 24 — CALEB'S REWARD

Many years had passed since Joshua and Caleb were spies in Canaan. They alone had been allowed to see the day when the people would settle in the land God had promised. They alone had believed God would keep his promises even when the other spies would not trust him. Joshua and Caleb had seen God help them conquer their enemies. Now it was time for Caleb to receive the reward Moses had promised.

"Moses promised 45 years ago that I would have a share of the land to pass on to my children," Caleb said to Joshua. "Now I am 85! But God has kept me fit and well for this day. Please give me the hill country of Hebron. I know the people there are unfriendly, but I am still strong. God will take care of me."

Joshua blessed his old friend Caleb. He knew that he loved God and trusted him still. He gave Caleb the area of Hebron as his special reward.

JOSHUA 14:6-15

Joshua blessed Caleb son of Jephunneh and gave Hebron to him as his portion of land.
Joshua 14:13

MARCH 25 — JOSHUA SAYS GOOD-BYE

JOSHUA 23–24

"But as for me and my family, we will serve the LORD."
Joshua 24:15

There was peace in the land of Canaan.

Joshua lived to be 110 years old. When he knew that his death was near, he called together the leaders of the people to say good-bye.

"I am old and must soon die," he said to them. "You have seen for yourselves how God has kept his promises and given us this land. Now you must be strong and always keep God's laws. You must keep yourselves separate from the other nations around you. You must love God with all your hearts."

Then Joshua brought together all the people with a message from God. "Remember that I, the Lord God, brought Abraham out of a land where they worshipped other gods. I brought him to Canaan and gave him Isaac. I gave

to Isaac his sons, Esau and Jacob. When Jacob's family went into Egypt, I sent Moses and Aaron to lead them out of slavery. Then I brought you across the Jordan River and helped you defeat all the Amorites and the other people who lived in Canaan. Now this land is yours."

Then Joshua challenged the people again to put away all foreign gods. "Choose today which god you will trust and worship. As for me and all my family, we will serve the Lord."

Then the people affirmed their faith in God and promised to trust and obey him alone. Joshua took a large stone and placed it under an oak tree at Shechem.

"This stone will be here always as a reminder of your promise to serve the living God."

Joshua died and the people buried him. Aaron's son Eleazar, the priest, died and was buried also. And the bones of Joseph that had been brought from Egypt were buried at Shechem.

MARCH 26—THE PEOPLE FORGET GOD'S LAWS

It was not long before a whole generation of Israelites who loved and served the Lord had died. Their children quickly forgot what they had been taught. They chose not to follow God's laws but worshipped the gods of the people around them.

Soon the Israelites began to marry people from the nations around them. They were no longer God's separate people. They worshipped Baal and Ashtoreth—the gods the Canaanites believed gave them rain to grow their crops and large families to carry on their family name.

The Israelites lived in ways that angered God, and they forgot the promises their ancestors had made.

Without God's help, their lands were robbed, and they were defeated in battle. Then Cushan-rishathaim, king of Aram, overpowered them and made them his subjects for eight years.

The Israelites were no longer free. They began to call out to God for help once more.

JUDGES 2:10-15; 3:5-8

The Israelites did evil in the LORD's sight. They forgot about the LORD their God, and they served the images of Baal and the Asherah poles.
Judges 3:7

MARCH 27—CALEB'S NEPHEW TO THE RESCUE

JUDGES 3:9-14

When the people of Israel cried out to the LORD for help, the LORD raised up a rescuer to save them.

Judges 3:9

God had compassion on his people; he did not forget them.

God brought them a judge, Othniel, who was Caleb's nephew. The Spirit of the Lord came to Othniel, and he was able to guide the people back to God's laws.

Othniel went to war against Cushan-rishathaim, and with God's help, he overpowered the king of Aram so that there was once more peace in the land of Canaan.

For 40 years Othniel guided the Israelites, but when he died, the people returned to their old ways. They rebelled against God's laws and did wicked things that angered God once more.

Then God allowed Eglon, the king of Moab, to make a pact with Israel's enemies, the Ammonites and the Amalekites. Eglon gathered an army and captured Jericho, the city of palms.

The Israelites were once more overpowered, and for 18 years they were Eglon's subjects.

Then, as before, they called to God for help.

MARCH 28—EHUD, THE LEFT-HANDED JUDGE

JUDGES 3:15-30

Moab was conquered by Israel that day, and there was peace in the land for eighty years.

Judges 3:30

God heard the cries of his people, and he sent Ehud, from the tribe of Benjamin, to rescue them.

When King Eglon demanded tax money from the Israelites, the people chose Ehud to take it to the king.

Ehud, a left-handed man, made a long double-edged sword and strapped it to his right thigh, underneath his clothes.

First Ehud bowed before the king and gave him the payment. He sent away the men who had helped him carry the money and gifts and then whispered, "I have a secret message for you, Your Majesty."

Eglon was curious and sent his attendants away. He invited Ehud to enter the upper room of his summer palace, not realizing that he was armed.

Ehud approached the king, who was a very fat man.

"I have a message from God for you," he said. Ehud reached for his sword

and plunged it into the king's belly, killing him. Quietly, Ehud left the room, locked the doors behind him, and made his escape.

When Ehud reached the hill country, he blew his trumpet. The Israelites rushed down the hills.

"Follow me!" cried Ehud as he led the people into battle. "God has helped us defeat the people of Moab!"

The Moabites were conquered by the Israelites, and there was peace in the land for 80 years.

MARCH 29—DEBORAH AND BARAK

When Ehud died, the Israelites stopped following God's ways again. It was not long before God let one of the kings who lived in Canaan rule over them.

King Jabin had a large and fierce army under the command of a man named Sisera. He equipped his troops with 900 iron chariots, and for 20 years he ruled harshly over Israel. The Israelites suffered and cried out to God.

Deborah, the wife of Lappidoth, led Israel at this time. She was a prophet who served the living God, and people would come to her for wisdom when they had arguments to settle.

JUDGES 4:1-10

Deborah, the wife of Lappidoth, was a prophet who was judging Israel at that time.
Judges 4:4

God spoke to Deborah about King Jabin. Then she sent for a warrior named Barak.

"I have a message for you from God," Deborah told Barak. "You must take 10,000 troops and march to Mount Tabor. God will bring Sisera and King Jabin's army toward the Kishon River. Then they will be trapped, and you can defeat them."

But Barak was frightened.

"I cannot do this alone," he said. "You must come with me."

Deborah was disappointed by Barak's response, but she agreed.

"But be warned!" she said. "Because you have not acted on God's instructions, a woman will have the victory over Sisera."

MARCH 30—JAEL'S TENT PEG

When Sisera heard that Barak was leading an attack, he gathered his army and 900 chariots by the Kishon River and waited.

Barak went up to Mount Tabor with his troops, where they were safe from the chariots.

"Attack!" called Deborah to Barak. "This is what God wants us to do. Today we will defeat our enemies."

Barak's troops charged down the hillside, attacking Sisera's army and slashing with their swords. God also sent a storm that caused the river to flood, and the chariots got stuck in the mud.

Sisera abandoned his chariot and ran away from the battle. He knew that his army could not win. He headed toward some tents belonging to a man named Heber.

I'll be safe here, thought Sisera. *Heber and King Jabin are friends.*

Heber's wife, Jael, saw Sisera. She knew who he was. "Don't be afraid," she said. "No one will find you here in my tent." Sisera went inside and asked for a drink. Jael gave him milk and hid him under some covers.

"Keep watch!" he pleaded. "If someone comes looking for me, don't tell them I am here!" He was exhausted and fell fast asleep.

But Jael was on God's side. She did not keep watch. Instead, she drove a tent peg through his head and killed him.

Barak charged through Heber's camp, looking for Sisera.

"Look no further," said Jael. "I will show you the man you have come for."

Barak saw the body of his enemy, killed by a woman, just as Deborah had prophesied. King Jabin was unable to fight back.

"Praise the Lord!" sang Deborah and Barak. "He has defeated our enemies."

JUDGES 4:11–5:31

Deborah said to Barak, "Get ready! This is the day the LORD will give you victory over Sisera, for the LORD is marching ahead of you."
Judges 4:14

MARCH 31 — THE CAMEL RIDERS

The Israelites enjoyed peace for another 40 years, but then they forgot all the things that God had done for them. They went back to their evil ways—and God left them to the mercy of the Midianites.

The Israelites hid in the mountains and were afraid to stay in the open. The Midianites would wait until the Israelites had grown their crops, then they would arrive on camels and spoil the land or steal what they had grown. So the Israelites were weak from hunger and frightened for their lives. They lived like this for seven years.

When the Israelites cried to the Lord for help, he sent them a prophet.

"We have disobeyed God!" the prophet warned the people. "That is why we are being attacked by our enemies."

JUDGES 6:1-10

When they cried out to the LORD because of Midian, the LORD sent a prophet to the Israelites.
Judges 6:7-8

APRIL 1 — GIDEON, THE RELUCTANT HERO

Gideon, the son of Joash, was trying to harvest wheat in secret, out of sight of the Midianites.

An angel came to sit under an oak tree and watched him.

"God is with you, mighty warrior!" the angel said to Gideon.

"Then why are we in so much trouble?" Gideon asked. "God brought our ancestors out of Egypt only to let us die under the Midianites!"

"You can change that," said the angel. "God wants you to save Israel from the Midianites."

"But why would God send me? I am no one! I belong to the smallest clan in my tribe. I am the least in my family!"

"You can do this because I will be with you," said the angel of the Lord. "We will save Israel together."

Gideon was amazed. "Please show me a sign," said Gideon. "Prove to me that this is not just a dream."

Gideon rushed home and returned with food as an offering.

"Put the food on a rock," said the angel.

Gideon did so, and the angel touched it with his staff. The food caught on fire, and the angel disappeared.

Then Gideon believed that he had been in the company of an angel sent by God, and he was afraid.

"You have nothing to fear, Gideon," said the Lord. "You will not die."

JUDGES 6:11-23

"But Lord," Gideon replied, "how can I rescue Israel! My clan is the weakest in the whole tribe of Manasseh, and I am the least in my entire family!"
Judges 6:15

APRIL 2 — GIDEON AND THE SHEEPSKIN

That night, God told Gideon to destroy the altar to Baal and the Asherah pole that belonged to his father. In their place, Gideon was to build an altar to the living God.

Gideon did this secretly at night, but in the morning, when the local men saw what had happened, they came to find him.

"Hand him over!" they demanded of Gideon's father. "Your son must die!"

"Whose side are you on?" asked Joash. "If Baal is really a god, surely he can defend himself!"

So the crowd left Gideon alone.

The Midianites joined forces with the Amalekites. They crossed over the Jordan River and set up camp.

Then Gideon was filled with God's Spirit. He blew his trumpet and gathered together the Israelite men from every tribe.

Gideon prayed for God's help.

"I need to be sure that you want me to save Israel," said Gideon. "I will put a sheepskin on the ground this evening. In the morning, if the sheepskin is wet and the ground is dry, I will know that you want me to lead Israel."

In the morning Gideon squeezed the sheepskin. It was wet, but the ground all around was dry.

"Don't be angry with me, Lord, but I must be sure. Let me put the sheepskin out again, only this time let the ground be wet and the sheepskin dry."

In the morning the ground was covered with dew, and the sheepskin was dry. God had answered Gideon.

JUDGES 6:25-40

Gideon said to God, "Please don't be angry with me, but let me make one more request. Let me use the fleece for one more test."
Judges 6:39

APRIL 3 — GIDEON'S SMALL ARMY

JUDGES 7:1-8

The LORD told Gideon, "With these 300 men I will rescue you and give you victory over the Midianites."
Judges 7:7

The Israelite army gathered together and set up camp.

"You have too many soldiers," said God to Gideon. "When the battle is won, the people will say that they did it in their own strength. Tell anyone who is afraid that they may go home."

That day 22,000 men went home. Only 10,000 remained.

"There are still too many," said God. "Ask the men to go to the river and drink."

Some of the men knelt down to drink, while others stood up and lapped the water out of their hands like dogs.

"I will use the men who stood up and lapped the water," said God. "Send the others home."

Gideon obeyed God. He now had an army of just 300 men to fight the Midianites.

APRIL 4 — BATTLE BY NIGHT

"It is time!" God said to Gideon during the night. "Now you will defeat your enemies! But first, go down to the enemy camp and listen to what is said. Then you will not be afraid to attack."

Gideon went silently with his servant to the enemy camp. There were

tens of thousands of men. There were more camels than grains of sand on the seashore. But Gideon had just 300 men.

"I've had a terrible dream!" Gideon heard one man say to another. "A huge, round barley loaf rolled into our camp and hit the tent so powerfully that the tent fell apart!"

"I know what that means," said the other. "God is on Gideon's side. They will win the battle."

Gideon thanked God for what he had heard. He returned and woke his men.

"Come! God has already won the battle!" he told them.

Gideon divided the men into three groups and gave each man a trumpet and a burning torch covered by an empty jar. In the darkness, the Israelites surrounded the enemy camp. At Gideon's signal, he and his men blew their trumpets and smashed the jars.

"For the Lord and for Gideon!" they cried.

The Midianites and the Amalekites were terrified. They stumbled and fell upon each other in the darkness. They killed each other with their swords. Those who remained ran to the hills.

It was just as God had said. God had rescued the Israelites once again.

JUDGES 7:9-25

They all shouted, "A sword for the LORD and for Gideon!"
Judges 7:20

APRIL 5 — ABIMELECH KILLS HIS BROTHERS

The people went to Gideon and asked him to rule over them.

"The Lord God will rule over you. You need no other," he said. "Neither I nor my sons will be your ruler." But one of Gideon's sons had other ideas.

Gideon had married many wives and had many children. One of his sons was named Abimelech. His mother was one of Gideon's slaves. Abimelech went to his mother's hometown of Shechem after Gideon's death and spoke to his relatives.

"Choose me as your leader. Don't let any of my half brothers rule over you."

Abimelech's relatives agreed, and he hired a band of men to follow him. Then he went to his father's hometown and killed all his half brothers. Only the youngest, Jotham, escaped. Then Abimelech returned to Shechem, and the people crowned him king.

JUDGES 8:22-23, 30-31; 9:1-24

[Abimelech] went to his father's home at Ophrah, and there, on one stone, they killed all seventy of his half brothers, the sons of Gideon.
Judges 9:5

When Jotham heard this he went to Shechem and climbed to the top of Mount Gerizim.

"Remember what my father did for you!" he cried. "Now think about what you have done to his family!"

Abimelech ruled Israel for three years, but God had seen the evil thing he had done.

APRIL 6—ABIMELECH'S PUNISHMENT

A man named Gaal came to Shechem. Before long he had a number of friends and supporters.

"What's so special about Abimelech?" he asked. "If you followed me, I would easily defeat Abimelech and his whole army."

Zebul, the governor of Shechem, was angry when he heard Gaal's bragging.

"Gaal is stirring up trouble," he warned Abimelech. "Make a surprise dawn attack and destroy him and his followers."

As Abimelech approached Shechem, Zebul went to Gaal.

"So, you think you can destroy Abimelech's entire army?" he sneered. "Well, now's your chance!"

Gaal and the citizens of Shechem fought Abimelech, but they were driven out of the city.

The next day, when Abimelech attacked Shechem again, the people hid in the temple. But Abimelech and his men chopped down branches and laid them against the walls of the temple and set fire to them so that the people inside were all killed.

Abimelech then marched on to Thebez. The people fled from their homes and locked themselves in a strong tower. Abimelech made his way toward the entrance to burn it as he had before, but this time one of the women saw what Abimelech was trying to do. She lifted a heavy grinding stone and flung it down on top of him. It landed on Abimelech's head and cracked his skull.

"Kill me with your sword," the wounded Abimelech begged his servant. "Don't let them say a woman killed me!"

The servant obeyed. When the Israelites saw what had happened, they left the city. God had punished Abimelech for the terrible things he had done.

JUDGES 9:26-57

A woman on the roof dropped a millstone that landed on Abimelech's head and crushed his skull.
Judges 9:53

APRIL 7—JEPHTHAH'S FOOLISH PROMISE

The Israelites continued to disobey the Lord God, and the Ammonites ruled over them.

The elders of Gilead went to Jephthah, who was a great warrior, and asked him to be their leader.

"If you defeat the Ammonites, we will make you our leader," they said.

So Jephthah agreed.

First Jephthah sent a peaceful message to the Ammonite king.

"What have we done to you that you rule over us in this way?" he asked.

"You took my land when God brought you out of Egypt," said the king. But Jephthah knew this was not true.

"We did not take your land but the land of those who would not let us pass safely through on our journey out of Egypt. Then we took the land that God gave to us. We have lived here now for hundreds of years. If you really had any claim on the land, why make it now?" he asked.

When the king of Ammon ignored him, Jephthah knew that God was leading him into battle.

"I will make a bargain with you," Jephthah foolishly said to God. "If you help me defeat my enemies, I will sacrifice the first thing I see when I return home!"

JUDGES 11

So it has become a custom in Israel for young Israelite women to go away for four days each year to lament the fate of Jephthah's daughter.
Judges 11:39-40

Jephthah led the Israelite army into victory. Then he went home. The first thing he saw was his only daughter, dancing. When Jephthah saw her, he remembered what he had promised God. He tore his clothes and wept. He knew that he had made a promise to God that he could not break.

APRIL 8—THE BIRTH OF SAMSON

JUDGES 13

When her son was born, she named him Samson. And the LORD blessed him as he grew up.
Judges 13:24

After Jephthah died, the people returned to their old ways. This time they were attacked by the Philistines, who then ruled over them for 40 years.

During this time, God sent an angel to a childless woman, the wife of a man named Manoah.

"I know you have no children," said the angel, "but God will give you a son. He will save Israel from the Philistines. You must drink no wine before his birth, and when he is born you must let his hair grow long as a sign that he has been dedicated to God."

The woman was amazed, and she told her husband. Manoah prayed to God to send the angel again so that they could be sure to do all that God asked of them. The angel came again and repeated all he had said, and Manoah realized that God had blessed them with a special task.

Some months later, the woman gave birth to a son and called him Samson. God blessed the child and prepared him for the work he had to do.

APRIL 9—SAMSON'S RIDDLE

When Samson grew up he wanted to marry a Philistine woman.

His parents were unhappy—why couldn't he find a wife from his own people? But the marriage was part of what God had planned for him.

His parents set off to make the wedding arrangements. Samson followed after them. As Samson walked through a vineyard, a young lion bounded toward him, ready to attack. God filled Samson with his Spirit and gave him amazing strength. He fought with the lion, killing it with his bare hands. But Samson told no one what had happened.

Some time later, Samson returned to the vineyard. Bees had made a

nest within the lion's dead body, and there was honey inside. So during the wedding feast, Samson told his Philistine companions a riddle.

"Out of the eater, something to eat. Out of the strong, something sweet. Tell me the answer to my riddle within seven days, and I will give you a prize. If not, you must reward me."

The Philistines had no idea how to solve the riddle, but they did not want to give Samson a reward either. Instead, they threatened Samson's new wife to find the answer. She wept and she cried and she begged him to tell her the secret of the riddle until finally Samson gave in. Then his wife told her people.

The Philistines gave Samson the answer to his riddle.

"What is sweeter than honey? What is stronger than a lion?" they cried.

Samson knew he had been tricked. He was very angry. He wanted to get his revenge.

JUDGES 14:1-18

"Out of the one who eats came something to eat; out of the strong came something sweet."
Judges 14:14

APRIL 10—SAMSON'S REVENGE

Samson went from the wedding feast and brought back the prize he had promised to give the Philistines. But he left to return to his father's house afterward. His father-in-law assumed he did not want his daughter, so he gave Samson's wife to another man.

When Samson returned to see his wife, he found that she was no longer his. In his anger, he took revenge on the Philistines.

He went out and caught 300 foxes and tied their tails together in pairs. Then he fastened a flaming torch to every pair of tails and let the foxes loose in the cornfields.

The Philistines soon came looking for Samson. They sent men from Judah to capture him.

Samson allowed himself to be tied up by the men, but as soon as the Philistines came toward him, God gave him enormous strength. Samson broke through the ropes as if through butter. Then he used the jawbone of a donkey to fight and kill 1,000 of his enemies.

Then Samson fell to his knees dying of thirst. He prayed to God to give him water after his victory, and God caused a spring to open up so that he could drink.

Samson led the Israelites against the Philistines for 20 years.

JUDGES 14:19–15:20

Samson judged Israel for twenty years during the period when the Philistines dominated the land.
Judges 15:20

APRIL 11 — DELILAH BETRAYS SAMSON

Time passed, and though the Philistines hated Samson, they could do nothing because God had given him such enormous strength.

Then Samson fell in love with a woman named Delilah. The Philistine leaders seized their chance. They offered Delilah bribes.

"Find out the secret of Samson's strength," they said to her, "and we will reward you."

Delilah was determined to find out the secret.

"Tell me the secret of your strength," she whispered to him one night.

"Tie me with seven new bowstrings, and I will be as weak as any man," Samson replied.

The Philistines brought Delilah the bowstrings, and while they hid in the room, she used them to tie Samson while he slept.

"The Philistines are here!" she screamed. Samson leaped up, and the strings snapped under his strength.

"You lied to me," said Delilah, some time later. "Show me you trust me. Tell me your secret."

"You need new ropes," he replied. "Then I will be weak."

Delilah tried the same trick again, but Samson snapped the ropes as if they were thread.

"Weave the seven braids of my hair into the fabric of your loom," said Samson, the next time she asked. This time he broke the loom.

Delilah continued to nag Samson every day.

"If you love me, you will tell me the secret of your strength," she said.

Eventually Samson could stand it no longer. "My hair has never been cut," he told her. "If my head is shaved, I will lose my strength."

Delilah made sure that Samson was asleep. Then one of the Philistines shaved the seven braids on his head. Samson's strength vanished. His enemies overpowered him, then blinded him and put him in prison. He could not fight back. His strength had gone.

JUDGES 16:4-22

Some time later Samson fell in love with a woman named Delilah, who lived in the valley of Sorek.
Judges 16:4

APRIL 12 — SAMSON DEFEATS HIS ENEMIES

The Philistines were delighted that at last they had captured their enemy. They organized a celebration to thank their god, Dagon, for their success.

"Let Samson entertain us!" cried the people.

So Samson was brought out from the prison to amuse them. All the Philistine rulers were there. The temple was filled with the laughter of people of all ages, including 3,000 on the roof. They had not noticed that Samson's hair had begun to grow again.

JUDGES 16:23-30

*[Samson] prayed,
"Let me die with
the Philistines."*
Judges 16:30

Samson could no longer see. He asked the servant who guided him to put him between the pillars of the temple.

Then Samson stretched out his arms.

"Remember me, Lord God," prayed Samson, "and give me strength once more. Punish the Philistines, and let me die as I have lived, destroying the enemies of your people."

Samson pushed at the pillars with all his might. God answered his prayer and gave him back his strength. The giant pillars toppled, pulling the walls inward and bringing the roof crashing to the ground.

Samson destroyed the Philistine temple and with it thousands of Philistines. He died in the attempt but killed more of his enemies by his death than he had in his lifetime.

APRIL 13 — ELIMELECH'S FAMILY SETTLES IN MOAB

There was a famine in Israel during the time of the judges.

Elimelech took his wife, Naomi, and left his home in the area around Bethlehem with his sons, Mahlon and Kilion. They went to the land of Moab to find food.

Elimelech died in Moab. Mahlon and Kilion married women from among the local people, and the family settled there for about 10 years. But then Naomi's sons died too, and the three women were left alone.

Naomi heard that the famine had ended in Israel. There was no reason for her to stay in Moab, so she decided to return to her home near Bethlehem.

"Stay here and return to your own mothers," Naomi told her sons' widows. "I will go back alone."

But the two young women, Ruth and Orpah, did not want to leave Naomi.

"But I have nothing to offer you," Naomi protested. "I am too old to give you husbands again, even if I could marry. You will do better to stay here in Moab."

So Orpah turned and went home. But Ruth clung to her mother-in-law.

"Don't tell me to go!" she begged. "I will never leave you. I will go with you to your country, and it will become my country. Your people will become my people, and your God will become my God. I will go where you go, and I will die where you die and be buried there."

Naomi saw that Ruth was serious, so the two women went on to Bethlehem, where they arrived at the beginning of the barley harvest.

Ruth 1

Ruth replied, ". . . Wherever you go, I will go; wherever you live, I will live. Your people will be my people, and your God will be my God."
Ruth 1:16

APRIL 14—RUTH WORKS IN THE FIELDS

With no one to provide for them, Naomi and Ruth were hungry.

"I will go and pick up the leftover grain in the fields," Ruth told Naomi.

God blessed Ruth, and she found herself working in the fields belonging to Boaz, a relative of Elimelech's. She worked hard, and Boaz asked one of his workers who she was.

"She is Naomi's daughter-in-law," the man replied. "She came from Moab to keep her mother-in-law company, even though her husband had died."

Boaz went over to talk to Ruth.

"Stay and gather grain in my fields," he said, "and take some water whenever you are thirsty."

"Why are you being so good to me?" Ruth asked.

"I have heard of your kindness to Naomi," he replied. "You have come to ask help from Naomi's God. May God now bless you and reward you for your loyalty to her."

Boaz provided Ruth with food that day, and there was enough for her to

Ruth 2

Ruth went out to gather grain behind the harvesters.
Ruth 2:3

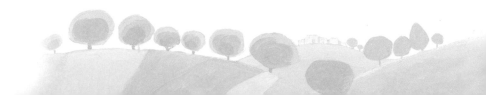

take some home to Naomi, as well as the barley Ruth had gathered. Boaz had made sure that plenty was left for her.

Naomi was amazed at the amount Ruth brought home.

"Where did you go?" she asked. "Someone has surely been kind to you."

Ruth told Naomi about the kindness of the landowner. "His name is Boaz," she added.

"He is a relative of ours!" exclaimed Naomi. "You must go to his fields again tomorrow."

APRIL 15 — RUTH AND BOAZ

RUTH 3

"Now don't worry about a thing, my daughter. I will do what is necessary, for everyone in town knows you are a virtuous woman."
Ruth 3:11

Ruth worked in Boaz's fields until the end of the harvest, and she and Naomi did not go hungry. But at the end of that time, Naomi spoke to Ruth about her future.

"It's my duty to try to find a better home for you," she said. "We know that Boaz has been kind to you, and we are also related to him. It is our custom that if a man dies leaving a young wife, a relative should marry her to care for his family."

"What must I do?" asked Ruth. "Tell me and I will do it."

Ruth did all Naomi told her to do. Ruth went to the threshing floor where Boaz had been celebrating the end of the harvest. She lay down at his feet while he slept, and waited. When he woke in the night, he was surprised.

"Who's there?" he asked.

Ruth told him why she had come.

"I will look after you," said Boaz kindly, "but there is another relative who should be asked first. If he is happy to let you go, I will take care of you and Naomi."

When Ruth returned home, she told Naomi all that had happened. Then together they waited.

April 16 — Naomi's Grandson

Boaz went to the town gate and found Naomi's relative. In front of the elders of the people, Boaz asked him if he wanted to buy Elimelech's land, marry Ruth, and raise children for her dead husband, Mahlon. The man decided that he could not do it and offered it to Boaz.

Boaz was happy. He married Ruth, and God blessed them all. Some time later, Naomi found herself not only happy in Boaz's household but proudly looking after her first grandchild.

"Everything was taken from me, but God gave me Ruth, who was better than all that was taken away. Now I have Obed, my grandson, too, and God has blessed me."

Obed grew up to have a son named Jesse, who had eight sons. The youngest son was called David.

RUTH 4

Boaz took Ruth into his home, and she became his wife. When he slept with her, the LORD enabled her to become pregnant, and she gave birth to a son.
Ruth 4:13

April 17 — Hannah's Sorrow

Every year Elkanah and his two wives, Hannah and Peninnah, went to Shiloh to worship God and make a special sacrifice.

Peninnah had many children, but though Hannah longed to have a baby of her own, she had none. Peninnah often teased Hannah, until Hannah cried so much she couldn't eat.

1 SAMUEL 1:1-20

In due time [Hannah] gave birth to a son. She named him Samuel, for she said, "I asked the LORD for him."
1 Samuel 1:20

One year, Hannah went to the place of worship and poured out all her sorrow.

"Lord God," she prayed in her heart, "if you will answer my prayer and let me give birth to a son, then I promise to give him back to you, to serve you all his life. Please hear me and help me!"

When Eli, the priest, saw Hannah's lips moving but heard no sound, he thought she had been drinking and rebuked her. But when Hannah told him of her unhappiness and what she had asked God, he was kind.

"May God answer your prayer and bless you," he said.

Hannah returned home. God did answer her prayer and bless her. Before long she found that she was expecting a baby. She gave birth to a son and called him Samuel.

APRIL 18—HANNAH KEEPS HER PROMISE

Hannah cared for her baby son for several years, and she loved him dearly. But then Hannah took Samuel to the place of worship in Shiloh and went to Eli, the priest.

"Do you remember the unhappy woman who came here and asked God to bless her with a baby son?" she asked him. "I am that woman, but I am no longer unhappy. God has blessed me, and now I must keep my promise. My son must live here in the temple and learn how to serve God."

1 SAMUEL 1:21–2:26

"Now I am giving him to the LORD, and he will belong to the LORD his whole life."
1 Samuel 1:28

Every year after that, Hannah came to visit Samuel and bring him a new robe that she had made for him.

Eli asked God to bless Hannah so she would have other children, and in time she had three more sons and two daughters.

Eli had two sons of his own named Hophni and Phinehas. They had grown up and become priests like their father. But both were selfish men who broke God's rules and did not serve God well.

Eli was sad when he saw how his sons behaved, and he warned them that God would be angry with them. But Hophni and Phinehas did not listen to him.

Samuel became Eli's helper. God watched as Samuel grew up, and he blessed him.

APRIL 19 — GOD SPEAKS IN THE NIGHT

As Eli grew older, his eyes became weak, and he depended more and more on Samuel's help.

One night, while the golden lamp stand was still lit and everyone was asleep, God called to Samuel.

"Samuel! Samuel!" God called.

Samuel woke at the sound of the voice, but he did not know who it was. He got up and went to Eli.

"Here I am!" said Samuel. "You called me!"

"No, I didn't call," said Eli. "Go back to sleep."

Before long Samuel heard the voice calling him again.

"Samuel! Samuel!" God called.

He went again to Eli.

"I didn't call you," said Eli. "Go back to your bed."

Then Samuel heard the voice for a third time.

He went once more to Eli. But this time Eli understood who was calling him.

"God is calling you," said Eli. "Go back to your bed. But this time, if the voice calls your name, reply, 'Speak, Lord, for your servant is listening.'"

God called Samuel again, and he answered. Then God told Samuel of his plans for his people and for Eli's sons.

1 SAMUEL 3

Samuel replied, "Speak, your servant is listening."
1 Samuel 3:10

From that day on, God spoke to Samuel, and Samuel learned to listen to and act on all that God asked him to do.

Eli and all the people saw that God was with him and that he spoke with God's authority. Samuel was the prophet that God had sent to help his people.

APRIL 20 — THE DEATH OF ELI

When the Israelites went into battle with the Philistines and were defeated, they returned to camp and decided to take with them the Ark of the Covenant.

I SAMUEL 4

"The people have been slaughtered, and your two sons, Hophni and Phinehas, were also killed. And the Ark of God has been captured."
1 Samuel 4:17

Eli's sons, Hophni and Phinehas, went with the Ark. They believed that if the Ark was with them in battle, God was with them too.

The Philistines saw how brave the Ark made the Israelite soldiers. They began to tremble and be afraid. These were the same people whose God had brought them out of Egypt!

Both sides entered into battle, but although the Ark was there, God was not with the Israelites that day. Hophni and Phinehas died along with 30,000 men. The Philistines captured the Ark of the Covenant and carried it away with them.

A young man ran from the battle line to tell the Israelites what had happened. When he told the people, they were all very afraid.

Eli was sitting at the gate, waiting. He was almost blind and very frail.

"What has happened?" Eli asked. "Tell me everything."

"Our people have fled from the enemy. We have lost a great many men today in battle. Your two sons are dead, and the Philistines have captured the Ark of the Covenant."

When Eli heard about the capture of the Ark, he was greatly shocked and fell down dead. His daughter-in-law, the wife of Phinehas, was expecting a baby at that time.

At the news, she went into labor and gave birth to a son. She named him Ichabod, because she believed that God had left his people.

APRIL 21 — THE ARK IN DAGON'S TEMPLE

The Philistines took the Ark of the Covenant to Ashdod, where they put it next to their god, Dagon, in the temple there.

The next day, the people went into the temple and found that the statue of their god had fallen on its face in front of the Ark of the Covenant. They lifted the statue and put it back again, but the next morning, it had not only fallen again but its head and hands had broken off.

Then there was a plague on the people of Ashdod, and the town was filled with rats. They suffered terribly and began to see that the Ark of the Covenant could not stay in their town. They moved it to Gath, but then there was a plague on the people of Gath. They moved it to Ekron, and the same thing happened there.

"Take the Ark away!" cried the people. "Send it back to the Israelites, or we will all die!"

So the Ark of the Covenant was put on a cart with some gifts of gold and hitched up to two cows. They put it on the road and set it on its way.

"If the cows go straight to the country of the Israelites, we will know their God has sent these plagues," they said. "But if not, then all our suffering has just been an act of chance."

But the cart went in the direction of the Israelites' country.

1 SAMUEL 5:1–6:15

[The Philistines] carried the Ark of God into the temple of Dagon and placed it beside an idol of Dagon.
1 Samuel 5:2

The Israelites rejoiced to see the Ark returned to them! They sacrificed the cows that had pulled the cart, and they worshipped God.

APRIL 22 — SAMUEL LEADS GOD'S PEOPLE

1 SAMUEL 7:2-15

Throughout Samuel's lifetime, the LORD's powerful hand was raised against the Philistines.
1 Samuel 7:13

After Eli's death, Samuel waited to see when the people would call out to God again. When he thought they were sorry that they had worshipped other gods and were ready to try again to follow God's ways, he called them all together.

"If you are ready to return to God and love him with all your hearts, then you must destroy all the idols you own and promise to serve God alone," he said. "Then God will drive out the Philistines."

The people destroyed all the images of Baal and the images of Ashtoreth they had collected, and they worshipped God once more.

Then Samuel told them he would pray for them.

"We have sinned, Lord, and we are sorry. Please forgive us. Be our God as you were the God of our ancestors."

When the Philistines threatened to attack the Israelites at Mizpah, the people were afraid.

But Samuel offered sacrifices to God and kept on praying.

God heard the prayers of his people. He sent thunder, which threw the Philistines into confusion and gave the Israelites the opportunity to attack and defeat their enemy.

Samuel set a stone in the ground and called it Ebenezer to mark the fact that God had helped his people there.

From that time on, Samuel became Israel's leader, and he judged the people wisely.

1 SAMUEL 8

"Look," they told [Samuel], "you are now old, and your sons are not like you. Give us a king to judge us like all the other nations have."
1 Samuel 8:5

APRIL 23 — THE PEOPLE WANT A KING

Samuel grew old, and although he had sons, they did not listen to God or obey him, just as Eli's sons had not.

"We want a king like all the other nations!" cried Israel's elders as they stood before Samuel. "You are old, and there is no good man to follow you who serves God."

Samuel was sad, and he was angry with the people. He prayed to God.

"Listen to the people," said God. "They are not rejecting you. They are rejecting me. A king cannot bring them what they want, but they are just as stubborn as their ancestors before them. They must learn this for themselves. They can have a king, but he will bring them great unhappiness."

Samuel warned the people as God told him to, but they refused to listen.

April 24—The First King of Israel

There was a man named Kish who had a son called Saul—a tall, handsome young man.

1 SAMUEL 9:1–10:1

Kish's donkeys had wandered off into the hills.

"Take one of the servants and go find the donkeys," Kish told his son.

So they went first to the hill country nearby, then, when they did not find them, farther away.

"We had better go back," Saul said to his servant after several days. "Soon my father will stop worrying about his donkeys and start worrying about his son!"

But the servant had heard that Samuel was in the area.

"There is a man of God nearby. Perhaps we could ask him about the donkeys."

Samuel took a flask of olive oil and poured it over Saul's head. He kissed Saul and said, "I am doing this because the LORD has appointed you to be the ruler over Israel, his special possession."
1 Samuel 10:1

Saul agreed to go and talk with Samuel before returning home.

God had already told Samuel that he had chosen the man who would be Israel's future king. When Samuel saw Saul walking toward him, he knew that this was the man God had chosen.

"We are looking for the seer, God's prophet," Saul said. "Can you direct us to him?"

"You have found him," Samuel answered. "Come and eat with me, and tomorrow I have something important to tell you. But don't worry anymore about your lost donkeys. They have been found."

The following day, Saul and his servant prepared to go back home. Samuel told Saul to order his servant to go on awhile without him.

When they were alone, Samuel poured some oil on Saul's head and anointed him to be the first king of Israel.

"God will change you and give you power to be the person who will be Israel's king. Don't be afraid, for God is with you."

APRIL 25 — SAUL, THE WARRIOR KING

Saul returned to his family, but he told no one about God's plans for him.

Then Samuel called all the people together.

"You have rejected the Lord God, who brought your ancestors out of Egypt," he said. "You have chosen to have a king rule over you instead. Now come so that we can see whom God has chosen to be this king."

Samuel went through the tribes of Israel until Benjamin was chosen. He went through the families until the family of Kish was chosen, and then Saul, his son. Saul was a tall, strong, fine-looking man.

"Long live the king!" shouted God's people when Samuel presented their new leader to them.

Meanwhile, the Ammonites attacked the Israelite city of Jabesh. The people of Jabesh wanted to make peace with them.

"We will make peace on one condition," agreed the Ammonites. "We will blind all your people in one eye."

When the Israelites heard this, they were afraid. But God gave Saul the power to lead them. He called them all together and led them in a surprise attack so that the Ammonites were defeated.

1 SAMUEL 10:16—11:15

Then Samuel said to all the people, "This is the man the LORD has chosen as your king. No one in all Israel is like him!" And all the people shouted, "Long live the king!"
1 Samuel 10:24

Then the people cheered for Saul as their warrior king. He had helped them to victory and made them brave in battle. The Israelites had what they had asked for: a king like the other nations.

April 26—Jonathan Fights the Philistines

God gave Samuel rules so that Saul would be a good king. At first Saul listened and did what God told him to do. But as time went on, Saul started to act without God's blessing.

1 Samuel 13:1–14:23

They killed some twenty men in all, and their bodies were scattered over about half an acre.
1 Samuel 14:14

"You have disobeyed God," Samuel told Saul. "Now he will look for another king, a man who listens to him and obeys him."

One day King Saul and his army were preparing themselves for a battle with the Philistines, who continued to attack Israel. Saul's son Jonathan left the group unnoticed, taking his armor bearer with him.

"Let's find out what the Philistines are doing," Jonathan said to him. "God can use just the two of us if he will bless us and give us victory."

They climbed up into the rocky mountains.

"We'll let the enemy see us," Jonathan told his armor bearer. "If they say,

'We're coming to get you!' we'll stay here. But if they say, 'Come here and get us!' we'll know God will help us defeat them."

As soon as the Philistines saw Jonathan, they dared him to come and fight. Then Jonathan knew what God wanted him to do. He climbed over the rocks, his servant following behind. The Philistine army fell back as Jonathan approached, and soon Jonathan and his armor bearer had killed many of their enemies. Then God sent an earthquake, causing the Philistines to panic and kill each other with their own swords.

God had given the Israelites victory through Jonathan.

APRIL 27—JESSE'S YOUNGEST SON

1 SAMUEL 15:1–16:13

The LORD was sorry he had ever made Saul king of Israel.
1 Samuel 15:35

Saul continued to do what he thought was right, even when it was the opposite of what God told him to do. He gave in when the people wanted to take what once belonged to their enemies. This brought Samuel sadness.

"God wants your obedience, not your sacrifices on altars," Samuel told

him. "God has warned me that because you have rejected his guidance, he is rejecting you as king."

Samuel wept about Saul's disobedience and stayed away from him, waiting to see what God would do next.

"Fill your horn with oil," God said one day. "I have chosen the man who will be king after Saul. Go to Bethlehem and invite a man named Jesse to a feast."

So Samuel went to Bethlehem and held a feast for all the people.

When Samuel saw Jesse's oldest son, he felt sure that he must be God's choice. But God said no.

"I have not chosen him, Samuel. You see what a person looks like on the outside, but I see what is inside the heart."

Samuel met Jesse's second son. But he was not the one God had chosen.

When Samuel had met seven of Jesse's sons and none of them was the one God had chosen, Samuel asked whether Jesse had any more sons.

"My youngest son is looking after the sheep," replied Jesse.

So they sent for David and brought him to the feast.

When Samuel saw him, God told him that this was his chosen king. So Samuel anointed David with oil in front of all his family, and God's Spirit filled him.

APRIL 28—THE KING'S UNHAPPY MOODS

Once God had stopped blessing Saul, the king suffered from depression, and his mind was full of bad, unhappy thoughts.

1 SAMUEL 16:14-23

"Let us find someone who plays soothing music," his servants offered.

Saul agreed and asked them to find someone.

"One of Jesse's sons plays well," suggested a servant. "He is a fine young man, and he loves the living God."

So King Saul sent a message to Jesse to bring his son to him.

Jesse loaded a donkey with gifts of bread and wine and a young goat and took David to see the king.

David played his harp whenever the king suffered from his unhappy moods, and Saul was happy to have David there. He asked Jesse to let David stay and become one of his armor bearers.

Whenever the tormenting spirit from God troubled Saul, David would play the harp.
1 Samuel 16:23

APRIL 29 — THE SHEPHERD'S SONG

David made up songs and sang them when he played his harp.

You, Lord, are my shepherd. I will never be in need.
You let me rest in fields of green grass.
You lead me where there are streams of cool water,
and you give me peace.
You lead me along the right paths,
because you can only do what is right.
I may walk through valleys as dark as death,
but I won't be afraid, because you are with me and care for me
as a shepherd makes his sheep feel safe.
You treat me as an honored guest at a feast
while my enemies watch.
You fill my cup until it overflows.
Your kindness and love will always be with me every day of my life,
and I will live forever in your house, Lord.

PSALM 23

The LORD is my shepherd; I have all that I need.
Psalm 23:1

APRIL 30 — THE GIANT'S CHALLENGE

The Israelite battle line was gathered on one hill; the Philistines were on the other. In between them was a valley, and in the valley was the Philistine champion, a giant of a man named Goliath.

His huge head and body were protected by a bronze helmet and bronze armor. He carried a long bronze spear on his back. In his hand was a spear with a heavy iron point. Day after day, Goliath walked up and down in front of the Israelites, challenging them to send a man to fight him.

The Israelites were terrified. No one would go.

One day David brought food supplies to the Israelite camp. He saw Goliath walking up and down and shouting, and he saw that no one stood up to him.

"How dare he challenge us!" said David to the men around him. "We have the living God on our side."

King Saul heard the rumors among his soldiers and sent for David.

"Our army should not be afraid of this warrior," David said. "I will go out and fight him."

"This giant is a professional fighter," Saul said. "You are just a boy."

"I look after my father's sheep," answered David, "and have to fight off lions and bears to protect them. If God can save me from the paws of the lion and the bear, he can surely save me from this Philistine."

David tried on the king's armor, but it was too big and heavy for him. Instead he took his sling and chose five small stones from the stream.

When Goliath saw him, he sneered.

David shouted back, "You have sword and spear, but I have the living God on my side! Today the whole world will know that there is a God in Israel who can save us."

David slipped a stone into his sling and whirled it around his head. The stone shot through the air and hit Goliath's forehead. He sank to the ground, and the Israelite army cheered. Their enemy's champion was dead, and his army had run away.

1 SAMUEL 17

David triumphed over the Philistine with only a sling and a stone.
1 Samuel 17:50

MAY 1 — SAUL, THE JEALOUS KING

After David had defeated Goliath, he became good friends with Jonathan, King Saul's son, and married one of Saul's daughters.

Saul gave David many things to do, and he saw that God blessed him in everything. Saul then gave him a position of great authority in his army, and David was both popular with the people and successful.

Saul watched all that happened. Soon Saul felt jealous that David was everything Saul thought a king should be.

One day when David was playing his harp, Saul felt so much anger and jealousy toward David that he picked up his spear and threw it at him. Saul missed and David was not hurt, but Saul had hoped to kill him.

Then Saul sent David away. He could not bear to have him close by. But Saul saw that God blessed David whenever David led the Israelites into battle with the Philistines.

1 SAMUEL 18

This was their song: "Saul has killed his thousands, and David his ten thousands!"
1 Samuel 18:7

MAY 2 — JONATHAN'S WARNING

Jonathan went to his friend David one day.

"David, you must hide," warned Jonathan. "My father wants to kill you. You are not safe here. I will speak to him and try to convince him that you mean him no harm."

King Saul listened to Jonathan and promised not to kill David. But at the next chance, Saul threw his spear at David again. Once more David escaped.

"I don't understand why your father wants to kill me," said David at one of their secret meetings. "How can I trust him and be safe?"

"He tells me everything," said Jonathan, "and you are my closest friend. I will not let him hurt you. Now, he will expect you at the new moon feast. If it is safe for you to come, I will send you a sign. But if your life is in danger, then you will also know."

When everyone except David came to the feast, King Saul asked his son where David was. Jonathan made excuses for his friend, but Saul burst into a furious rage.

1 SAMUEL 19:1-10; 20

At last Jonathan said to David, "Go in peace, for we have sworn loyalty to each other in the LORD's name."
1 Samuel 20:42

"What kind of son are you to side with my enemy! I know you are protecting him! Now go! Bring David here so I can kill him!"

Jonathan went out into the field and shot some arrows. He sent a boy to fetch them, giving the agreed sign. Then David knew his life was still in danger. Jonathan was warning him to run away.

May 3 — David, the Outlaw

David could think of only one place where he could hide from King Saul. He went to the priests who lived at Nob.

"I'm here on a secret mission from the king," David said. "I left in a hurry and have no weapon. I need something to eat and a sword or spear, if you have one."

Ahimelech the priest only had the special holy bread, but he gave this to David to eat. The only weapon there was Goliath's sword. David took the sword with him.

David moved on, but Saul's head shepherd, Doeg, was there that day. He went to tell Saul the way David had gone. He also told Saul that the priest had helped David.

"I will have all the priests killed for their part in David's escape," Saul said in his anger.

1 SAMUEL 21–22

David left Gath and escaped to the cave of Adullam.
1 Samuel 22:1

Saul's own men would not hurt the priests, but Doeg went and killed not only Ahimelech and the other priests but everyone who lived in the town of Nob. Only one man escaped. He was Abiathar, Ahimelech's son.

Abiathar fled and found David and the men he had gathered around him. David was angry when he heard what Saul had done, and he was very sad for all the lost lives.

"This is all my fault," he told Abiathar. "You must stay here, and I will keep you safe."

MAY 4—DAVID SPARES SAUL'S LIFE

1 SAMUEL 24

[David] said, "I will never harm the king— he is the LORD's anointed one." 1 Samuel 24:10

David and his men kept on the move to escape from King Saul. But when he heard that the Philistines were attacking the town of Keilah, David asked God what he should do.

"Go and protect the town," said God. "They need your help against their enemies."

So David and his men fought and defeated the Philistines and saved the people of Keilah. But Saul heard of the victory and came looking for David with 3,000 men.

David was camping in the hills of En-gedi when Saul came searching for

him. Saul entered the cave where David's men were hiding, but he did not realize that they were there deep inside the dark cave.

"Look," one of his men whispered to David. "God has given you this opportunity to kill your enemy!"

David crept up to Saul and cut off a part of his cloak without him knowing. But he would not kill the man God had made king. He waited until Saul had left the cave, then went out and called to him.

"King Saul!" David called as he went on his knees. "Look here at the cloth cut from your cloak. Now do you believe that I have done nothing to harm you and I don't want to kill you?"

Saul wept at the sound of David's voice. "You have been good to me today, and I don't deserve this. God has blessed you, and he will make you king after me. But promise that you will not kill all my family."

David promised, and Saul returned home. But David continued to hide from Saul.

MAY 5 — ABIGAIL'S WISDOM

The prophet Samuel died and was buried at Ramah. He did not live to see David become king. Instead, David and his men were living in the wilderness, hiding from King Saul.

For some time they had protected the shepherds of a rich but foolish man named Nabal. As the time for sheep shearing and feasting came near, David sent some of his men to ask if any food could be spared for them.

Nabal was known for his bad manners, and he saw no reason to be kind to David and his men. He sent the men away rudely and with nothing.

David was angry. He told his men to arm themselves to fight.

Meanwhile, a servant went to tell Nabal's wife, Abigail, how rude and unkind her husband had been. Abigail was beautiful, and she was also wise. She knew what danger Nabal had placed them all in.

Abigail prepared a feast for David's men—bread, wine, roasted sheep, plenty of grain, clusters of raisins, and fig cakes—and without telling her husband, she went out on a donkey into the mountains to meet David.

"Please forgive my husband's bad manners," she said to David. "Don't be

1 SAMUEL 25

David replied to Abigail, "Praise the LORD, the God of Israel, who has sent you to meet me today!"
1 Samuel 25:32

angry with us, but accept these gifts of food. We know that God has blessed you and protects you from your enemies. Now please—shed no blood in anger."

David accepted her gift and praised God for preventing him from killing the men there.

"Thank you," he said to Abigail. "Go home in safety."

Nabal was drunk when Abigail returned home. The next morning she told him what she had done. But soon after, Nabal became ill and died.

David did not forget what Abigail had done to help him. When he heard that Nabal had died, he asked her to be his wife.

MAY 6—DAVID'S NIGHT RAID

1 SAMUEL 26

"God has surely handed your enemy over to you this time!" Abishai whispered to David.
1 Samuel 26:8

Again Saul took his 3,000 men to search for David.

David's spies watched while Saul and his army set up camp. The king was surrounded by his troops, and Abner, the commander of Saul's army, was by his side.

"Who will come with me to see Saul?" David asked his friends.

"I will," offered Abishai.

When it was dark, the two men crept down to Saul's camp, where everyone was sleeping deeply. Close to King Saul's head lay his spear, its point stuck in the ground. By his side was a water jug.

"Let me kill Saul while we have the chance," whispered Abishai to David. "God has given his life to us."

"No!" ordered David. "Don't touch him! He is still God's chosen king."

Instead, David told Abishai to pick up the spear and water jug, and they left the camp as quietly as they had come.

"Speak to me, Abner!" shouted David from a safe distance. "You haven't been protecting your king! Where are your master's spear and water jug?"

Saul recognized David's voice and realized what had happened. He knew that once more David had spared his life.

"May God bless you for not killing me," cried the king.

Then David asked the king to send a man to collect his spear.

MAY 7 — SAUL'S FINAL DEFEAT

David knew that King Saul would soon be searching for him again.

He took 600 of his men and escaped to the land of the Philistines. The Philistine king, Achish, knew that Saul and David were enemies. He let David settle in his land. Achish preferred to have David as a friend rather than an enemy.

Meanwhile, Saul prepared to lead the Israelite army. He wanted Samuel's advice—but Samuel was dead. So Saul disguised himself and went to Endor to find a woman who claimed to be able to speak to the dead.

1 SAMUEL 28–29; 31

When Saul saw the vast Philistine army, he became frantic with fear.
1 Samuel 28:5

"I must talk to Samuel," he told her.

"Surely you know that King Saul has forbidden anyone to talk to the dead! It is against God's law," she said.

Saul reassured her that she would be safe, and she called to Samuel. But as soon as she saw the dead prophet, she knew that the disguised man in front of her was King Saul himself.

"Tell me what Samuel says," Saul commanded. "You need fear nothing from me."

But Samuel had no good news for Saul.

"Why do you call me?" asked Samuel. "You have done all those things God told you not to do. Now God has left you. Tomorrow you will be defeated by the Philistines. You and your sons will all die."

King Achish gathered his army to fight the Israelites. He had told David to fight with him against David's own people, but the Philistine commanders were unhappy about this. They told King Achish that they did not want David fighting on their side.

So when the Philistines defeated the Israelites the next day, David was not there to watch his friend Jonathan be killed in battle or to see King Saul fall on his own sword rather than be killed by the Philistines.

Israel's first king was dead.

MAY 8—DAVID, KING OF JUDAH

2 SAMUEL 2:1-11

David asked the LORD, "Should I move back to one of the towns of Judah?"
2 Samuel 2:1

After Saul's death, David wanted to return to his own land.

"Should I go back to Judah?" David asked God.

"Yes," said God. "Go to the town of Hebron."

So David took his two wives, the men who had fought with him, and their families, and they all settled in Hebron. Men from the southern tribe of Judah came to Hebron and welcomed David and made him their king.

Meanwhile, Abner, the commander of Saul's army, had made Saul's son Ishbosheth king over the northern part of the land. The people in the north did not accept David as their king. So the land was divided. Israel included the tribes in the north and Judah those in the south.

MAY 9—THE FIGHTING COMMANDERS

David's army, under the command of Joab, sat on one side of the pool of Gibeon. Ishbosheth's army, under the command of Abner, was on the other side.

"Let's choose 12 champions and let them fight!" said Abner. "Whichever side does best will win the battle."

There was a fierce contest between the two sides, but all the soldiers died. There was no winner. Then war broke out with both armies fighting each other. David's men were stronger, and Ishbosheth's army was defeated.

Abner fled from the battle, chased by Asahel, Joab's brother.

Abner turned and tried to talk sense into Asahel.

"Stop chasing me!" shouted Abner. "I don't want to have to kill you."

2 SAMUEL 2:12-32

*Abner shouted
down to Joab,
"Must we always
be killing each
other! Don't
you realize that
bitterness is the
only result!"*
2 Samuel 2:26

But Asahel would not give up, and Abner killed him with a spear.

Abner then tried to make a peace agreement with Joab. At sunset, he and his men called to Joab from the hilltop.

"We should be on the same side," Abner said. "This fighting is senseless. Let's stop now!"

So Joab agreed to end the battle, but he did not forget that Abner had killed his brother.

MAY 10—ABNER CHANGES SIDES

Over time David married more wives and had six sons. Each child had a different mother.

The trouble between the lands of Judah and Israel continued, but David's side was stronger. Soon Abner decided to go over to David's side because King Ishbosheth made him very angry.

When Joab discovered that King David had made peace with Abner, he was furious. He found an opportunity to be alone with Abner, and then he murdered him as revenge for his brother's death.

David was very sad when he heard how Abner had died. He knew that he had been a brave soldier, and he mourned his death openly. So all the people knew that he had not been involved in Abner's death.

2 SAMUEL 3

*Joab and his
brother Abishai
killed Abner
because Abner had
killed their brother
Asahel at the battle
of Gibeon.*
2 Samuel 3:30

MAY 11 — THE MURDER OF ISHBOSHETH

When Ishbosheth heard that Abner was dead, he was afraid. All of Israel was afraid.

Then one day, while Ishbosheth was taking his rest in the heat of the afternoon, two strangers arrived. They crept into the house and found the king lying on his bed. They stabbed and killed him, then cut off his head. Thinking that this would please King David, they took his head as a trophy and brought it to Hebron.

"We have brought you the head of your enemy," they told David.

David could not believe what they had done.

"You murdered an innocent man while he slept in his own bed!" he cried. "You must die for your crime."

The two men were taken out and executed, but David made sure that Ishbosheth's head was buried with Abner.

2 SAMUEL 4

When they arrived at Hebron, they presented Ishbosheth's head to David.
2 Samuel 4:8

MAY 12 — THE CAPTURE OF JERUSALEM

Once people realized that Ishbosheth was dead, they met together at Hebron.

"Years ago we were one nation, and we fought together against our enemies," they said to David. "God promised that you would look after us as a shepherd looks after his sheep. We want you to be our king now."

So when David was 30 years old, he was made king of all Israel.

David gathered together an army and marched toward the protected city of Jerusalem, which was set on a hill. The city was controlled by the Jebusites, a Canaanite tribe.

"You are no match for us here!" they bragged. "Not even David will be able to defeat us."

But David found the tunnel that had been dug under the city to bring in water from the Gihon spring.

He surprised the Jebusites by entering the city through the water tunnel and was able to capture Jerusalem.

David made the fortress his capital, and from then on it became known as the City of David.

2 SAMUEL 5:1-9

David was thirty years old when he began to reign, and he reigned forty years in all.
2 Samuel 5:4

MAY 13—DAVID DANCES

Now that he was king and living in Jerusalem, David wanted to bring the Ark
of the Covenant there as a sign of God's presence. So the Ark was placed on a
new cart and was carefully guided along the road.

Suddenly one of the oxen pulling the cart stumbled. Uzzah put out his
hand and touched the Ark to stop it from falling. But at that moment he fell
down, dead.

David was angry. He knew that the Ark was holy and that the instructions
were clear about not touching the Ark, but David thought it was unfair that
Uzzah had been struck dead.

"I can't bring the Ark back to Jerusalem now," said David. "The day is
ruined."

So David left the Ark in Obed-edom's house.

Three months later, David was told how much God had blessed Obed-
edom because he was looking after the Ark of the Covenant. Then David
knew he had to bring the Ark back to Jerusalem so that God would bless the
whole nation.

Everyone gathered as the Ark was carried into Jerusalem. They sang to
God, and David celebrated by joining the people and dancing before God.

Michal, David's wife, saw him dancing in the streets.

2 SAMUEL 6

*David went there
and brought the
Ark of God from
the house of
Obed-edom to
the City of David
with a great
celebration.*
2 Samuel 6:12

What a fool he is making of himself! she thought.

When the celebrations were over, Michal went out to meet David.

"I saw you dancing with the people today!" she sneered. "You didn't behave the way a king should."

"It doesn't matter what you think of me," said David to his wife. "I was praising God and dancing for God. And he chose me to be king rather than your father, Saul, because God knew what was in my heart."

MAY 14—GOD'S DWELLING PLACE

2 SAMUEL 7

"The LORD declares that he will make a house for you—a dynasty of kings!"
2 Samuel 7:11

David built a palace made of cedar wood in Jerusalem. His enemies knew that God was with him, and Israel enjoyed a time of peace.

One day David spoke to Nathan, the prophet, about the Ark of the Covenant.

"It does not seem right that I live here in a palace while the Ark lives in a tent," said David. "I think I should build a Temple fit for God."

That night Nathan heard God speaking to him.

"I don't want David to build a Temple for me," said God. "I have been happy to move from place to place with my people. My plan for David is to make Israel into a great nation. I will make him a great king, and I will never stop loving him. After David will come one of his sons. I will also love him, and he can build me a Temple. David's family will be kings for a long time to come."

Nathan told David everything that God had said. David was amazed at the plans God had for him, and he was humbled.

"I don't know why you have chosen me or looked after me," said David, "or why you have told me your plans. But I do know that you are a great God, and you always keep your promises."

MAY 15 — THE GOD WHO KNOWS EVERYTHING

David wrote this song as a prayer to God.

You have looked deep into my heart, Lord, and you know all about me. You know when I am resting and when I am working, and from heaven you discover my thoughts.

You notice everything I do and everywhere I go. Before I even speak a word, you know what I will say, and with your powerful arm you protect me from every side.

I can't understand all of this! Such knowledge is far above me. Where could I go to escape from your Spirit or from your sight?

If I were to climb up to the highest heavens, you would be there. If I were to dig down to the world of the dead, you would also be there.

Suppose I had wings like the dawning day and flew across the ocean. Even then your powerful arm would guide and protect me.

Or suppose I said, "I'll hide in the dark until night comes to cover me." But you see in the dark, because daylight and darkness are all the same to you.

You are the one who put me together inside my mother's body, and I praise you because of the wonderful way you created me. Everything you do is marvelous!

Nothing about me is hidden from you! I was woven together in a secret place, but with your own eyes you saw my body being formed. Even before I was born, you had written in your book everything I would do.

Your thoughts are far beyond my understanding, much more than I could ever

PSALM 139

O LORD, you have examined my heart and know everything about me.
Psalm 139:1

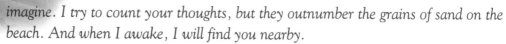

imagine. I try to count your thoughts, but they outnumber the grains of sand on the beach. And when I awake, I will find you nearby.

Look deep into my heart, God, and find out everything I am thinking. Don't let me follow evil ways, but lead me in the way that is true.

MAY 16 — DAVID IS KIND TO JONATHAN'S SON

David often thought of his friend Jonathan, who had died in battle.

"Does Saul have any family still living?" David asked one day. "I would like to be kind to his relatives for Jonathan's sake."

"There is one called Mephibosheth," Ziba told the king. "He is Jonathan's son. He was dropped when he was five years old, and both his feet are damaged."

"I'd like to help him," said David. "Bring him here."

Mephibosheth was nervous about being brought before King David.

"Don't be afraid, Mephibosheth," David told him. "Your father was my greatest friend. I promised to look after his family. Come and live in the palace with me, and I will give you the land that belonged to your family."

Mephibosheth was amazed that a great king like David would keep his promise and take care of him. He lived in Jerusalem and was treated as part of David's family from that time on.

2 SAMUEL 9

The king then asked him, "Is anyone still alive from Saul's family? If so, I want to show God's kindness to them."
2 Samuel 9:3

MAY 17 — DAVID BREAKS GOD'S RULES

One evening in springtime, when the Israelite army was away fighting, King David went out onto the palace rooftop.

As he looked across the city, he saw a woman bathing in the courtyard of a nearby house. She did not know she was being watched. She was a very beautiful woman.

David called a servant and asked who she was.

"That's Bathsheba," the servant replied, "Uriah's wife."

David knew Uriah. He was a soldier in his army. But at that moment, David did not care whose wife she was. He wanted Bathsheba for himself.

"Bring Bathsheba here," he ordered.

2 SAMUEL 11:1-5

As [David] looked out over the city, he noticed a woman of unusual beauty. . . . He sent someone to find out who she was.
2 Samuel 11:2-3

Bathsheba came to the palace, and David slept with her.
Some time later, Bathsheba sent a message to David.
"I'm pregnant," she said. "The baby I am carrying is yours."

MAY 18 — URIAH DIES IN BATTLE

David was anxious about Bathsheba's news. He quickly thought of a plan
to cover up the wrong he had done. David sent a message to Joab at the
battlefront, asking him to send Uriah home.

Uriah returned to Jerusalem, and David asked him about the progress of
the war with the Ammonites.

Afterward David told him to go home and relax and spend time with his
wife. But Uriah would not go home.

"How can I enjoy myself while all my fellow soldiers are fighting?" he said.
"It would be wrong."

Sadly, David let Uriah return to the battlefield. He asked him to take with
him a letter for Joab.

"Make sure Uriah fights on the front line," the letter said. "Leave him
without protection so that he will die."

Joab had surrounded the city. He let Uriah fight close to the city walls so
that he was killed by an arrow, along with a number of the other soldiers.

A messenger was sent from the battlefront to King David, telling him that
some of his men had died. Uriah was one of them.

2 SAMUEL 11:6-27

*When Uriah's
wife heard that
her husband
was dead, she
mourned for him.
. . . But the LORD
was displeased
with what David
had done.*
2 Samuel 11:26-27

David felt relieved. Now he thought he could hide what he had done wrong.

Bathsheba mourned her husband's death. But then David brought her to the palace, and she became his wife.

Time passed, and Bathsheba gave birth to a baby boy. But God knew all that had happened—from David's lying to his arranging Uriah's death. God was angry with David.

MAY 19—NATHAN'S MESSAGE

God sent the prophet Nathan to David with a message.

"There were once two men," said Nathan. "One of them was a wealthy farmer with many sheep and cattle. The other man was poor with just one little lamb. It was very special to him.

"One day a guest came to stay with the rich man. Instead of killing one of his own sheep for their meal, he stole the little lamb from the poor man and cooked it."

David was furious.

"That's a terrible thing to do," he said. "The rich man must be punished!"

2 SAMUEL 12:1-25

Nathan said to David, "You are that man!"
2 Samuel 12:7

"But you are the rich man," said Nathan. "This is God's message for you. God has given you so much. He made you king over his people and saved you from Saul's anger. He gave you wives and children of your own. Yet you took another man's wife and made sure that the man himself died. God is angry, and you must be punished for this."

Then David put his head in his hands. He knew that everything Nathan had said was true.

"I am so sorry," said David. "I have sinned against God."

"God forgives you," said Nathan. "But there will still be consequences for the wrong that you have done."

Not long after this, Bathsheba's son became very ill, and although for a whole week David did nothing except pray to God for his life, the little boy died. David comforted Bathsheba as best he could. In due time, she had another little boy. They named him Solomon.

May 20—David's Sorrow

David prayed to God after Nathan had come to him.

Have mercy on me, dear God,
because of your great and constant love.
Wash away my sin, and let me feel your forgiveness.
I know that what I have done is wrong.
I cannot forget how terrible it is, and I am so sorry.
I know, too, that you are holy,
and it is you that I have wronged.
I have betrayed your trust and let you down.
Wash away my sin, dear God; take away my guilt.
Forgive me, and do not hold this wrong against me forever.
I know you don't want empty offerings
or outward signs of my guilt.
You just want to know that I am really sorry
and that I will not sin in this way again.
Make my heart pure,
and help me to do only what is right.
Give me back the joy I had in loving and serving you
so that others may know and love you too.

Psalm 51

Create in me a
clean heart, O God.
Renew a loyal spirit
within me.
Psalm 51:10

MAY 21—DAVID IS BETRAYED

David had many sons, and they were often jealous of each other.

Amnon, David's oldest son, fell in love with his half sister Tamar. When Tamar's brother Absalom found out that he had forced her to sleep with him, he was angry and hated Amnon. He waited for an opportunity and had him killed.

When David heard what had happened to his oldest son, he was filled with sadness. Absalom fled the country quickly and stayed away from his father. But David loved his sons. He missed Amnon because he was dead. But although he was angry with Absalom, he also missed him.

Joab saw how sad David was. After some years had passed, he convinced David to let Absalom come home.

Absalom was strong and handsome and popular with the people. He was also determined. Absalom dreamed of being king one day. He moved to Hebron and gathered a group of men around him.

Before long a messenger came to David in Jerusalem.

"Absalom has been proclaimed king in Hebron," he announced.

"Then we must go from here quickly!" said David to his men. "Absalom will let nothing stand in his way. He will kill us all."

So David and his friends fled from Jerusalem. But when he found out that Ahithophel had also joined Absalom, David wept. He had been betrayed by his son and by his trusted adviser.

"Oh, God," prayed David. "Please make Ahithophel give Absalom bad advice."

Then David turned to Hushai. "Return to Jerusalem and pretend to join Absalom. You will be able to advise against any plans Ahithophel may have."

MAY 22—HUSHAI TRICKS ABSALOM

When Absalom arrived in Jerusalem, Hushai came to meet him.

"Long live the king!" said Hushai.

Absalom was suspicious.

"Why are you here?" he asked. "Is this how you serve your friend— my father, David?"

2 SAMUEL 13–15

A messenger soon arrived in Jerusalem to tell David, "All Israel has joined Absalom in a conspiracy against you!"
2 Samuel 15:13

"I will serve the man God and all the people have chosen as king," Hushai replied. "I will serve you now as well as I served your father in the past."

Absalom then turned to Ahithophel and asked him what he should do next.

"Let me choose 12,000 men to attack David tonight," said Ahithophel. "He and his men will be tired and anxious. It will be easy to kill David. Then I will lead his troops back to Jerusalem, and there will be peace."

It was a good plan, but Absalom was undecided.

"What do you think?" he asked Hushai.

Hushai thought quickly. "Ahithophel has not given you good advice," he said. "David will know you will try to come after him. He will hide away from his men. Wait for a while, and then go after him. But make sure you lead the army yourself."

Absalom liked Hushai's plan. Secretly, Hushai sent a message to David and warned him.

2 SAMUEL 16:15–17:16

The LORD had determined to defeat the counsel of Ahithophel, which really was the better plan, so that he could bring disaster on Absalom!
2 Samuel 17:14

MAY 23 — THE DEATH OF ABSALOM

David prepared for battle. He divided his men into three groups and planned to go with them to fight.

"You must stay here," they told him. "If anything happens to you, everything is lost. You can send us help if we need it."

David decided to do as they wanted, but he had one request. He made sure everyone heard it. "Do what you have to do, but please do not harm Absalom!"

The two armies met in the forest, and the fighting was fierce. David's soldiers defeated Absalom's men, and thousands of men died.

Then Absalom came riding through the forest, weaving his way through the trees, his hair flowing behind him. Suddenly, his thick hair caught in the branches of a big tree, and he was pulled from his mule and left dangling in midair. His mule ran on without him.

"I saw Absalom hanging from a tree," said one of the soldiers to Joab.

"What do you mean you saw him? Why didn't you kill him?" asked Joab. "I would have rewarded you."

"King David gave instructions that we shouldn't hurt his son," the man said. "I wouldn't dare disobey such an order."

2 SAMUEL 18

Ten of Joab's young armor bearers then surrounded Absalom and killed him.
2 Samuel 18:15

But Joab wasted no time. He and his 10 armor bearers found Absalom and killed him.

Two men ran to David with the news of their victory. But Joab warned them not to say that Absalom was dead.

"The victory is ours!" cried Ahimaaz, who got there first.

"Is Absalom alive?" asked David. But Ahimaaz claimed not to know.

"Is Absalom alive?" David asked the other messenger.

"I wish all your enemies would end up like he did," the messenger replied.

Then David wept for his son.

"Oh, my dear son, Absalom," cried David. "How I wish I could have died instead of you!"

MAY 24—DAVID KEEPS HIS PROMISE

King David grew old and unwell, and soon the affairs of the nation were of less importance to him. He kept to his room and was nursed day and night by a beautiful woman named Abishag.

David's fourth son, Adonijah, decided to take over from his father and rule the people.

Joab supported him, but Zadok the priest, Benaiah, and Nathan the prophet remained loyal to David.

Nathan went to see Bathsheba.

"Have you heard that Adonijah has made himself king?" Nathan asked her. "You had better warn King David. Didn't he promise you that Solomon would be king after him?"

Bathsheba went to see King David and told him what she knew. Nathan confirmed it.

"I will keep my promise," David assured Bathsheba. "Solomon will be king. Let Benaiah take Solomon to Gihon, riding on my mule so that he can be anointed."

Solomon was prepared and taken to Gihon, where Zadok took oil and anointed him king.

1 KINGS 1

"Your son Solomon will be the next king and will sit on my throne this very day, just as I vowed to you before the LORD, the God of Israel."

1 Kings 1:30

"Long live King Solomon!" shouted the people. Then there was a great joyful procession, with the people making music and singing and shouting.

Adonijah had been feasting with his friends and supporters. They heard the sound of music and celebration and came to find out what was happening.

"David has made Solomon king!" a messenger announced. "Zadok the priest has anointed him."

Adonijah's supporters realized they might now be in danger for taking the rival king's side. They quickly made their way to their own homes, leaving Adonijah alone. Adonijah was certain Solomon would kill him, and he fled to the sacred tent.

"I will not harm my brother as long as he does not betray me," promised King Solomon.

MAY 25 — DAVID'S LAST DAYS

1 KINGS 2:1-12

David died and was buried with his Ancestors in the City of David.
1 Kings 2:10

When David knew that he was dying, he sent for Solomon.

"I will soon die and go the way that all of us must. The throne of Israel will belong to you and to your descendants. Remember to obey God and to follow all the laws that Moses left us. If you do as God says, he will bless you in everything you do."

"Watch Joab," warned David. "Remember that he is a murderer. Make sure that he is punished."

Solomon listened carefully to his father. Not long afterward, David died and was buried in Jerusalem. He had ruled for 40 years, and under his leadership Israel had become a strong nation.

MAY 26 — ADONIJAH'S REQUEST

1 KINGS 2:13-35, 46

So the kingdom was now firmly in Solomon's grip.
1 Kings 2:46

Solomon sat on David's throne and ruled as king. But Adonijah still hoped to take some power for himself.

Adonijah went to Bathsheba with a request.

"Solomon will listen to you," he said. "Please ask if I may marry Abishag now that our father is dead."

Bathsheba told Solomon what Adonijah had asked for, but Solomon knew he wanted much more.

"Adonijah cannot be trusted," Solomon told his mother. "We will not be safe until he is dead."

Solomon sent Benaiah to kill Adonijah, and when he was dead, Joab ran away and hid, knowing that he was in danger for supporting him. But Solomon had also given the order for Joab's death for the murders he had committed.

Benaiah found Joab and killed him too.

Then Solomon promoted Benaiah so that he was commander of the army in Joab's place. He also made Zadok the priest.

Solomon was now properly in control of Israel.

MAY 27 — GOD'S GIFT TO SOLOMON

1 KINGS 3:1-15

Solomon loved God and followed his father's advice by keeping all God's commandments.

One night, after a day of worshipping God at Gibeon, Solomon had a strange dream in which God appeared to him.

"Give me an understanding heart so that I can govern your people well."
1 Kings 3:9

"Ask for anything you want," God said, "and I will give it to you."

Solomon replied, "You blessed my father, David, and you gave him a son who would rule after him. You have already been so good to me, allowing me to be king in his place. But I know nothing—I am young and inexperienced. What I want most of all is the ability to make wise judgments so that I can rule the people fairly."

God was pleased with Solomon's answer.

"You have asked for wisdom," said God, "when you could have chosen wealth or revenge over your enemies or a long life. I will give you what you have asked for, so that everyone will be amazed and you will always be remembered for your wisdom. But I will also give you wealth and power. And if you obey me, I will give you a long life too."

When Solomon woke up, he clearly remembered his dream and all that God had promised him.

MAY 28—SOLOMON'S WISDOM

One day two women came to see Solomon.

"Your Majesty," cried one of the women. "This woman and I live in the same house. I gave birth to a baby son while she was in the house with me. Then three days later, she also had a baby son.

"We both went to sleep with our babies cuddled up next to us. But this woman rolled onto her baby while she was sleeping, and he died. She came to me while I slept and switched her dead baby with my living son. When I awoke, I knew that the dead baby was not mine."

"That's not true!" shouted the other woman. "My son is alive; yours is dead!"

"Bring me a sword!" ordered Solomon. "Divide the baby into two parts so that each woman can have a share!" But Solomon knew that the real mother would not let her child suffer and die in this way.

"Don't harm him!" the first woman pleaded with the king. "Let her have the baby."

"No, what the king says is fair!" replied the other woman. "Then neither of us can have the baby!"

Immediately Solomon knew which woman was the baby's mother.

"Give the first woman her baby," Solomon ordered. "She is his mother."

1 KINGS 3:16-28

Then [Solomon] said, "Cut the living child in two, and give half to one woman and half to the other!"
1 Kings 3:25

Everyone in Israel was amazed. They knew that God had given him wisdom to judge between them fairly.

May 29 — Wisdom about Families

Solomon wrote down many of his wise sayings:

Listen to what your parents tell you. Their teaching will fit you well and look good on you, like the nicest of clothes. PROVERBS 1:8-9

A wise child pays attention when his parents correct him, but a foolish one never admits that he is wrong. PROVERBS 13:1

If you love your children, you will correct them when they do something wrong. PROVERBS 13:24

The start of an argument is like a hole in a dam. Stop it quickly before it gets out of control. PROVERBS 17:14

There is nothing but sadness and sorrow for a parent whose child does foolish things. PROVERBS 17:21

Discipline your children while they are young enough to learn. If you don't, you are helping them to destroy themselves. PROVERBS 19:18

Children are blessed if their parents are honest and do what is right. PROVERBS 20:7

Anyone who thinks it isn't wrong to steal from his parents is no better than a murderer. PROVERBS 28:24

MAY 30—WISDOM ABOUT FRIENDS

PROVERBS 15:1

A gentle answer can turn anger away, but a fierce reply can make things worse.

PROVERBS 16:28

Gossip is spread by wicked people. They stir up trouble and break up friendships.

PROVERBS 17:1

It is better to eat bread and water with your friends than to eat a feast with your enemies.

PROVERBS 17:9

If you want people to like you, forgive them when they do something wrong. Remembering wrongs can break up a friendship.

PROVERBS 21:23

If you want to stay out of trouble, be careful about what you say.

PROVERBS 22:24-25

Don't make friends with people who have hot tempers. You might learn their habits and find it hard to change.

PROVERBS 27:6

A friend means well, even if he hurts you. But if an enemy starts pretending to be your frirend, trouble is sure to follow.

MAY 31 — WISDOM FOR LIFE

Trust in the Lord with all your heart. Don't rely on what you think you know. Ask for God's help in all you do, and he will guide you. PROVERBS 3:5-6

Do good to those who are in need whenever you can. Don't tell someone you will help them tomorrow if you can help them today. PROVERBS 3:27-28

Be careful how you think. Your life is shaped by your thoughts. Speak only the truth, and have nothing to do with lies. PROVERBS 4:23-24

Be generous, and you will do well. Help others, and you will be helped. PROVERBS 11:25

Wise people are careful to stay out of trouble, but foolish people act without thinking. PROVERBS 14:16

If you want to be happy, be kind to the poor. Never look down on other people. PROVERBS 14:21

If you mistreat poor people, you insult God, who made them. But kindness to the poor is an act of worship. PROVERBS 14:31

Do what is right and fair. That pleases God more than any gift you could offer him. PROVERBS 21:3

Wise people will see trouble coming and avoid it, but a foolish person will walk into trouble and regret it later. PROVERBS 22:3

Don't wear yourself out trying to get rich. Your money can disappear in an instant, as if it had grown wings and flown away. PROVERBS 23:4-5

It is better to have no money and be honest than to be rich and dishonest. PROVERBS 28:6

You will never succeed in life if you try to hide your sins. Confess them, and God will show mercy and forgive you. PROVERBS 28:13

JUNE 1 — A TEMPLE FOR GOD

While Solomon was king, there was peace in Israel. The time was right for Solomon to build a Temple for God.

King Hiram of Tyre had been a friend of King David. When Hiram sent ambassadors to David's son, Solomon sent back a message.

"God told my father, David, that a Temple would be built after his reign when there was peace in the land. Now that time has come, and I want to build a Temple for God. I want you to chop down the best cedar trees in Lebanon so I can start building. I will pay you whatever you ask."

1 KINGS 5–8:21

So Solomon finished building the Temple.
1 Kings 6:14

The king of Tyre was happy to make an agreement, and he gave Solomon all the wood he needed. The logs of cedar and pine were made into rafts and were floated down the coast to Solomon.

God told Solomon how the Temple should be designed and built. The stones were prepared in the quarry and brought to the chosen site. Solomon had the inside walls lined with beautifully carved wood and covered with gold. The Temple was filled with all the things that God wanted, taken from the tent of meeting.

Finally, in front of all Israel's elders, the Ark of the Covenant, which contained the stone tablets with God's laws, was brought to the Temple and put into the Most Holy Place. The cloud of God's presence filled the Temple so that the priests were dazzled by the light.

Then Solomon asked God's blessing on the people.

JUNE 2 — SOLOMON'S PRAYER

"Lord God of Israel, you are like no one else," prayed Solomon. "No one in heaven above and no one beneath the earth shows such love and kindness. No one else keeps promises as you do.

1 KINGS 8:22–9:9

"O LORD, God of Israel, there is no God like you in all of heaven above or on the earth below."
1 Kings 8:23

"Lord, I have built this house for you, but I know that even heaven cannot contain you, for you are a great God! Let this Temple be a place where your people can come when we need your help. Whether we bow before the altar here, or whether we bow in its direction when we are far away, hear our prayers.

"We will come if we fear our enemies. We will come if there is no rain or no food. We will come when we have sinned—for there is no man, woman, or child who does not sin and break your laws—and we will ask your forgiveness. Then Lord, hear us from heaven and have mercy on us. Keep the promises that you made to Moses and our ancestors, that we will be your people and that you will be our God."

Then Solomon turned to the people and prayed again. "We ask that God will be with us and bless us and help us to keep his laws, so that all the people on earth will know that the Lord is God and that there is no other."

God appeared to Solomon some time after this and spoke to him. "I have heard your prayers, and I will bless you and this house that you have made for me. But if you disobey me and neglect to follow my laws, your children will not be kings, and this Temple will be ruined. People will pass by and know that it is because you did not obey my laws and because you did not love the God who brought you out of Egypt."

JUNE 3 — THE VISIT OF THE QUEEN OF SHEBA

Reports about Solomon's wealth and wisdom were carried to people far from Israel through the traders who passed through his land.

Far away, the queen of Sheba heard stories of Solomon's greatness. She prepared for the long journey across the desert sands of Arabia and along the Red Sea coast. She rode by camel on a beautiful chair covered in cushions, with a roof to protect her from the sun. She rode up into the land of Moab and crossed the Jordan River to arrive in Jerusalem. She journeyed for months to see Solomon for herself.

Her arrival was greeted with great interest. The queen had brought with her camels, mules, and donkeys, all carrying gifts for King Solomon—gold, precious stones, and exotic spices.

1 KINGS 10:1-13

When the queen of Sheba heard of Solomon's fame, which brought honor to the name of the LORD, she came to test him with hard questions.
1 Kings 10:1

The queen saw the magnificent, ornamented palace that Solomon had built with fancy crimson and purple curtains. She walked in his fruitful vineyards and beautiful gardens and by his refreshing pools. She saw his many fine horses and chariots, and she tasted good food and wine. She noticed the expensive clothing his servants wore and listened to singers with exotic musical instruments.

She watched Solomon worship God in the Temple and found that he could answer questions about so many things—his wisdom was endless.

"I heard all about you in my country," the queen said to Solomon, "but I couldn't believe it was true. Now I know that you are even greater than your reputation. Let me praise your God for making you such a great and wise king!"

JUNE 4—SOLOMON'S POWER AND WEALTH

Solomon planted olive, spice, and nut trees and studied the ways of spiders, locusts, and harvesting ants. He knew about plants, animals, birds, reptiles, and fish.

As Solomon's reputation grew, he became richer and richer. Many visitors came to ask for his advice and help. Each one brought expensive gifts. He traded with many different nations, and his fleet of ships brought back gold, silver, ivory, apes, and peacocks.

1 KINGS 10:14–11:3

King Solomon became richer and wiser than any other king on earth.
1 Kings 10:23

Soon Solomon had so much gold that everything in his palace was made of it. Silver was worthless because there was so much gold. Solomon's throne was made out of ivory, with golden armrests and golden stitching. On each side of the throne was a huge golden lion. Six steps led up to the throne, and on each side of each step was another golden lion. No one had ever seen anything so spectacular before.

But Solomon had a weakness. He married foreign wives, who bowed down to idols and did not know the one true God. He had forgotten God's warnings.

JUNE 5 — THE BROKEN PROMISE

As the years passed, Solomon not only loved his many wives, he also began to worship their gods.

God was angry with Solomon.

"I warned you not to worship these idols as the other nations do—and you have broken your promise to me," said God. "I will not take the kingdom from you yet, because I made a promise to your father, David. But I will take the kingdom from your son."

A young man named Jeroboam worked very hard for Solomon. One day as Jeroboam was walking on the road outside Jerusalem, the prophet Ahijah came to him. Ahijah took off the new cloak he was wearing and ripped it into 12 pieces.

"Take them!" he said, giving 10 pieces to Jeroboam. "This is a picture of what God will do for you. Once Solomon is dead, God will make you king over 10 of the tribes of Israel. Remember to follow God's commandments and serve him well."

Solomon heard what had happened and tried to kill Jeroboam. But Jeroboam escaped to Egypt and hid there.

1 KINGS 11:4-13, 26-40

In this way, Solomon did what was evil in the LORD's sight; he refused to follow the LORD completely, as his father, David, had done.

1 Kings 11:6

JUNE 6 — THE DIVIDED KINGDOM

When Solomon died, Jeroboam left Egypt and joined with the people from the northern tribes of Israel at Shechem.

Solomon's son Rehoboam also went to Shechem, hoping that the people would proclaim him king. Instead they challenged him.

"Your father, King Solomon, made us work hard. If you want us to make you king now, you must promise to make our work easier."

Rehoboam didn't know what to do. He told the people to return in three days. Meanwhile, he consulted his father's old officials.

"It's the only thing to do," they advised him. "Make their work easier."

Rehoboam listened, but he didn't like their advice. So he went and asked his friends what he should do.

"Don't give in!" said his friends. "Tell them that you will make them work harder, and they'll regret it if they don't!"

So when the men returned after three days, Rehoboam gave them the answer his friends had suggested. It was not the right answer!

1 KINGS 11:41–12:20

Rehoboam rejected the advice of the older men and instead asked the opinion of the young men who had grown up with him and were now his advisers.
1 Kings 12:8

"You are not one of us—you are not our king! We will not serve you or work for you."

Rehoboam had made his first mistake. He returned to Jerusalem, where only the tribe of Judah followed him. The 10 northern tribes of Israel made Jeroboam their king.

The kingdom of Israel was divided. Now there was no longer one nation but two.

June 7 — King Jeroboam's Disobedience

Jeroboam was anxious. He had built two cities at Shechem and Peniel, but the Temple was in Jerusalem—under Rehoboam's control. If he let the people return to worship God, they might decide to follow King Rehoboam instead. He couldn't let that happen.

So Jeroboam made two golden calves.

"These are your gods!" he said to the people. "Now you don't need to go to Jerusalem to worship."

Jeroboam placed one of the statues in each of his two cities and went to worship them himself. He made priests out of the common people instead of the Levites, and he introduced new feast days.

He was challenged one day by a prophet from Judah.

"Be warned!" the man shouted. "God has seen these things you have done. He has chosen Josiah, one of King David's descendants, to overthrow all the bad things you have done. And so you will know that what I say comes from God, your altar will crumble, and the ashes of the sacrifice will fall on the ground."

Jeroboam was angry.

"Grab him!" he said, pointing at the prophet. But at that moment Jeroboam's hand was paralyzed. He could not move it.

Jeroboam watched helplessly as the altar cracked and crumbled before his eyes, scattering the ashes over the ground.

"Ask God to help me!" he begged. "Give me back the use of my hand."

The prophet prayed for Jeroboam, and his hand was restored. But Jeroboam soon forgot the prophet's warning. He continued to disobey God.

1 KINGS 12:25–13:34

At the same time a wide crack appeared in the altar, and the ashes poured out, just as the man of God had predicted in his message from the LORD.
1 Kings 13:5

JUNE 8—A TERRIBLE WARNING

1 KINGS 14:1-20

"Then the LORD will shake Israel like a reed whipped about in a stream."
1 Kings 14:15

Jeroboam's son Abijah was ill. It became clear that he might die.

"Go to Ahijah, the prophet in Shiloh," Jeroboam told his wife. "Ask him what will happen to our son. But disguise yourself—don't let him know that you are the king's wife."

Jeroboam's wife took some bread, cakes, and honey as gifts for the prophet, and she went to Shiloh.

Ahijah was an old man and could no longer see. But God told him that Jeroboam's wife was coming and that she would be disguised. God gave Ahijah a message for her.

"I know who you are, wife of Jeroboam," said Ahijah. "I have bad news for you, given to me by God himself. He knows everything your husband the king has done. Your family will be punished because of his sins—terrible things will happen! But God has seen that your child is good. God will take him now so that he will be spared a worse fate. When you get home, your son will die, and his death will sadden everyone."

Jeroboam's wife returned home to find that her son had died.

June 9 — War and Defeat

The kingdom of Judah was strengthening at this time. Rehoboam protected his cities against attack and gave each of his sons a city to rule over.

But Rehoboam also built many shrines and altars to other gods, and his people followed him. He did all the things his ancestors had done that had made God angry. He did not follow God's commandments or love him as his grandfather David had done.

God allowed Shishak, the king of Egypt, to attack Jerusalem. Shishak looted the Temple and the palace, removing the golden treasures that Solomon had made.

Israel and Judah fought each other. Peace between the nations was over.

1 Kings 14:21-31

In the fifth year of King Rehoboam's reign, King Shishak of Egypt came up and attacked Jerusalem.
1 Kings 14:25

June 10 — The Wicked King Ahab

Kings came and went in Israel. Nadab, Jeroboam's son, was overthrown by Baasha. Elah, Baasha's son, was overthrown by Zimri, and Omri overthrew Zimri. Each king was worse than the one before. Not one of them served God as King David had. All God's commandments were broken again and again.

When Omri's son Ahab became king, the evil in the land was greater than it had ever been. Ahab married a woman named Jezebel, daughter of the king of Sidon, who worshiped the fertility god, Baal.

Ahab openly worshiped Baal too and made a temple for his statue.

The people who had once worshiped God as creator of all the world now bowed down to idols they had made with their own hands.

1 Kings 15:25–16:34

Ahab son of Omri did what was evil in the LORD's sight, even more than any of the kings before him.
1 Kings 16:30

JUNE 11 — ELIJAH BRINGS BAD NEWS

1 KINGS 17:1-7

The ravens brought [Elijah] bread and meat each morning and evening, and he drank from the brook.

1 Kings 17:6

In the mountains of Gilead, there lived a man named Elijah.

Elijah was a prophet. He heard God speak and, unlike so many of the people of Israel at that time, he tried to follow God's ways.

God chose Elijah to go to see King Ahab.

"God—the one true God—has sent me here," said Elijah. "There will be no rain, not even any early morning dew, for some years. There will be a drought until God chooses to send rain again."

The king was angry at the news, but Elijah did not stay to see what he would do.

"Leave this place now and go eastward," God told Elijah. "You will find all you need by Kerith Brook."

Elijah found the brook on the eastern side of the Jordan River. He made himself a shelter there and drank water from the brook. God sent ravens with food for him to eat, and Elijah had everything he needed.

It did not rain. Day after day, the hot sun beat down, and the dawn brought no dew. The ground became dry and thirsty. After a while, the water in the brook dried up.

JUNE 12 — THE OIL THAT DIDN'T RUN OUT

God had already provided for Elijah's needs.

"Go to Zarephath," God told Elijah. "There is a woman there who will give you food."

Elijah traveled to Sidon, and when he reached the city gates of the place called Zarephath, he saw a woman gathering sticks for firewood.

"May I have some water, please?" Elijah asked her. "And a little bread to eat?"

"I have no bread baked," she replied, "for the drought has made us all hungry. I have just a little flour and oil left, and I am here gathering these few sticks to make a fire. I will cook the last meal for myself and my only son. Then we will die, for there is no more."

"Don't be afraid," said Elijah. "Go and bake this bread as you were planning to do. Only share a little of it with me, and God will bless you. Your flour and oil will not run out until God sends rain again."

The woman went home and baked the bread. She shared it with Elijah and her son—and there was still enough flour and oil for another meal.

Again the woman used the flour and oil so they could share their last meal. Again there was just enough left. Many days passed, and God made sure that the woman and her son and Elijah had enough to eat.

1 KINGS 17:8-16

"There will always be flour and olive oil left in your containers until the time when the LORD sends rain and the crops grow again!"
1 Kings 17:14

JUNE 13 — ELIJAH SAVES A LITTLE BOY

1 KINGS 17:17-24

Elijah stayed in a room in the woman's house.

After some time had passed, the woman's son grew ill. She sat by his bedside, watching him and holding him in her arms until he drew his last breath and died.

The woman was overcome by grief and anger.

The woman told Elijah, "Now I know for sure that you are a man of God, and that the LORD truly speaks through you."
1 Kings 17:24

"Why did you come here?" she sobbed. "What have I done to you that my son should die like this?"

Elijah took the dead boy in his arms and carried him upstairs to his own room. He laid the boy on his bed and prayed.

"Lord God," he cried, "why have you allowed this to happen to the woman whose home I have shared? Please give the boy back his life!"

God heard Elijah's prayer. Suddenly, the boy started to breathe again. Elijah lifted him gently and carried him back to his mother.

"Look! Your son is alive!" Elijah said.

The woman hugged her son and smiled at Elijah, the tears still in her eyes.

"Now I know you are God's friend," she said.

JUNE 14—THE THIRD YEAR OF DROUGHT

1 KINGS 18:1-20

When Ahab saw him, he exclaimed, "So, is it really you, you troublemaker of Israel?"
1 Kings 18:17

It had not rained for nearly three years.

King Ahab sent the prophet Obadiah to search for any green place left in the land where food might be found for the animals. If none could be found, the animals would have to be killed.

But before long, Obadiah met Elijah. Elijah asked him to bring the king to him, because he had a message from God.

"My lord," said Obadiah, "you must know that King Ahab has had people searching the whole country for you! I cannot go tell him I have found you now! You are sure to disappear, and he will kill me!"

But Elijah promised he would stay until Ahab came to meet him.

Obadiah brought King Ahab, who was very angry.

"You are a troublemaker!" the king shouted at Elijah.

"You are the one who has brought trouble to the land," said Elijah, "because you stopped worshipping God and started to worship idols. Now we will settle this matter. Call all the people to Mount Carmel, and bring all the false prophets who are your wife's friends."

King Ahab sent for all the people and all the prophets of Baal and Asherah. The word went out that there would be a contest between them and the one true God, who had protected Elijah through the years of drought.

So the people came, and with them the 450 prophets of Baal. They gathered on Mount Carmel.

JUNE 15 — THE CONTEST ON THE MOUNTAIN

Elijah stood on Mount Carmel in front of King Ahab and all the people.

"Today you must choose whom you will serve," said Elijah. "If the living God is the real God, then choose him––and follow him! If Baal is the real God, then serve and follow him. It is time to make up your minds and do what is right.

"I am the only prophet here who worships the one true God," he said, "while there are 450 prophets here who worship Baal. We will each prepare a sacrifice. You call upon Baal to send down fire to burn yours up, and I will ask my God to do the same for mine. Then we will see which is the one true God who can send down fire."

The prophets agreed. They prepared a bull for the sacrifice, and all day they prayed to Baal to send down fire.

Nothing happened.

"Is your god asleep?" Elijah asked. "Is he on vacation so he can't answer?"

1 KINGS 18:21-29

"Call on the name of your god, and I will call on the name of the LORD. The god who answers by setting fire to the wood is the true God!" And all the people agreed.
1 Kings 18:24

The prophets prayed and shouted even louder, but still there was no answer. The prophets of Baal had failed. There was no fire on the altar they had prepared. Now it was Elijah's turn.

JUNE 16—THE ONE TRUE GOD

1 KINGS 18:30-45

When all the people saw it, they fell face down on the ground and cried out, "The LORD—he is God! Yes, the LORD is God!"
1 Kings 18:39

Elijah did not just make an altar as the other prophets had done. He used 12 stones to represent the 12 tribes of Israel and to remind the people that they were God's people. He dug a deep ditch around the altar and then prepared his sacrifice. Finally, Elijah asked for large jars to be filled with water and poured all over the wood and the sacrifice so that it ran down into the ditch. Elijah's sacrifice was soaking wet. No accident could cause it to burn.

Then Elijah stepped out in front of the people and prayed. Elijah prayed that God would hear him so that the people would believe once more that he was their God too and would worship him.

When Elijah stopped praying, God answered.

God sent down fire. God sent down fire that burned the bull, the stones, and the water from the ditch. The people fell on their knees and cried out, "The Lord is God! The Lord—he is God!"

Elijah called for the false prophets to be put to death. Then he watched as black clouds began to form and the wind rose—and God sent rain once more upon the land.

JUNE 17—JEZEBEL'S DEATH THREATS

When Ahab told Queen Jezebel that Elijah had killed all her prophets, she was furious. She threatened to kill Elijah, too. He was terrified and ran away into the desert.

Elijah found a solitary tree and sat under it in the shade. He was tired and frightened. He felt he couldn't take any more.

"Let me die," he said to God. "I have had enough." In his exhaustion, Elijah fell asleep.

After a while, an angel came and touched him.

"Get up. Have something to eat," said the angel.

Elijah looked up and saw some water and freshly baked bread. He ate the bread and drank the water. Then he fell asleep again.

The angel touched Elijah for a second time.

"Eat some more and refresh yourself for the journey ahead," the angel said.

Elijah ate again. Then he set out for Mount Sinai, the mountain of God.

1 KINGS 19:1-9

Jezebel sent this message to Elijah: "May the gods strike me and even kill me if by this time tomorrow I have not killed you just as you killed them."

1 Kings 19:2

JUNE 18—EARTHQUAKE, FIRE, AND WHISPER

When Elijah reached Mount Sinai, he found a cave and stayed there for the night.

"What are you doing here, Elijah?" asked God.

Elijah had been thinking about all that had happened since he had been serving God as his prophet. He had tried to encourage God's people to obey him, but still they seemed to disobey and go their own ways.

"I have done my best to serve you," said Elijah, "but no one listens. No one hears and tries to follow you. And now they are trying to kill me!"

God heard what was in Elijah's heart and understood that he was discouraged and frightened.

"Stand on the mountain," said God, "and watch me pass by."

A powerful wind suddenly stirred and ripped through the mountains, shattering the rocks in its path. But God was not in the wind.

1 KINGS 19:9-18

After the earthquake there was a fire, but the LORD was not in the fire. And after the fire there was the sound of a gentle whisper.
1 Kings 19:12

Then there was an earthquake, cracking open the rocky ground and moving everything in its path. But God was not in the earthquake.

Then there was a fire. But God was not in the fire.

Finally, there was a gentle whisper.

Elijah left the cave and stood on the mountain with his cloak wrapped around him.

But Elijah was still unhappy. He did not understand God's message.

"Go back the way you came," said God. "Anoint Jehu to be king of Israel and Elisha to succeed you as prophet. Those who have disobeyed me will be punished. But there are some left who have remained faithful and have not worshipped foreign idols. I will save them."

JUNE 19 — GOD'S NEW PROPHET

Elijah went to find Elisha. He was plowing a field with a pair of oxen.

Elijah went to him, took off his cloak, and threw it around Elisha's shoulders. The young man knew what this meant: He was to serve God by helping Elijah and learning from him.

Elisha left his oxen and ran after Elijah.

"Let me first go back to say good-bye to my parents, and then I will come with you," he said.

Elisha burned his plows, killed the oxen, and cooked them. He gave the cooked meat to the people to eat. Now his past life was over. He was ready to follow Elijah and serve God as a prophet.

1 KINGS 19:19-21

Elisha left the oxen standing there [and] ran after Elijah.
1 Kings 19:20

JUNE 20 — QUEEN JEZEBEL'S PLAN

Near King Ahab's palace lived a man named Naboth who owned a vineyard.

Ahab wanted a garden near the palace and thought Naboth's vineyard would work out very well.

"Your vineyard would make an ideal garden for me," the king said to Naboth one day. "Name your price and sell it to me, or I will give you a better vineyard somewhere else."

But Naboth's vineyard had belonged to his father and his grandfather. He didn't want to sell it to anyone.

Ahab had set his heart on the vineyard. He had not expected Naboth's answer to be no. He went home, shut himself away in his room, and pouted.

Queen Jezebel couldn't believe what she was seeing.

"What are you doing here, feeling sorry for yourself? You're the king! You can have anything you want!"

So Jezebel plotted against Naboth to get the king what he wanted. She arranged for Naboth to be invited to a feast where two men would be paid to lie about him and accuse him of being a traitor in front of all the people.

The plan worked. Naboth was taken and stoned to death.

Now there was no one to stop King Ahab from taking the vineyard for himself. But God sent Elijah to him with a message.

1 KINGS 21

Ahab immediately went down to the vineyard of Naboth to claim it.
1 Kings 21:16

Ahab was walking around the vineyard making plans when he saw Elijah. He knew it could only mean trouble.

"Did you really think God would be happy if you killed a man to take what he owns?" said Elijah. "You will die for what you have done to Naboth. Your queen will die for her part in this, and your family will be punished."

Ahab listened to Elijah and was sorry and afraid. God decided to give him another chance. For the next few years, there was peace in the land.

JUNE 21 — A WICKED KING'S DEATH

In Judah, King Jehoshaphat had become not only powerful but feared by all the nations around him. Unlike King Ahab in Israel, Jehoshaphat destroyed foreign idols and tried to follow God's ways as David had before him.

One day he went to visit King Ahab. Ahab prepared a great feast for him. He wanted Jehoshaphat's help.

"Join with me and fight against Ramoth-gilead!" Ahab asked.

"I will help you," Jehoshaphat replied. "But what does God say? Is there a prophet here we can consult?"

1 KINGS 22:1-37

The king died, and his body was taken to Samaria and buried there.
1 Kings 22:37

King Ahab brought various prophets to Jehoshaphat, all of whom said that God would give them victory. But Ahab said that there was one man, Micaiah, who always brought bad news. Jehoshaphat wanted to hear what he had to say.

"Go to war, and you will be successful!" Micaiah said. But Ahab did not trust his message.

"You never bring good news," he said. "Tell me what God has told you!"

"God wants you to be lured into battle and to your death. He has told all your prophets to tell you to fight so that this will happen."

Ahab was angry and had Micaiah locked up. He would fight, with or without God's help. He told Jehoshaphat to wear his royal robes into battle, but Ahab rode his chariot in disguise. He did not want the enemy to know he was the king.

The enemy wanted only King Ahab's death. With God's help, they found him. An arrow pierced the holes in his armor and wounded him. King Ahab watched the battle, propped up in the chariot until sunset, when he finally died.

JUNE 22 — A CHARIOT TO HEAVEN

It was time for Elijah's ministry to end. Elisha knew that this would be the last day he would spend on earth with the prophet he had learned so much from.

Elisha walked with Elijah from Gilgal.

"Stay here!" Elijah said to his friend. "God has sent me to Bethel."

But Elisha refused. "I will come with you," he said.

When they reached Bethel, the prophets there spoke to Elisha.

"Do you realize that God will take Elijah today?" they asked.

"Yes, I know," he replied.

The same thing happened when they walked on to Jericho and then again to the Jordan.

Then Elijah took off his cloak, rolled it up, and hit the water with it. A pathway appeared through the river so that the two prophets could cross safely to the other side.

"Soon I must leave you. Is there anything I can do for you before I go?" asked Elijah.

"Give me twice as much of your faith and power," said Elisha.

"This is something only God can give. If you see me leave this earth, you will have what you asked for," said Elijah.

2 KINGS 2:1-15

As they were walking along and talking, suddenly a chariot of fire appeared, drawn by horses of fire. It drove between the two men, separating them, and Elijah was carried by a whirlwind into heaven.
2 Kings 2:11

Then a chariot and horses made of fire appeared in the sky and separated Elijah from Elisha. Elijah was taken up into heaven in a whirlwind.

Elisha picked up Elijah's cloak and rolled it up. He hit the Jordan River as Elijah had done. A pathway appeared through the water.

Some prophets had been watching from a distance.

"God has given to the prophet Elisha the faith and power of Elijah," they said to each other.

JUNE 23—GOD SENDS WATER IN THE DESERT

2 KINGS 3

King Jehoshaphat of Judah asked, "Is there no prophet of the LORD with us? If there is, we can ask the LORD what to do through him."
2 Kings 3:11

When Ahab's son Joram became king after his father's death, the king of Moab refused to send him the lambs and wool that the Moabites used to send Ahab in return for peace.

Joram joined with King Jehoshaphat and the king of Edom, and they rode together across the desert to fight against Moab. Before long they had run out of water for themselves and their animals.

"Is there no prophet here so that we can find out what God wants us to do?" asked King Jehoshaphat.

"Elisha is here," an officer answered. "He used to help the prophet Elijah."

The three kings went down to Elisha, but he would not speak to King Joram.

"Bring a harp player here, so that I may hear what God has to say. But understand that I do this because of King Jehoshaphat only," he said.

Then God spoke to Elisha. He told the kings that God would both send water and give them victory over the people of Moab.

The next morning, as God had promised, water was flowing from the land of Edom, and it filled the desert. The people had plenty to drink and to water their animals. But when the people of Moab came to fight, they saw the sun shining on the water, red as blood. It seemed to them that the kings had killed each other in battle. They thought it would be easy to come and loot what remained of their camp. When they did so, the armies chased them away, invaded their land, and had victory over Moab, just as Elisha had told them.

JUNE 24—THE WIDOW'S DEBT

One day a woman came to ask for Elisha's help. Her husband had been a prophet, but when he died, he owed money.

"I cannot pay back the man he owed," she told Elisha. "He wants to take my two sons to be his slaves as payment for the debt."

"What do you have in your home?" Elisha asked her. "Tell me how I can help you."

"I have nothing," replied the woman desperately. "I have just a little olive oil left."

"Go to your neighbors," Elisha told her. "Ask them to give you as many empty jars as they have. Collect as many as you can. Then go home to your sons, shut the door, and pour oil into all of the jars."

The woman did as Elisha told her. She collected the jars and filled each one with oil.

"Give me another jar," she said to her son.

"There are none left," he told her. Then the oil stopped flowing. But she had many jars full of oil.

The woman returned to Elisha and told him what had happened.

"Now go and sell the oil. You will be able to pay your debt, and you and your sons can stay together."

2 KINGS 4:1-7

When she told the man of God what had happened, he said to her, "Now sell the olive oil and pay your debts, and you and your sons can live on what is left over."
2 Kings 4:7

JUNE 25 — THE GIFT OF A CHILD

Whenever Elisha passed through Shunem, a rich woman there offered him a meal and a place to stay. She and her husband had prepared a room for him on their roof. The room had a bed, a table, a chair, and a lamp.

One day, when Elisha was staying at their house, he told his servant Gehazi to ask the woman to come to see him.

"You have been very kind to me," Elisha said. "Is there anything I can do to show my thanks?"

The woman shook her head. She felt she had all she needed. But Elisha's servant saw that the woman's husband was old and she had no child to look after her. He told Elisha that she might want a son.

"This time next year you will hold your baby son in your arms," Elisha told her.

The woman was anxious—she did not want her hopes raised. But everything happened just as Elisha had said. A year later the woman gave birth to a baby boy.

2 KINGS 4:8-17

"Next year at this time you will be holding a son in your arms!"
2 Kings 4:16

June 26 — A Miracle in Shunem

The rich woman from Shunem loved her son dearly. Her life was completely different now God had blessed her.

One day the boy was out with his father at harvesttime when suddenly he complained of pains in his head. His father sent him home in the arms of a servant. His mother took the boy on her lap and held him, but around noon her son died.

The woman carried him up to Elisha's room and laid him on the bed. Then she asked her husband for a donkey and one of the servants so she could visit Elisha at Mount Carmel.

When Elisha saw her coming, he was worried. He asked Gehazi to go to meet her and ask what was wrong.

She would not tell him, but when she reached Elisha, she threw herself at his feet and took hold of him.

"Why did you give me a son just to take him away? I could live with the pain of having no child, but I cannot live with the agony of loving him and having him die!"

Elisha was very concerned and sent his servant to her home with his walking stick. He told him to lay it across the boy's face to restore him. But the woman would not move until Elisha went with her.

As Elisha approached the woman's house, Gehazi came to meet him.

"There is no change," he told him. "The child is still dead."

So Elisha went into the room and prayed to God to restore the boy. Then he breathed into his mouth and warmed him with his own body. He went out of the room, returned, and did the same thing again.

Then the boy sneezed seven times. He opened his eyes. Elisha called the woman into the room.

"Here is your son," said Elisha to the woman.

2 KINGS 4:18-37

When she came in, Elisha said, "Here, take your son!"
2 Kings 4:36

June 27 — The Captive Servant Girl

In the land of Aram, an Israelite girl had been taken captive in one of the raids on nearby villages.

She worked as a servant in the home of an army commander named Naaman.

2 KINGS 5:1-8

Naaman was a brave and respected soldier. But his skin was covered in the deadly white patches of leprosy.

"I wish my master could see the prophet in Samaria!" the Israelite girl told her mistress. "I am sure he would cure his leprosy."

[Elisha] sent this message to him: "Why are you so upset? Send Naaman to me, and he will learn that there is a true prophet here in Israel."

2 Kings 5:8

Naaman went to the king of Aram and told him what the girl had said. So the king wrote a letter to King Joram of Israel and sent Naaman with silver, gold, and other gifts.

"I am sending Naaman to you with this letter so that you can cure him of his leprosy," the letter said.

King Joram was upset at the letter. He thought it was a trick so that the king of Aram could wage war against him. He didn't think of Elisha. He didn't consider that God could help him.

Elisha heard of King Joram's trouble.

"Send him to me," Elisha said. "Then he will know that there is a prophet who serves God in Israel."

JUNE 28 — NAAMAN IS CURED

Naaman went with his servants, his horses, and his chariots, and he stopped outside the place where Elisha lived. A servant came out from Elisha's house with a message from the prophet.

2 KINGS 5:9-15

"Go to the Jordan River and wash there seven times."

Naaman was angry. Elisha had not even come out to greet him.

"Go and wash yourself seven times in the Jordan River. Then your skin will be restored, and you will be healed of your leprosy."

2 Kings 5:10

"Surely there are better rivers in Damascus where I could wash!" he said. "I thought he would come and wave his hand over my skin and pray to his God!"

But one of Naaman's servants spoke wisely to him.

"Sir," he said, "if the prophet had asked you to do something difficult, you would have done it. Don't be too proud to do this simple thing."

Naaman listened and decided to go down to the Jordan River and wash. When he came out of the river the seventh time, his skin was clean and new and unmarked, like that of a child. He was cured.

"Now I know there is no God except the God of Israel," he said.

JUNE 29 — JEHU IS ANOINTED KING

The time had come for King Ahab's family to die, just as Elijah had
prophesied. No one in Ahab's family remembered or obeyed God.

Elisha sent one of the young prophets on a mission.

"Take this bottle of oil and find Jehu, the son of Jehoshaphat," he said.
"Ask to speak to him secretly, and then anoint him king of Israel. Don't wait
to explain further—come back as fast as you can."

The prophet found Jehu and drew him away from his fellow soldiers. Once
they were on their own, the prophet poured the oil on Jehu's head.

"God has chosen you to be the king of Israel. You must kill all who remain in
Ahab's family as punishment for their disobedience." Then the prophet fled.

"What did he want?" asked one of the soldiers when Jehu returned.

"Nothing that makes much sense," he replied. But when his friends pressed
him further, he told them, "God has anointed me king."

The men took off their cloaks and spread them on the steps under Jehu's
feet. They blew on the trumpet and shouted, "Jehu is king!"

2 KINGS 9:1-13

*They quickly spread
out their cloaks
on the bare steps
and blew the ram's
horn, shouting,
"Jehu is king!"*
2 Kings 9:13

JUNE 30—THE DREADFUL END OF QUEEN JEZEBEL

2 KINGS 9:14–10:17

*When Jehu arrived
in Samaria, he
killed everyone
who was left
there from Ahab's
family, just as
the LORD had
promised through
Elijah.*
2 Kings 10:17

Joram and Ahaziah, the kings of Israel and Judah, were both in Jezreel. Jehu gathered his troops and set out to find them.

The guard on the watchtower saw Jehu's chariot approaching.

King Joram sent out a soldier on horseback to meet him and find out what he wanted. But when the man caught up with him, Jehu told him to follow behind him. A second soldier was sent out, but Jehu made him follow behind as well.

"The man leading the troops is driving his chariot like a crazy person!" the guard reported. "Only Jehu drives like that!"

So King Joram of Israel and King Ahaziah of Judah went out to meet Jehu, each in his own chariot.

They met him at the place that used to be Naboth's field. Queen Jezebel had planned out Naboth's death so that Ahab could steal the field from him.

"Have you come in peace?" asked King Joram.

"How can there be peace while your mother, Queen Jezebel, rules us with witchcraft and idol worship?" demanded Jehu.

"He's a traitor!" King Joram shouted out to Ahaziah as he turned in panic. Jehu aimed his arrow at Joram's back. His aim was right on, and he killed Joram with a single shot. Then Jehu made sure the body was left in Naboth's field to fulfill the prophecy that God made when Naboth was murdered.

Meanwhile, King Ahaziah had also turned and fled. Jehu's men chased after him and wounded him, and he died later in the city of Megiddo.

But Jehu had not yet finished his work. Queen Jezebel was still in Jezreel.

She painted her eyes and brushed her hair, then watched for Jehu from a window in the palace.

"What are you doing here, you murderer?" she demanded.

Jehu looked around to see who was on his side. He looked to some palace officials.

"Throw her down!" he called.

The men took hold of Jezebel and threw her out of the window so that she fell to her death.

Everyone in Ahab's family was dead. Their rule was ended. King Jehu was free to rule Israel as God intended.

July 1 — Jehu's Trick

King Jehu knew that there were still many worshippers of Baal in the land. He went to Samaria and called them all together for a feast.

"You know how well King Ahab served the god Baal," he told the people. "Well, now you will see how well I can serve him. Let all Baal's priests and all those who worship him come together for a celebration. Anyone who does not come will be found and put to death!"

All the Baal worshippers came to the temple so that it was filled from end to end. Jehu made sure that no one who worshipped the one true God was there.

Then Jehu ordered his soldiers to put to death all those who were inside. He destroyed the sacred pillar inside the temple and then the temple itself. In this way he made sure that the evil of Ahab's family was wiped out from the land of Israel forever.

2 Kings 10:18-28

In this way, Jehu destroyed every trace of Baal worship from Israel.
2 Kings 10:28

July 2 — A Wicked Grandmother

In Judah, Athaliah, the mother of King Ahaziah, ruled for six years. One by one, she had killed the entire royal family after her son's death, so that no one could take power from her.

But her baby grandson, Joash, had escaped. He was taken to the Temple, where Athaliah would never find him. A priest named Jehoiada looked after him there, and as Joash grew up, Jehoiada taught him all about God.

2 KINGS 11

Joash was seven years old when he became king.

2 Kings 11:21

In the seventh year, Jehoiada secretly sent for the palace and Temple guards and asked for their support. Then he put the crown on Joash's head and a copy of God's law in his hands. He made sure the guards surrounded him with their swords drawn.

"Stay close to your king," he ordered the guards as they led Joash out to face the people. Then he told everyone that Joash was king of Judah.

The crowd that had gathered cheered and shouted.

"Long live the king!"

Athaliah came to see what all the noise was about. When she saw that Joash was alive and had been made king, she was furious.

"Traitors!" she cried.

But the people had a new king. No one listened to her now.

Jehoiada made sure Athaliah was removed from the celebrations and then killed at the horse gate, out of the way of the crowds and of her grandson. Joash was seven years old when he became king.

JULY 3 — JOASH REPAIRS THE TEMPLE

Jehoiada made sure the people knew that everything would be different now in Judah. The people came back to God and renewed their promise to him so that they would once more be his people and he would be their God.

The altars and the idols of Baal were smashed. The temple of Baal was destroyed as it had been in Israel.

2 KINGS 12

All his life Joash did what was pleasing in the LORD's sight because Jehoiada the priest instructed him.

2 Kings 12:2

Joash had listened to everything Jehoiada had taught him about God. He told the priests to collect money from the people so that the Temple could be repaired.

Jehoiada found a large chest. He made a hole in the top of it and put it by the side of the altar for the people to put money in. Then when it was full, the silver would be melted down and weighed and used to pay the carpenters, the builders, and the stonecutters. It would also buy the wood and stone needed to make the repairs.

So repairs were made to the Temple, and Joash tried to lead his people back toward God.

July 4 — The Death of Elisha

In Israel, Jehu's son Jehoahaz became king, and after him, Jehoahaz's son Jehoash. During this time the prophet Elisha became very ill.

King Jehoash went to Elisha and wept. He knew that Elisha had served God faithfully but also that he and his people had failed to do so.

Elisha spoke to the king from his bed.

"Take some arrows and shoot one out of the window toward Syria," he said. The king did so.

"You are the Lord's arrow," Elisha told him. "You will fight and defeat the Syrians."

Then Elisha told the king to strike the ground with the other arrows. The king did so three times.

"If only you had struck the ground five or six times!" said Elisha. "You will defeat the Syrians, but only three times, not completely."

Elisha died and was buried.

Time passed, and king after king in Israel turned from God and failed to obey him. Evil men had power, and the people worshipped the gods of the nations around them again.

2 Kings 13:1-20

*Then Elisha died
and was buried.*
2 Kings 13:20

July 5 — Jonah Runs Away

The Assyrians were a growing threat to God's people. Their country bordered the lands of Israel to the north, and they were greedy to take more land for themselves and become even more powerful.

JONAH 1:1-3

The LORD gave this message to Jonah son of Amittai: "Get up and go to the great city of Nineveh."
Jonah 1:1-2

So when God called on Jonah, one of his prophets, to go to Nineveh and warn the people there to repent of their wickedness, Jonah was not happy. Why did Israel's God want anything to do with the Assyrians?

Jonah was so unhappy that he went to the port of Joppa to look for a ship going to Tarshish, about as far in the opposite direction as he could go.

Jonah paid for his ticket, boarded the ship, and then went inside the ship, where he fell into a deep sleep.

JULY 6—THE RAGING STORM

The ship had not been out to sea long when the wind grew stronger and a violent storm arose. Waves battered the sides of the ship, and it rocked back and forth so dangerously that the sailors on board were sure they would drown.

The men prayed to their gods and threw their belongings over the side to lighten the ship. They clung to one another in fear.

JONAH 1:4-12

"Throw me into the sea," Jonah said, "and it will become calm again. I know that this terrible storm is all my fault."
Jonah 1:12

Then the captain noticed that Jonah was missing. He went inside the ship to find him.

"Wake up!" he cried, shaking Jonah. "How can you sleep through this storm? Get up and pray! Perhaps your God can save us."

By this time the sailors were sure that the storm was someone's fault. They finally figured out that Jonah was responsible. Then they stood back and stared at him. It was clear that he was the guilty one.

"What terrible thing have you done that your God is punishing us?" they asked Jonah. "Who are you?"

"I worship the God who made the land and the sea," Jonah replied. "But I have run away from him. This is all my fault. There is only one thing you can do: You must throw me overboard."

JULY 7 — MAN OVERBOARD!

The sailors listened in horror. They did not want to kill Jonah, but they did not want to die either.

At first they tried to row back to shore, but the sea was too strong for them.

Then the sailors prayed to the living God. "Do not blame us for taking this man's life! We can do nothing else!"

They picked up Jonah and threw him over the side.

The wind stopped right away; the waves grew calm. The sailors were amazed and fell to their knees. They had seen the power of the living God.

Jonah, meanwhile, had sunk beneath the waves and felt himself falling down, down, down and strangled by seaweed. Then, as he felt his life slipping away from him, he called to God for help. And God answered.

God sent a huge fish to swallow him whole—and saved him.

Jonah stayed inside the body of the fish for three days and three nights. He thought about what had happened and how he had tried to run away from God. He remembered that he had once promised to serve God and do whatever he asked. Then he praised God and promised to serve him again because only his God had the power to save.

Then God spoke to the huge fish and commanded it to spit Jonah out onto dry land.

JONAH 1:13–2:10

The LORD had arranged for a great fish to swallow Jonah. And Jonah was inside the fish for three days and three nights.
Jonah 1:17

JULY 8 — THE GOD WHO FORGIVES

God had given Jonah a second chance. This time when God said, "Go to Nineveh," Jonah went.

Jonah went through the streets of the great city, and he preached the message that God had given him. He warned the people that they must ask

Jonah 3

The LORD spoke to Jonah a second time: "Get up and go to the great city of Nineveh, and deliver the message I have given you."
Jonah 3:1-2

for God's forgiveness and change their ways or their land would be destroyed in 40 days.

The people did not need to be told more than once! They heard what Jonah said, and they believed his message.

Even the king listened and acted. "No one is to eat or drink. Everyone must wear mourning clothes and ask God to forgive them. Everyone must stop doing evil and violent deeds. Perhaps even now it is possible that God may change his mind and forgive us."

God watched the people of Nineveh, and he heard their prayers. And because of God's kindness, he forgave them. He did not destroy the people of Assyria.

July 9—Jonah's Anger

Jonah 4

God said to Jonah, "Is it right for you to be angry because the plant died?" "Yes," Jonah retorted, "even angry enough to die!"
Jonah 4:9

Jonah was furious that God had listened to the prayers of the Assyrians.

"I knew this would happen," he told God angrily. "I knew you were kind and forgiving and that you would love these people if they changed their ways. That's why I ran away! They are evil people, and they deserve to die! Now I might as well be dead!"

Jonah went outside the city and pouted. God let a vine grow over his head to give him shade from the hot sun. But the next day, a worm ate the vine so that it died, and Jonah grew weak from the heat.

"Let me die!" he cried to God.

Then God spoke to Jonah. "Why are you so angry? I let the vine grow, and I let the vine die. You are unhappy about the death of the vine, even though you did nothing to help it grow and did not look after it. It is only a vine, but still you are angry. Now try to understand how I feel about the thousands of people who live in the city of Nineveh. They hardly know right from wrong, but I made these people. I know them and care about them. I do not want them to die, Jonah. You must not be angry because I choose to save them."

July 10—The God of the Poor

During the time when Uzziah was king of Judah, there was a shepherd named Amos who also looked after fig trees.

"Amos," God said, "I want you to give my people a message. Go to them and speak for me."

"Be warned!" Amos said to his own people in Judah. "God has seen what you do. You are no different from other nations. Although you know God's laws, you don't keep them. You have sinned again and again. For this you will be punished, and Jerusalem will be burned to the ground."

Then Amos spoke to the people of Israel. "Be warned! You are God's people, and he cares for you. Yet you ignore God's laws and you worship idols. You have plenty of money and enjoy many possessions, but you have become rich by ruling over others and cheating the poor people around you. Change your ways! Put what you believe into practice. Learn to love what is good and hate what is evil.

"This is what God says: 'You offer me gifts when you come to worship me. You sing noisy songs and play your harps. But I will accept none of this. I would rather you lived your lives in the right way, being fair and kind to those around you. Let all that is fair flow like a stream through a dry land, and let all that is right flow like a river that never runs dry.'"

Then God gave Amos a vision of a wall beside a plumb line, which checks to see if the wall is straight.

"I will put a plumb line in the middle of my people. I will judge them and see that they are not like a wall that is built straight. Instead they are crooked and out of line. The time is coming soon when they will lose what they have and be taken from their homes to live in a foreign land."

AMOS 1–9

The Lord replied, "I will test my people with this plumb line. I will no longer ignore all their sins."

Amos 7:8

JULY 11 — THE LOVING HUSBAND

HOSEA 1–14

When the LORD first began speaking to Israel through Hosea, he said to him, "Go and marry a prostitute."
Hosea 1:2

Then God chose another man, Hosea, to be his messenger.

"Your whole life will be a picture for my people in Israel," said God. "I want you to marry a woman who will make you sad. She will leave you and love other men. She won't care how much you love her, and she will forget all about you, no matter what you do for her. But you will not leave her. You will keep on loving her."

So Hosea married Gomer, and they had children. Gomer left him for another man, and eventually she became a slave.

"Now go and get your wife back," said God. "Buy her out of slavery. Live with her and keep on loving her."

Hosea paid the price to get his wife back, and he loved her.

"I love the people of Israel just as much as you love Gomer," explained God. "My people have hurt me and made me sad. They have ignored me and left me for other things. I have not left them. They will be punished, but I will keep on loving them."

JULY 12 — THE PROMISE OF PEACE

MICAH 1–7

O people, the LORD has told you what is good, and this is what he requires of you: to do what is right, to love mercy, and to walk humbly with your God.
Micah 6:8

It was about this time that the prophet Micah brought God's message to the people of Israel, warning them of the coming invasion of the Assyrians.

"You have sinned and rebelled against God!" said Micah. "You are supposed to be concerned about justice, yet you hate what is good and go on doing evil things. The time is coming when you will call out to God for help, but it will be too late! All your idols will be destroyed—everything will be smashed to pieces. Your enemies will defeat you, and you will be taken captive. You will be taken away from your home and be forced to live in a foreign land."

But Micah also promised that there would be a time after God's punishment when he would bring someone to save them.

Micah told the people, "God says to Bethlehem: 'You are one of the smallest towns in Judah, but I will bring from your people a ruler for Israel whose ancestors go back to ancient times. You will be defeated by your

enemies until the time when a woman gives birth to her son. Then those who have remained faithful to the Lord will come together.'

"God will stand among his people. He will lead them and care for them as a shepherd cares for his sheep. And there will be peace. Do you know what God wants of you? Do you know how to live so you can please him? He has already told you the answer. You must treat others fairly, you must always be kind, and you must be humble before God, your maker."

JULY 13 — ISAIAH'S VISION

ISAIAH 6:1-8

At the end of the rule of King Uzziah, God spoke to the people through the prophet Isaiah.

Isaiah was in the Temple when he had a vision of God and knew that God was calling him to serve him. Isaiah wrote down what he saw.

"God sat upon his throne, high above everyone else, and his long robe filled the Temple. Around him were heavenly creatures, each of which had six wings. With two wings they covered their faces. With two wings they covered their feet. And with two wings they flew.

"They called out to each other saying, 'Holy, holy, holy! The Lord God is full of power and glory!'

"The Temple shook from top to bottom at the sound of their voices, and it filled with smoke.

It was in the year King Uzziah died that I saw the Lord. He was sitting on a lofty throne, and the train of his robe filled the Temple.

Isaiah 6:1

"I felt so sinful, so unworthy, to be in God's holy presence. I knew that all my people and I are so far from the holiness of the God we claim to know and worship.

"Then one of the heavenly creatures flew down to me carrying a burning coal from the altar. He touched my lips with it and said, 'Your guilt is gone; your sins are forgiven.'

"Then I heard the voice of God: 'Whom shall I send?' he asked. 'Who will take my words to the people?'

"I answered, 'I will go! Send me!'"

JULY 14 — THE FUTURE KING

ISAIAH 1–9

A child is born to us, a son is given to us. The government will rest on his shoulders.
Isaiah 9:6

God sent Isaiah to his people with a message.

"God has seen all the terrible things you have done, and no one will escape God's punishment. Time is running out. Turn away from your wrong ways now," Isaiah told the people of Judah. "Tell God how sorry you are before it is too late."

No one wanted to hear bad news. But Isaiah also had good news. He told them about a time in the future when God would do something very wonderful.

"God will punish his people because they will not listen to him. But he will not be angry forever. God will remember his people.

"God will give his people his son. A child will be born who will rule over all people by doing what is fair and right. He will bring light into dark places. He will bring peace that lasts forever.

"He will be called Wonderful Counselor, Mighty God, Eternal Father, and Prince of Peace. He will be born into the family of King David, and God's own Spirit will be with him."

JULY 15 — ISRAEL FALLS TO THE ASSYRIANS

When Hoshea became king of Israel, King Shalmaneser of Assyria attacked Israel and defeated Hoshea's army. Hoshea was allowed to remain king as long as Israel paid heavy taxes to Assyria.

Hoshea tried to escape from Shalmaneser's rule with the help of the king of Egypt. Hoshea asked him to be on his side, so that together they could overthrow the Assyrians. But the plan was discovered, and the Assyrian army came into Israel. Shalmaneser arrested King Hoshea and had him put in prison. Then he marched on toward Samaria, where the people defended themselves for three years before they were defeated.

King Shalmaneser captured the people of Israel and had them taken away to Assyria. Then he filled the land that God had given to the Israelites with people from other tribes who bowed down to gods of wood and stone.

The warnings given by the prophets had begun to come true. God's people were being punished for rebelling against God and not following his ways.

2 KINGS 17:1-23

Israel was exiled from their land to Assyria, where they remain to this day.
2 Kings 17:23

JULY 16—HEZEKIAH TRUSTS GOD

In Judah, there was at last a king who loved God and followed his commandments. Hezekiah destroyed all the idols and places of false worship in the land, and he trusted God to help him and his people.

Hezekiah defeated the Philistines, and unlike the people of Israel, he refused to pay the Assyrians the taxes they demanded.

The Assyrian army swept through Israel, taking over some of Judah's major towns, before Hezekiah acted. To raise the money he needed, Hezekiah stripped the Temple of its treasures. But it was not enough. The Assyrian king, Sennacherib, demanded more.

"Surrender to Assyria!" shouted Sennacherib's official so that everyone could hear. "Don't listen to King Hezekiah! He thinks your God will help you! But your God is no different from the gods of all the nations around you. He has no power. He cannot save you."

Hezekiah put on mourning clothes and prayed. Then he sent messengers to the prophet Isaiah for advice.

Isaiah sent back a message for King Hezekiah: "God says that you must not let the Assyrians frighten you. Trust God. He will cause the commander to hear a rumor that will make him go home to his own country—and there he will be killed."

It happened just as God had told Isaiah.

The Assyrian commander received news of another attack and left Jerusalem. Before he went, he gave King Hezekiah a letter warning him not to trust in God.

2 Kings 18–19;
Isaiah 36–37

Hezekiah trusted in the LORD, the God of Israel. There was no one like him among all the kings of Judah, either before or after his time.
2 Kings 18:5

Then Hezekiah prayed, "Mighty Lord, you alone are God. You created the earth and the sky. Now Lord, look what is happening to us. Rescue us from the Assyrians, so that all the nations of the world will know that you alone are God."

"God has answered your prayer," said Isaiah. "The Assyrians will not enter the city, nor even shoot an arrow. God will defend us."

An angel went to the Assyrian camp, and that night 185,000 soldiers died. Sennacherib returned home to Nineveh, where he was killed by two of his sons.

July 17—The Shadow of the Sundial

Some time later, King Hezekiah became very ill. The prophet Isaiah went to visit him with a message from God.

"It is time for you to die," Isaiah told him. "Make sure you have put everything in order."

King Hezekiah turned to face the wall with tears rolling down his cheeks.

"Lord God, please remember me. Know that I have tried to serve you as best as I could."

As Isaiah left the palace, he heard God speaking to him again.

"Go back and give Hezekiah this message: I have seen his tears and heard his prayer. I will heal the king and let him live for another 15 years."

Isaiah rushed back to give the king this news. Isaiah told Hezekiah's servants to put a medicine made out of figs on the sores on his body.

"How can I be sure?" Hezekiah asked Isaiah. "Will God give me a sign of this?"

"Do you want the shadow of the sundial to move 10 steps backward or forward?" asked Isaiah.

"Backward!" exclaimed Hezekiah. "It always moves forward."

Isaiah prayed, and the shadow of the sundial (an ancient clock) moved 10 steps backward. Hezekiah went to the Temple to praise and worship God three days later.

God had given Hezekiah more time. In that time God blessed Hezekiah with wealth and riches. Hezekiah built more cities and had a tunnel dug from a spring so that fresh water flowed into Jerusalem.

When he died, Hezekiah was buried in the tomb of the kings.

2 Kings 20;
Isaiah 38–39

Isaiah the prophet asked the LORD to do this, and he caused the shadow to move ten steps backward on the sundial of Ahaz!
2 Kings 20:11

July 18 — Words of Hope

God gave messages of hope and comfort to Isaiah to pass on to his people.

"'Comfort my people,' says our God. 'Tell them that they have suffered long enough and now I will forgive them.'

"God himself is coming to rule his people. He will take care of them as a shepherd takes care of his sheep. He will gather the lambs together and carry them gently in his arms.

"Comfort, comfort my people," says your God.
Isaiah 40:1

"How can we describe our God? Can we take the ocean and measure it in our hands? Can we take all the soil from the earth and put it in a cup? Can we pick up a mountain and weigh it on a scale?

"At the beginning of time, God stretched out the sky like a curtain. He brought out the stars like an army and counted them.

"Do you think this God doesn't know about your troubles? Do you believe he doesn't care if you suffer? Haven't you heard about him? The Lord is God forever. He created the whole world. He doesn't grow tired or weary. Instead, he helps and supports all those who are weak. All those who put their trust in God will find new strength. They will rise on wings like eagles. They will run and not get tired. They will walk and not grow weak."

JULY 19—GOD'S LOVE FOR HIS PEOPLE

ISAIAH 43; 55

You will live in joy and peace. The mountains and hills will burst into song, and the trees of the field will clap their hands!
Isaiah 55:12

Another time Isaiah spoke to the people about God's love for them.

This is the message he gave them from God: "Do not be afraid, because I will save you. I have called you by your name. You belong to me.

"When you pass through deep waters, I will be with you. I will not let the floodwaters cover you. When you walk through fire, I will not let you be burned. The flames will not destroy you.

"I am the Lord your God, the Holy One of Israel, who will save you. You are precious to me, and I love you.

"Come to me, everyone who is thirsty. I have cool water for you! Come to me, everyone who has no money—I have a feast to share with you. Why do you want to spend your money on things that cannot make you happy? Why buy things that leave you hungry again tomorrow? Come to me and listen. Come to me and I will give you life!"

JULY 20—GOD'S PLAN TO SAVE HIS PEOPLE

Isaiah also told the people about the child God promised to send.

"This child will be rejected by his people. He will suffer and know pain. But his pain will be our pain. He will suffer in our place. He will die because we have sinned—not for any sin of his own. He will take the punishment that we deserve for our sins so that we can be forgiven.

"We are all like lost sheep, wandering away from the right path and going our own way. But he will be like a lamb that goes to be killed. He will be arrested and sentenced to death. He will be led away to die, though he will not commit any crime.

"It is God's will that he should suffer for us. He will go to his death willingly in our place. But after all he suffers, he will again have joy. He will know that his death has brought about something good. His one death will mean life for many people."

ISAIAH 53

All of us, like sheep, have strayed away. We have left God's paths to follow our own. Yet the LORD laid on him the sins of us all.
Isaiah 53:6

JULY 21—KING MANASSEH'S PUNISHMENT

Hezekiah's son Manasseh became king after his father's death. But instead of worshipping God, he started to worship the sun, the moon, and the stars. He sacrificed his own son to foreign gods and practiced witchcraft. He brought idols into God's Temple, and he was even guilty of killing many innocent people.

Manasseh would not listen to the warnings of the prophets God sent to him. When the Assyrians attacked Judah, they took Manasseh prisoner. They

embarrassed him and put a ring in his nose. They locked him up in bronze chains and took him to Babylon.

Finally, after all his suffering, Manasseh remembered God and how he had disobeyed him.

2 Kings 21:1-22;
2 Chronicles 33:1-23

While in deep distress, Manasseh sought the LORD his God and sincerely humbled himself before the God of his ancestors.
2 Chronicles 33:12

"I have been wicked! I am so sorry for all the things I have done," he cried. Then he asked God to forgive him.

God heard Manasseh's prayer. God let him return to Jerusalem, where Manasseh destroyed the altars and the idols he had made. Then Manasseh told the people that they must follow God's ways.

Some of the people listened, but others—including his own son Amon, who became king after him—continued to sin. They rejected God and disobeyed his commandments.

July 22 — King Josiah's Sorrow

After a plot against him by his own officials, Amon was killed. His son Josiah was only eight when he was made king of Judah.

Josiah wanted to serve God as his ancestor King David had done. He set about repairing the Temple so that he could lead the people in worshipping God again.

When the work was underway, the high priest, Hilkiah, discovered an old scroll that had not been read for years. In it was the promise God had made with his people, and the prophecy of how God would destroy Jerusalem because of the people's disobedience.

When Josiah heard the laws written on the scroll, he wept and showed how sad he was.

He told the people, "Pray to God. Find out what God wants us to do. We have broken all his laws, and he must be so angry with us."

Hilkiah hurried to find the prophetess Huldah.

"God says that he will destroy Jerusalem," she said. "The people have abandoned him and worshipped idols. But God has also seen the king's sorrow. Judah will be destroyed, but not in King Josiah's lifetime."

Josiah summoned the people to the Temple. The scroll was read out loud so that everyone could hear it.

"I promise to serve God with all my heart," declared Josiah.

"We promise too," declared the people.

Josiah started removing and destroying all the idols and altars to foreign gods in the land. When it was done, he led the people in celebrating the Passover and remembering how God had led the Israelites out of slavery in Egypt.

Josiah served God with all his heart, all his mind, and all his strength, and he obeyed God's commandments.

2 KINGS 21:23–23:25

When the king heard what was written in the Book of the Law, he tore his clothes in despair.
2 Kings 22:11

JULY 23 — GOD'S CHOSEN MESSENGER

The evil of King Manasseh could not easily be forgotten. There would be peace in Josiah's time, but not for those who came after him. When Josiah had been king for 12 years, God spoke to a priest's teenage son, Jeremiah.

"Before you were created in your mother's womb, I knew you, Jeremiah. Before you were born, I chose you and set you apart to be my messenger."

Jeremiah could hardly believe God's words.

"But I'm only a child," he answered. "I don't know how to serve you and be your prophet!"

"I will tell you what to say," said God. "You must not be afraid—I will be with you, and I will keep you safe."

Then Jeremiah felt a hand touch his lips.

"I have put my words in your mouth," said God. "Speak for me."

A picture started to form before Jeremiah's eyes, and in his vision he saw

JEREMIAH 1

*"I knew you before
I formed you in
your mother's
womb. Before you
were born I set you
apart and appointed
you as my prophet
to the nations."*
Jeremiah 1:5

a pot, full of boiling water. It was tilting toward the south, and the hot liquid was ready to gush out.

"The people of Judah have been disobedient. They have worshiped idols, and they have not obeyed my laws. Soon they will be destroyed by an enemy from the north," said God.

"Now Jeremiah, go and tell them what you have seen. They will be angry—they will not want to hear it. But remember that I am with you."

JULY 24 — A REBELLIOUS PEOPLE

Jeremiah went to the people of Jerusalem with God's words.

"I remember when I first brought you out of Egypt," said God. "You were my special people, and I was your God. You loved me and wanted to follow me with all your hearts. I protected you from your enemies, and you trusted me alone.

"What went wrong? Why did your ancestors forget their promise? What made them turn from me to worthless idols? When they were in trouble, I was there to help them. They only needed to ask, and I would have rescued them. But they preferred gods made out of wood and stone. They preferred a god made with hands rather than the God who had made them and the world they lived in. Now you are in real trouble. Where are your gods now? Let them save you if they can!

"But it's not too late to be sorry. It's not too late to come back to me and keep the agreement we had. Act now, people of Judah! Weep for your sins, and show you are sorry. Turn from your wicked ways and love me again.

JEREMIAH 2–17

*The LORD gave
another message
to Jeremiah. He
said, "Remind the
people of Judah
and Jerusalem
about the terms
of my covenant
with them."*
Jeremiah 11:1-2

"The time is coming soon when there will be no chance to make things right. Your enemy in the north is preparing for battle. His war chariots are coming like a whirlwind! His horses are faster than eagles and will swoop down and destroy you! They have taken up their bows and swords. They are cruel and without mercy. Change your ways now. You have brought the trouble upon yourselves, but it is not too late to turn back to me."

Jeremiah wept for the people. He went to them time and time again and warned them of the punishment that was awaiting them. He told them that God would listen if they came back and said they were sorry. But the people laughed at Jeremiah. They would not believe what he said.

JULY 25 — THE POTTER'S CLAY

One day, God told Jeremiah to go down to the potter's house.

Jeremiah stood and watched the potter at his wheel. He molded a lump of clay, carefully cupping his wet hands around it, pulling the clay up and out into the shape of a pot. But suddenly the wheel stopped spinning. The potter was unhappy with the shape of the pot. He picked up the clay, threw it back on the wheel, and began to reshape it into something better.

"I am like that potter," said God. "My people are like the clay. If they fail to be the nation I planned because they are rebellious and disobedient, then I will start again. I will reshape them into something useful and perfect. The people of Judah will suffer, and the suffering will shape them into the people I want them to be."

Then God told Jeremiah to buy a clay pot and go out to the valley of Ben-Hinnom with some of the elders and priests. There he was to warn them about the terrible things that were to happen.

"God's people have filled this place with the blood of innocent people," Jeremiah told them. "Now God will punish them. Soon this will be called the Valley of Slaughter. The enemy will come and take over the city, and the suffering will be terrible."

Then Jeremiah smashed the clay pot in front of the men.

JEREMIAH 18:1–20:2

The jar he was making did not turn out as he had hoped, so he crushed it into a lump of clay again and started over.
Jeremiah 18:4

"This is what God says he will do to this rebellious people," he said. "They will be broken into so many pieces that they cannot be put back together."

Still the people did not believe Jeremiah. Pashhur the priest had him beaten and chained up by one of the gates in the Temple.

JULY 26—JEREMIAH BUYS A FIELD

JEREMIAH 32

Then I knew that the message I had heard was from the LORD. So I bought the field at Anathoth, paying Hanamel seventeen pieces of silver for it.
Jeremiah 32:8-9

The Babylonians were making attacks on Jerusalem when God told Jeremiah to buy a field from his cousin Hanamel.

So when Jeremiah received a visit from his cousin, he bought the field and had the papers signed in front of witnesses. But Jeremiah did not understand. Why buy land when God had said that everything would be destroyed?

"Lord God," said Jeremiah. "I know that nothing is impossible for you, but why did you want me to buy that field?"

"It is a sign of what will happen," said God. "Jerusalem will be destroyed because my people have refused to listen to me. But one day, some of them will return. They will come back to live here, and fields will once more be bought and sold. This is my promise for the future. I will look after my people. I will give them good things, and I will be their God."

JULY 27—THE WORDS IN THE FIRE

When Jehoiakim was king of Judah, the prophecies about the destruction of Jerusalem began to come true. The attacks made on Judah by King Nebuchadnezzar of Babylon became more fierce. But still no one took Jeremiah seriously.

"Buy a scroll," said God to Jeremiah, "and write down everything I have ever told you. Perhaps when the people hear it and understand all that is going to happen, they will see how wicked they have been, and I will be able to forgive them."

Jeremiah told everything to Baruch, who wrote Jeremiah's words on the scroll.

"Take this scroll to the Temple," said Jeremiah. "I have been banned from going there. Go on a special day, when there will be lots of people there. Read to them everything that you have written."

Baruch went to the Temple and read from the scroll. The people listened to all the things God had told Jeremiah about what would happen. When Jehudi heard about it, he told Baruch to come and read it to him and the other court officials.

When these men heard God's words, they were terrified. They realized the warning must be taken seriously.

"We must tell the king," they said. "But you and Jeremiah must hide."

It was almost winter, and King Jehoiakim was sitting by an open fire as Jehudi unrolled the scroll and read to him. But he had read only a few columns before Jehoiakim told him to stop. Then the king took a knife, cut the words from the scroll, and threw them carelessly into the fire. The more Jehudi read, the more Jehoiakim cut from the scroll and threw into the flames, until the whole scroll was burned.

Then the king sent his men to find Jeremiah and Baruch. He would not listen to God's warning. He wanted the prophets to be punished.

"Start again," said God to Jeremiah. "Write on another scroll. I will punish Jehoiakim because he has refused to listen to me."

JEREMIAH 36

Each time Jehudi finished reading three or four columns, the king took a knife and cut off that section of the scroll. He then threw it into the fire, section by section, until the whole scroll was burned up.
Jeremiah 36:23

JULY 28 — THE BABYLONIANS TAKE CAPTIVES

Nothing could stop the Babylonians from attacking Judah. They had captured officials, builders, and craftsmen. They had captured King Jehoiakim and taken him away to Babylon in chains. King Nebuchadnezzar had stripped the palace and taken away many of the beautiful treasures from the Temple.

Then in the spring, the Babylonians returned. All the remaining treasures were taken from the Temple. Jehoiakim's son Jehoiachin, who was now king, was captured and taken to Babylon, along with 10,000 others. Among these was a man named Ezekiel.

Once they were captives in a foreign land, the people remembered the words of warning the prophets had given them. They wished they had listened. They began to be sorry they had disobeyed God. But the people who were left unharmed in Jerusalem thought they had escaped God's punishment. Despite what had happened, they were pleased with themselves.

JEREMIAH 24;
EZEKIEL 1:1-2

"This is what the LORD, the God of Israel, says: The good figs represent the exiles I sent from Judah to the land of the Babylonians."
Jeremiah 24:5

Nebuchadnezzar made Zedekiah king of Judah.

Jeremiah was one of those left behind in Jerusalem. One day he was near the Temple.

"Look at those two baskets of figs," said God. "What do you see?"

"One basket is full of good, ripe figs," replied Jeremiah. "The other figs are rotten. They are not worth anything."

"Think about those figs," said God. "The people who are in captivity in Babylon are like the good figs. I will watch over them and look after them until the time is right for them to return. But the rotten figs are like King Zedekiah and all those who are left behind in Jerusalem. They are so bad that they are not worth saving."

JULY 29 — JEREMIAH IN PRISON

Outside the walls of Jerusalem, King Nebuchadnezzar had built extra walls of protection. Day after day, month after month, the soldiers camped outside. Inside the city, food became scarce. King Zedekiah asked Jeremiah to pray to God for help.

"The Babylonians will retreat when they see that the Egyptians are coming to help you," said God. "But it will not last long. They will return and take over the city and then burn it down. Only those who surrender will be safe."

Knowing that the enemy had retreated for a while, Jeremiah went out through the city gates to look at the field that God had told him to buy.

"Why are you leaving the city?" demanded one of the soldiers. "You traitor! You are going to join the Babylonians!"

He dragged Jeremiah back and had him beaten and imprisoned in an underground cell. He was still there when King Zedekiah sent for him to see if there were any messages from God.

"God has said that you will be handed over to the Babylonians," Jeremiah told him. "But why am I in prison? Please don't send me back there, or I am sure it will kill me."

Zedekiah had Jeremiah locked up in the palace courtyard instead, but while he was there, he continued to tell all who would listen what God had told him.

"Surrender to the Babylonians and you will escape with your life! Stay here and you will starve to death or get deathly sick! God has given Jerusalem to the Babylonians—he is punishing his people because they have turned from him to foreign idols."

"Stop that man!" the officials told the king. "He is spreading fear among the soldiers! How can they put up a fight when he tells them there is no hope left?"

Zedekiah waved them away.

"Do what you like with him!" he said.

JEREMIAH 37:1–38:5

King Zedekiah commanded that Jeremiah not be returned to the dungeon. Instead, he was imprisoned in the courtyard of the guard in the royal palace. The king also commanded that Jeremiah be given a loaf of fresh bread every day as long as there was any left in the city.
Jeremiah 37:21

JULY 30—AT THE BOTTOM OF THE WELL

JEREMIAH 38:6-13

The officials took Jeremiah from his cell and lowered him by ropes into an empty cistern in the prison yard. . . . There was no water in the cistern, but there was a thick layer of mud at the bottom, and Jeremiah sank down into it.

Jeremiah 38:6

Jeremiah was thrown into the well. There was no water there, but he sank down into the mud. As he sat in the darkness, he thought he was going to die.

Ebed-melech, one of the king's officials, heard what had happened.

"Your Majesty," he said, "Jeremiah will die if he is left in the well."

King Zedekiah was weary.

"Bring him out before he dies," he said.

So Ebed-melech found some rope, some worn-out clothing, and some men to help him. He made sure Jeremiah put the clothing under his arms so the rope would not hurt him, and he gently hauled Jeremiah up out of the well and into the light.

JULY 31—THE FALL OF JERUSALEM

"Tell me what you know!" said King Zedekiah. "What will happen to me?"

"I have told you many, many times," said Jeremiah, "but you do not listen. Unless you surrender to the Babylonians, you and your family will die."

"But I'm afraid!" wailed Zedekiah. "What will they do to me if I surrender?"

"If you obey God, you will live," Jeremiah assured him.

But Zedekiah did not listen. The Babylonians attacked Jerusalem once more. The people were starving. King Zedekiah and his soldiers tried to escape by leaving the city at night and going through the royal garden.

The Babylonians chased after the king and took him prisoner. They killed his sons in front of him, murdered his officials, and then blinded him. They locked him up with chains and took him to Babylon, where he remained in prison until he died.

The Babylonians raided the Temple of anything left that was valuable and could be carried away. They set fire to all the buildings and broke down the city walls. They put the people in chains and took them away to Babylon. Only a few poor people were left behind to work in the fields.

A captain in the Babylonian guard saw Jeremiah, who was in chains.

"All this happened just as you said it would, because your people ignored your God," said the captain. "I will let you go free. You can come with me to Babylon, or you can stay here if you prefer."

Jeremiah knew that God had kept his promise and kept him safe. Jeremiah made his decision. He chose to stay with the people who were left in his homeland.

JEREMIAH 38:14–40:6

Jeremiah returned to Gedaliah son of Ahikam at Mizpah, and he lived in Judah with the few who were still left in the land.
Jeremiah 40:6

AUGUST 1 — CAPTIVES IN BABYLON

The captives who had been taken to Babylon were not treated badly. King Nebuchadnezzar asked his chief officer to choose some of the best young men to be educated and trained to work for him in the palace.

Among those chosen were four young men from the royal palace in Judah: Daniel, Hananiah, Mishael, and Azariah. They were given new names—Belteshazzar, Shadrach, Meshach, and Abednego—and were given food and wine from the king's own table. They were to be trained for three years.

Daniel was unhappy. Although he was a captive in a strange land, he did not want to eat any of the foods that were forbidden by God. He asked the king's chief officer to give him only water to drink and vegetables to eat.

"The king himself has decided what you must eat to make you strong and healthy," he answered. "I will lose my life as well as my job if you get sick!"

So Daniel spoke instead to the guard.

"We won't get sick. Try it and see. Give us just water and vegetables. If we look weak after 10 days, then we will eat whatever you give us."

The guard agreed, and 10 days later, Daniel and his friends looked healthier than the other young men. So they were allowed to eat the food they

DANIEL 1

The king talked with them, and no one impressed him as much as Daniel, Hananiah, Mishael, and Azariah. So they entered the royal service.
Daniel 1:19

had chosen. Then God blessed them and gave them special abilities, so that they were the best among the captives who had been chosen. God also gave Daniel the ability to understand dreams and visions.

When the four young men had finished their training, they were presented to King Nebuchadnezzar. He was amazed at their wisdom and understanding.

AUGUST 2 — NEBUCHADNEZZAR'S DREAM

King Nebuchadnezzar did not sleep well. His mind was troubled, and he had strange dreams that worried him.

He called his magicians and wise men and told them the problem.

"Tell me what I dreamed and what it means, so that I will once more be able to sleep!" said the king.

"Tell us your dream, and we will explain it to you," his wise men replied.

But the king became angry. "No! I will reward the person who tells me what I dreamed and its meaning. But if you cannot, then you will all be killed!"

"It's impossible!" they cried. "There is no one on earth who can do what you ask!"

So Nebuchadnezzar sent them away and ordered that they be killed.

When the king's official came to find Daniel and his friends to carry out the order, Daniel asked what had happened to make the king so angry. Then he went to King Nebuchadnezzar and asked for more time to find the meaning of the dream.

"Pray!" Daniel urged his friends. "We must ask God to show the king's dream to us, or we will die with all the wise men in Babylon."

The four men prayed and asked God to help them, and during the night, God gave Daniel a vision so that the mystery was clear to him.

"We praise you, Lord God!" Daniel prayed. "All wisdom and power are yours. You give wisdom to the wise and show things hidden in darkness, mysteries that no one can understand. You have answered my prayer and given me wisdom. You have shown me the king's dream."

DANIEL 2:1-23

That night the secret was revealed to Daniel in a vision. Then Daniel praised the God of heaven.
Daniel 2:19

August 3 — The Mystery Revealed

The next day, Daniel went to the king.

"Can you tell me what I dreamed?" asked Nebuchadnezzar.

"Your majesty," said Daniel, "there is no wise man alive who can tell you what you dreamed. But there is a God in heaven who can reveal mysteries, and he has shown you what the future holds.

"You dreamed of a huge statue. Its head was made of gold, its chest and arms were made of silver, its belly and thighs were made of bronze, its legs were made of iron, and its feet were made of iron and clay.

"Then a rock was cut out of a mountain. It fell down and shattered the statue so that the gold, silver, bronze, iron, and clay all lay in pieces. Then a wind came and blew it all away, while the rock became a mountain as big as the earth.

"This is what it means," continued Daniel. "God has given you everything you have. God has given you power over all you see around you. You are the golden head of the statue. After you will come other powerful kingdoms, but in time they will all fall away.

"The rock that became a mountain, stronger than everything else, is the Kingdom that God will make. God's Kingdom will be greater than any of them, and it will last forever. It will never end."

King Nebuchadnezzar fell at Daniel's feet.

DANIEL 2:24-49

The king said to Daniel, "Truly, your God is the greatest of gods, the LORD over kings, a revealer of mysteries, for you have been able to reveal this secret."

Daniel 2:47

"Your God is the true God!" he cried. "He is the King of all kings!"

Then King Nebuchadnezzar gave Daniel many fine gifts and made him ruler over Babylon and all the wise men in the kingdom. And Daniel gave his friends Shadrach, Meshach, and Abednego important jobs in Babylon, while he continued to stay in the palace.

AUGUST 4—THE GOLDEN STATUE

King Nebuchadnezzar made a huge statue of gold. It was placed in an open field in Babylon and was so tall and wide that it could be seen for miles around.

DANIEL 3:1-7

King Nebuchadnezzar made a gold statue ninety feet tall and nine feet wide.
Daniel 3:1

Nebuchadnezzar called everyone of any importance in the area to stand before the statue.

An announcer stood up and gave this message: "The king has commanded all people, whatever language you speak, to bow down and worship the golden statue that King Nebuchadnezzar has made. As soon as you hear the sound of music, you must bow down and worship. Anyone who fails to do this will be thrown into a blazing furnace of fire!"

The music sounded. All the people fell down to worship the statue as they had been commanded—except Shadrach, Meshach, and Abednego.

AUGUST 5—THE BLAZING FURNACE OF FIRE

Some of the king's advisers were troublemakers.

"Your Majesty," they said one day to the king, "you have commanded that everyone should fall down and worship the golden statue that stands in the field. But there are some men you have put in charge who do not obey your order or worship your gods. There are three Jews—Shadrach, Meshach, and Abednego—who refuse to bow down and worship the statue."

The king was very angry. He sent for Daniel's three friends.

"I have heard that you refuse to obey me," the king said. "But I will give you one more chance. Bow down and worship the statue—or you will be thrown into the blazing furnace of fire. Then no god will be able to save you!"

"King Nebuchadnezzar," the friends replied, "you are a great man, but our God is even greater. If you throw us into the blazing furnace of fire, our God is able to save us. But whether he decides to rescue us or not, we will worship only him. We will not bow down and worship your golden statue."

In a rage, the king ordered that the furnace be heated to the highest temperature and that the three men be tied up and thrown, fully clothed, into the fire.

Nebuchadnezzar watched. Then he stared in amazement.

"Didn't we tie up three men and throw them into the fire? Yet I can see four men, and they are walking around in freedom! Get them out, quickly!"

The three men stepped out of the fire. They were completely unharmed and no longer tied up. They were not burned by the fire, their clothing was not scorched, and they did not even smell of smoke.

"Praise the living God!" exclaimed Nebuchadnezzar. "He sent an angel to rescue you, because you were prepared to die rather than worship the statue I had made."

Then Nebuchadnezzar issued another command: "No one of any language may say anything against the God of Shadrach, Meshach, and Abednego. For he alone has the power to save."

DANIEL 3:8-30

"Look!" Nebuchadnezzar shouted. "I see four men, unbound, walking around in the fire unharmed! And the fourth looks like a god!"
Daniel 3:25

AUGUST 6 — THE KING LOSES HIS MIND

King Nebuchadnezzar dreamed again and called all his advisers to help him. As before, none could help him except Daniel.

"I dreamed that I was looking at a tree that grew so tall it touched the sky. It could be seen from all the ends of the earth. Its leaves were beautiful, and it produced enough fruit for everyone to eat. It was so strong that all the creatures on earth lived under it, and all the birds made nests in its branches.

DANIEL 4

"Now I, Nebuchadnezzar, praise and glorify and honor the King of heaven. All his acts are just and true, and he is able to humble the proud."
Daniel 4:37

"But while I watched, an angel came from heaven. It called for the tree to be chopped down, its branches to be cut off, its leaves to be stripped, and its fruit to be scattered. The animals fled from under it, and the birds flew away. But its stump was tied up with chains, and it was drenched with dew."

Daniel understood the meaning of the dream, but he was afraid to tell the king. King Nebuchadnezzar encouraged him to hold nothing back.

"The dream is a nightmare, O King!" said Daniel. "I wish it applied to someone other than you. But you are that tree that has grown as tall as the sky so that all the nations around know how great and powerful you are.

"God has seen all this but now wants you to know that you are nothing compared to him. He wants you to change and do what is right. He wants you to be kind to those you have ruled over harshly. Until you do this, your mind will be destroyed, and you will live among the animals and eat grass like the cattle."

It all happened as Daniel told the king. Nebuchadnezzar endured a time when he lost his mind. But at the end of it, he realized that God is indeed the God of all the earth. He praised God and understood that he loves kindness and justice and hates unfairness and cruelty.

AUGUST 7 — THE WRITING ON THE WALL

When King Nebuchadnezzar died, Daniel and his friends were forgotten. Years passed and the new king, Belshazzar, held a magnificent feast.

All the great men in Babylon were invited, and Belshazzar ordered that the wine be served in the gold and silver goblets that Nebuchadnezzar had taken from the Temple in Jerusalem.

The guests ate and drank; they raised their goblets and shouted, "Praise be to the gods of gold, silver, bronze, iron, wood, and stone!"

Suddenly the fingers of a human hand appeared and started moving against the wall. One by one people stopped eating and drinking. Their mouths dropped open in amazement and fear. They looked at the king. His face turned the color of ashes, his hands shook, and finally he collapsed on the floor.

The fingers wrote, "MENE, MENE, TEKEL, PARSIN."

"Find someone to tell me what this means!" said Belshazzar weakly. "I will make him the third most powerful person in the land."

None of the magicians or wise men could tell him the meaning of the writing on the wall.

Then the king's mother remembered that Daniel had helped Nebuchadnezzar with the meaning of his dreams, and he was sent for.

"Tell me what it means, and I will reward you," said the king.

"I don't want a reward," said Daniel. "God sent this hand to write on the wall because he has seen your wickedness. He has weighed you on the scales, and you have been judged unworthy. Now your rule is at an end. Your kingdom will be taken by the Medes and the Persians."

Belshazzar knew he had heard the truth, but it was too late. That night the Persian army attacked Babylon. Belshazzar was killed.

DANIEL 5

"This is the message that was written: MENE, MENE, TEKEL, and PARSIN."
Daniel 5:25

August 8 — A Plot against Daniel

When Darius the Mede became ruler, he saw that Daniel was gifted and experienced, so he made Daniel one of his top three officials.

Daniel 6:1-9

They concluded, "Our only chance of finding grounds for accusing Daniel will be in connection with the rules of his religion."
Daniel 6:5

Daniel worked hard, and Darius was so impressed with him that he wanted to put Daniel in charge of the whole kingdom. But there were other officials who were jealous of Daniel. They wanted to remove him from power. They wanted to find something—anything—that would make him lose his job.

"It's useless!" they said to one another. "The only way we will ever get rid of Daniel is if it has something to do with his God."

They started making plans, and slowly an idea began to take shape. They went to see Darius.

"Your Majesty, may you live forever!" they said. "We all think that you should issue an order. No one may pray to anyone but you for the next 30 days. If they do, they should be thrown into a den of lions!"

Darius was proud and pleased. It was a good idea, he thought. He even put it in writing so that it became law. And the law of the Medes and Persians could not be changed.

August 9 — Daniel and the Lions

When Daniel heard about the new law, he went as usual to his upstairs room, where the windows faced Jerusalem. There he knelt down and prayed three times a day to God, asking him for help.

The men who wanted to bring Daniel down were watching. Their plan had worked.

"Your Majesty," they said, "are we right in thinking that anyone who disobeys your order will be thrown into a den of lions?"

King Darius nodded.

"This law cannot be changed," he said.

"But Daniel, the man who has such power in your kingdom, ignores the command. He does not pray to you. Instead he prays three times a day to his God."

Darius was very sad. He realized that the men had set out to trap him, and now he was powerless to rescue Daniel. Darius had no choice. He ordered his men to throw Daniel into the lions' den.

"May your God save you," he said to Daniel.

That night Darius could not sleep. As soon as it was morning, he returned to the lions' den.

"Daniel!" he cried. "Has your God saved you from the lions?"

"Yes, Your Majesty!" shouted Daniel from the den. "My God has saved me! He sent an angel to close the mouths of the hungry lions. I am unharmed."

"Release Daniel from the den!" cried Darius, overjoyed to find Daniel alive. "And punish those men who have tried to hurt him."

Then Darius made another law.

"All the people in my kingdom must worship and respect Daniel's God. For he is the living God, whose kingdom will last forever. He is the God who rescues and saves; he is the God who performs signs and wonders. And he has the power to save, even from the mouths of lions!"

Daniel continued to be faithful to God for the rest of his life.

DANIEL 6:10-28

"My God sent his angel to shut the lions' mouths so that they would not hurt me."
Daniel 6:22

AUGUST 10—A VISION OF GOD

Ezekiel was a priest. When Nebuchadnezzar attacked Jerusalem, Ezekiel had been taken as a prisoner along with many other Jewish people and forced to live on the banks of the Kebar River in Babylon.

One day God spoke to Ezekiel in a vision. First Ezekiel saw a storm cloud moving toward him, with lightning flashing around it in every direction. In the center was a fire that glowed with extreme heat. Within the fire, Ezekiel saw four winged creatures that shot through the sky at lightning speed.

Then Ezekiel saw the four creatures moving on the ground, each with a crystal wheel that was full of eyes. The sound of their wings was as loud as a marching army or the roar of rushing water.

As Ezekiel watched, he heard a voice. The creatures lowered their wings, and above a sapphire throne, Ezekiel saw something like the shape of a man. He glowed with brilliant, fiery light and shone with all the colors of the rainbow.

Ezekiel fell to the ground. He knew this was a vision of God in all his glory.

"Stand on your feet, and I will speak to you," said the voice. Then the Spirit of God helped Ezekiel get up off his knees. "I have chosen you as a messenger to my rebellious people, the Jews. You must not be afraid but must give them my message, even though they will not want to hear it. Now open your mouth and eat what I will give you."

Ezekiel opened his mouth, and God gave him a scroll to eat, which had many words written on it. It tasted as sweet as honey.

"Go now and speak to my people, and I will help you, even when they refuse to listen," said God.

EZEKIEL 1:1–3:9

The voice said to me, "Son of man, eat what I am giving you—eat this scroll! Then go and give its message to the people of Israel."
Ezekiel 3:1

AUGUST 11—EZEKIEL'S OBEDIENCE

God spoke through Ezekiel by letting him act out his message. The people watched the prophet and understood by his actions the message that God had for them.

Ezekiel drew a picture of Jerusalem on a clay brick. Then he made armies, military equipment, and ramps, and he acted out an attack. He ate only wheat, barley, beans, lentils, and grains, and he drank only water. He had only a little bit, day after day, so that he became thin and weak.

The people understood that Jerusalem would be attacked by their enemies.

Ezekiel shaved off his hair and beard and divided it into three piles. He took a third of the hair and burned it inside a model of the city of Jerusalem. He took another third and chopped it up around the outside of the model with his sword. The rest, apart from a few strands of hair, he scattered to the wind. Then Ezekiel tucked the few remaining strands carefully inside his cloak.

God's message was clear: Many of his people would die by fire or by sword in the attack on Jerusalem. Others would be taken out of their homeland and scattered. But there would still be a few, a remnant, who would survive. And these few would one day return safely to their home in Jerusalem.

EZEKIEL 4–5

"Therefore, I myself, the Sovereign LORD, am now your enemy. I will punish you publicly while all the nations watch."
Ezekiel 5:8

AUGUST 12 — DRY BONES

Ezekiel continued to speak to the people through the events in his life for many years. Then, just as God's people in Babylon were ready to give up hope, Ezekiel had another vision.

God's Spirit took Ezekiel to the middle of a valley, where there were dry, lifeless bones scattered all around him. As Ezekiel walked through them, God asked him whether he thought the bones could ever live again.

"Lord, only you know that," replied Ezekiel.

"Speak to these bones!" said God.

So Ezekiel spoke to them with the words God gave him. "Dry bones, hear the word of the Lord! God says that he will put you together again and cover you with skin. He will give you breath so that you will once more breathe and have life. Then you will know that he is God."

EZEKIEL 37:1-14

*He said to me,
"Speak a prophetic
message to these
bones and say, 'Dry
bones,' listen to the
word of the LORD!'"*
Ezekiel 37:4

A rattling sound echoed through the valley, and one by one the bones moved and locked together to form skeletons. Slowly the bones were held together with muscles, and then they were covered with flesh and wrapped in new skin.

"Tell the wind to give these bodies breath!" said God.

Ezekiel spoke to the wind, and the lungs of the lifeless bodies filled so that they could breathe again and come to life. They stood up, and there were so many that they formed a large army.

"This is what I will do for my people," God told Ezekiel. "I will breathe new life into them. I will take them back to the land of Israel, the land I promised would be their home. Then everyone will know that I am God."

AUGUST 13 — THE EXILES RETURN TO JERUSALEM

The Jewish exiles had been living under the rule of the Persians since the Persians had overthrown the Babylonians. It was time for God's promises to come true. The messages for his people, spoken by Isaiah, Jeremiah, and Ezekiel, were about to take place.

The king of Persia, Cyrus, sent this order to the Jewish people: "I know that the Lord, the God of heaven, has put me in charge of many people and many nations. He has told me to rebuild the Temple in Jerusalem. Any of you who wish to return to Jerusalem may now go and help with this work. Those who want to stay here can help in other ways, by making donations of gold or silver or animals."

God's people could hardly believe what was happening. After all the years of suffering, all the years when they were living in a foreign land, they were being allowed to go home—and instructed to rebuild God's Temple.

Preparations were made. Silver and gold were collected. The first group of excited people, led by Zerubbabel, prepared to leave.

"I will give back to you all the things Nebuchadnezzar took from your Temple," said King Cyrus. "They don't belong here."

So God's people took back with them not only the riches they had been given, but also 5,400 pieces of gold and silver—in bowls and dishes and pans.

More than 50,000 people made the journey to Jerusalem, along with horses, mules, camels, and donkeys.

EZRA 1–2

[The LORD] stirred the heart of Cyrus to put this proclamation in writing and to send it throughout his kingdom.
Ezra 1:1

AUGUST 14—THE REBUILDING BEGINS

When God's people reached their land, they went first to the places that had been their homes. They stayed there for a few months before meeting together in Jerusalem.

There they made plans for rebuilding the Temple, and Jeshua and Zerubbabel started to rebuild the altar. As soon as it was made, they started to offer sacrifices to God. They celebrated the festivals as they had before they were captured, even though they were afraid of the people around them. They worshipped God even before the foundation of the Temple was laid.

Then they ordered logs from Tyre and Sidon, as Solomon had before them. They paid the builders and the carpenters to start building the foundations, and when the foundations were finished, the people met together to praise and thank God.

"God is good!" they sang. "His love and goodness last forever!"

EZRA 3–6

The Temple was finally finished, as had been commanded by the God of Israel and decreed by Cyrus, Darius, and Artaxerxes, the kings of Persia.
Ezra 6:14

But the people of Samaria and others living in the land of Judah were not happy. In the years that followed, they made up stories about God's people and wrote letters full of lies to the kings who were ruling at the time. After the death of King Cyrus, they questioned whether the Jews had any right to be there at all and stopped the work of rebuilding.

God spoke through the prophets Haggai and Zechariah to encourage the people.

"Keep on building!" they said. "This is God's will for his people. Do not give up, and he will bless us. Jerusalem will once more be a place where God is worshipped."

King Darius of Persia supported them against their enemies.

"Do not stop the rebuilding work," ordered King Darius. Then he warned their enemies that if they blocked the work on the Temple, they would be punished. So the people continued to build the Temple until it was finished.

AUGUST 15 — ESTHER IS MADE QUEEN

ESTHER 1:1–2:18

The king loved Esther more than any of the other young women.
Esther 2:17

When Xerxes had been king in Persia for three years, he prepared a wonderful banquet in Susa. All the important people in the land were invited. On the seventh day of the party, Xerxes sent for his wife, Vashti, so he could show off her beauty. But Vashti refused to come.

Xerxes was embarrassed in front of his guests. He was so angry that he decided never to see Vashti again. Instead he sent letters to every province in his kingdom to find himself a new wife. He ordered that all the most beautiful women should come and take a year of beauty treatments, after which he would choose one of them to be his queen.

Esther was one of the women chosen. Esther, who was very beautiful, was descended from the Jewish captives who had been taken from Jerusalem by the Babylonians. Her cousin Mordecai had looked after her when both her parents died.

"Don't tell them that you are Jewish," Mordecai warned when Esther was taken to the palace.

When Xerxes saw Esther, he loved her more than all the other beautiful women. He chose her to be his queen.

AUGUST 16—A PLOT AGAINST KING XERXES

Mordecai worked as a palace official. One day he overheard two of King Xerxes' officers planning an attempt on the king's life.

Mordecai told Esther what he had heard, and Esther told the king. The two officers were killed, and the event was written down in Xerxes' palace records.

Some time later, King Xerxes chose to give great power to a man named Haman, who was known in the palace. The king ordered that everyone should bow down to Haman and pay him respect. Everyone did this except Mordecai, Esther's cousin.

The king's attendants asked Mordecai why he would not bow down to Haman, and they tried to change his mind. But still Mordecai would not bow down. He was a Jew, one of God's people, and he would only worship the true God.

When Haman realized what was happening, he was very angry. He hated Mordecai. He wanted revenge—not just against Mordecai but against all the

ESTHER 2:19–3:15

[Haman] looked for a way to destroy all the Jews throughout the entire empire of Xerxes.
Esther 3:6

Jewish people, for he knew that they loved God. So he went to the king with a plan of his own.

"Your Majesty," said Haman, "there are people scattered throughout your kingdom who have different customs from us and do not obey your laws. I think you should make a law ordering that every one of them be destroyed. I will personally reward the men who carry out the order."

"Keep your money," said King Xerxes. "But do what you like with these people."

So the law was made, and a date was set for the deaths of every Jewish man, woman, and child. The law was posted in Susa, and all the people wondered how such a terrible thing could happen.

AUGUST 17—ESTHER PRAYS FOR GUIDANCE

Mordecai put on mourning clothes and ashes when he heard about the new law of King Xerxes. Jewish people all over the kingdom showed their sadness too.

Mordecai sent a message to Esther, asking her to beg the king for mercy.

"I cannot go to the king unless he sends for me," Esther replied. "Anyone who breaks this rule is put to death!"

Mordecai sent back his answer: "Even a queen will not escape this law. Perhaps God has made you queen in Persia so that you can save your people."

"Pray for me," replied Esther. "I will do the same. Then I will go to the king, even if I die because of it."

The next day, Esther went to see the king. When he saw her, he was pleased she had come and was happy to talk to her.

ESTHER 4–5

Esther replied, "If it please the king, let the king and Haman come today to a banquet I have prepared for the king."
Esther 5:4

"What can I do for you, Queen Esther?" he asked. "Ask anything—I will give you half my kingdom."

Esther was waiting for the right moment.

"I have prepared a banquet for you and Haman. Please come," she said.

The king agreed. When Haman received his invitation, he was delighted. But when he walked past Mordecai, who did not bow, Haman burned with anger.

"Build a hanging post and ask the king to hang Mordecai on it tomorrow!" his friends said. So Haman ordered the hanging post to be built. After that he felt much happier.

AUGUST 18—GOD'S ANSWER TO PRAYER

That night, King Xerxes could not sleep.

"Read me the history of my rule as king," he said to one of his attendants.

The man read. When he came to the part where Mordecai had overheard the plan to kill the king and the men were stopped, King Xerxes interrupted his attendant with a question.

"How was Mordecai rewarded?" asked the king.

"He wasn't," said the attendant. "There is no record of it here."

"Who is in the court at the moment?" Xerxes asked.

Only Haman was there. He had arrived early to ask the king to agree to Mordecai's hanging.

"What do you think is a fitting reward for someone the king wishes to honor?" Xerxes asked Haman.

Haman smiled. He was sure the king was planning to honor him.

"Dress him in the king's robe," said Haman. "Let him ride one of the king's horses through the streets. Announce in a loud voice so that everyone can hear, 'This is how the king rewards the man he is pleased with!'"

ESTHER 6

Haman took the robes and put them on Mordecai, placed him on the king's own horse, and led him through the city square, shouting, "This is what the king does for someone he wishes to honor!"

Esther 6:11

"Excellent!" said the king. "Please do all this for Mordecai without delay."

Haman felt sick. He went from the palace and obeyed the king, but as soon as he could, he rushed home to tell his wife and friends what had happened.

"But this must put you in great danger," they said. "You cannot plan to kill someone the king has honored!"

Before Haman had time to think of another plan, the king's servants arrived to take him to Esther's banquet.

AUGUST 19—ESTHER'S REQUEST

"Well, my queen," Xerxes said to Esther as the banquet began. "What is it that you would like me to give you? Ask for whatever you wish, and I will be happy to grant your request."

"Your Majesty," said Esther. "Please save my life—please save the lives of all my people. For there is a man who has planned their destruction, and we are all to be killed. If we were only to be sold as slaves, I would have said nothing, but our lives are on the line."

"Who is this man? Who wants to destroy your people?" demanded the king.

"This man! This evil Haman!" said Esther, pointing at him.

Haman was terrified. The king and queen stared at him in their anger. Xerxes stormed out of the palace in a rage while Haman begged the queen for mercy. King Xerxes had already made up his mind.

"Haman has built a hanging post on which to hang Mordecai," said a servant.

"Take him! Hang him on his own hanging post!" said the king. "Get him out of my sight!" Haman was dragged from the room.

Then King Xerxes spoke to Esther.

"I cannot undo Haman's order, for the law cannot be changed. But I can help the Jews fight their enemies and defend themselves," he said.

Xerxes gave to Mordecai all the power that he had once given to Haman. He put a ring on his finger as a sign of his authority, and he put a gold crown on his head. Mordecai left the palace wearing the clothes of royalty—a blue and white robe and a purple linen coat.

The Jews were safe. Every year after that they met to celebrate and to remember how Queen Esther had saved them.

ESTHER 7–9

They impaled Haman on the pole he had set up for Mordecai, and the king's anger subsided.
Esther 7:10

August 20 — The Patience of Job

There was once a man named Job. He had a large and happy family and many servants to look after him. He was very wealthy, and he owned thousands of sheep and camels, and hundreds of cows and donkeys.

Job was also a good man. He loved God and did all he could to obey him and live honestly.

One day Satan came into God's presence. Satan was God's enemy.

"Where have you been?" asked God.

"Roaming the earth," replied Satan. "Going here and there."

"Have you seen Job?" asked God. "He is rare among men. He is a truly good man."

"Of course he's good," sneered Satan. "You make it easy for him to be good. He has everything he could possibly want. But if all he has were to be taken away from him, no doubt he would not love you as much. He'd probably be as bad as the next person."

"We will see," said God. "You may take away all that he loves, but do not harm the man himself."

Satan went to work. He caused lightning to fall from the sky and burn up Job's sheep and servants. Robbers carried off Job's camels, and a whirlwind caused the roof to fall in on Job's children and kill them.

JOB 1:1–2:10

There once was a man named Job who lived in the land of Uz. He was blameless—a man of complete integrity. He feared God and stayed away from evil.

Job 1:1

Job cried out in his sadness and fell down to worship God.

"I had nothing when I was born, and I shall take nothing with me to my grave. The Lord has given me all that I have, and he has taken it all away. Praise the name of God!"

Satan came again to God.

"Job may have nothing, but he is still healthy and strong. He would soon curse you if he became ill and was in pain!" said Satan slyly.

"We will see," said God. "You may take away his health and strength, but you must not let him die."

Satan caused Job to be covered all over with painful sores.

"Curse God and die!" urged his wife. "You cannot still love him!"

"No," replied Job. "We were happy to accept the good things that God gave us; we must also accept suffering when it comes."

AUGUST 21 — GOD ANSWERS JOB

JOB 2:11–42:17

The LORD blessed Job in the second half of his life even more than in the beginning.
Job 42:12

When Job's three friends heard what had happened, they came and sat with him. They felt very sorry for him. They had never seen him in such a bad state.

"Why was I born?" Job asked after some days. "The worst that could have happened has now happened!"

"Perhaps God is punishing you for some terrible sin," said the first friend. "Confess your sin and God may make you well."

"But I can think of no such sin," said Job.

"Well that must be it!" said his second friend. "You cannot admit you have done something wrong!"

"I will ask God to tell me what I have done wrong," replied Job.

"Maybe your sin is so huge God will make you suffer even more!" said the third friend.

"You are no help to me at all!" said Job to his friends, and he continued to pray in the hope that God would answer him. Then God spoke.

"You want to know why you are suffering, Job? Let me ask you some questions.

"Where were you when I laid the foundations of the world? Have you ever called the morning into being or formed the stars into constellations? Have you given strength to a horse or clothed its neck with a flowing mane? Have you taught the hawk to fly or the eagle where to build its nest? You have asked me questions, but do you think you can understand the answers?"

Job realized how great and marvelous God was. He did not need to know why he was suffering. He knew that he could trust God, no matter what happened.

"I am sorry," replied Job. "There are things that are too wonderful for me to know."

"Your friends were wrong," said God. "You did not suffer because you sinned. They must ask you to forgive them."

Job forgave his friends. Then God blessed Job even more than he had before, and Job enjoyed a long and happy life.

AUGUST 22—EZRA RETURNS TO JERUSALEM

More than 60 years had passed since the first group of Israelites had returned to Jerusalem to rebuild the Temple. Now another group followed, with Ezra the priest as their leader.

King Artaxerxes of Persia had given Ezra permission to return.

"I say that you may return to Jerusalem with anyone who wants to go. Take a copy of God's law, and my treasurers will give you what you need. You must teach the people God's laws and report back to me," he wrote.

EZRA 7:1–10:1

Ezra arrived in Jerusalem in August of that year.
Ezra 7:8

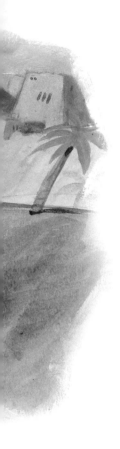

Ezra was amazed. He called the people to get ready.

"I have told the king that God will protect us on our journey," he said. "We must fast and pray before we go and ask God to help us."

They journeyed safely to Jerusalem and met the others who had returned. Then some of the leaders came to Ezra, embarrassed.

"Since we returned, some of our people have married wives who do not believe in the living God."

"What?" cried Ezra in sorrow and anger. He fell on his knees. "After all God has done for us in bringing us back here?" Then Ezra wept and prayed to God for the forgiveness of all the people.

"I am so sorry, Lord," he prayed. "We are your people, and we should know the laws you have taught us. But we never learn. We make the same mistakes again and again. Please forgive us."

Some of the people heard Ezra's prayer. They knew he was right. A large group of men, women, and children joined him and wept and prayed with him.

"We have sinned," they said. "Forgive us and show us how we can obey you."

August 23 — Nehemiah's Prayer

Nehemiah was still away from his homeland, working as cupbearer for King Artaxerxes.

Nehemiah 1:1–2:8

I replied, "If it please the king, and if you are pleased with me, your servant, send me to Judah to rebuild the city where my ancestors are buried."
Nehemiah 2:5

One day he heard news from his brother Hanani that the walls of Jerusalem were still in ruins. Nehemiah wept in sorrow and could not eat.

"Lord God, please listen to my prayer," he said. "I know that we, your people, have disobeyed you. I am sorry for all the wrong things we have done. I know that we were sent away from our country because of our disobedience. But you also promised to return to Jerusalem those people who were obedient. Please let me go back to Jerusalem to help rebuild the walls."

Four months passed. Then, as Nehemiah was serving the king one day, Artaxerxes noticed that something was wrong.

"Why do you look so sad, Nehemiah?" asked Artaxerxes.

Nehemiah knew that God was answering his prayer.

"The walls surrounding the place where my ancestors are buried need to be rebuilt. I cannot help but be sad," he said. "Please let me go to Jerusalem."

"When will you get back?" asked the king. "How long will you be away?"

Nehemiah saw that the king was agreeing to let him go and that God was on his side. He named a time.

"And if you agree to let me go, please provide me with protection for my journey and the materials to rebuild the city gates and walls."

God answered Nehemiah's prayer. Artaxerxes agreed to everything.

AUGUST 24—REPAIRING THE CITY WALLS

Nehemiah arrived safely in Jerusalem and started inspecting the walls at night so that no one would know why he was there. All that remained were piles of rubble where there should have been walls. And the gates had been burned.

The next day he went to the city officials and told them his plans and how King Artaxerxes had given him permission to rebuild the walls.

The people started working right away. They organized themselves into groups, each working on different sections of the wall. But not everyone was happy. Two Samaritans, Sanballat and Tobiah, did not want God's people to succeed. At first they laughed and made fun of them.

"If a fox were to walk along the top of that wall, the whole thing would collapse!" Then they tried to raise an army to come and attack the builders.

But Nehemiah kept on praying that God would help them. He told the workers to take weapons with them so they were prepared to defend

NEHEMIAH 2:9–4:23; 6:1-16

I said to them, "You know very well what trouble we are in. Jerusalem lies in ruins, and its gates have been destroyed by fire. Let us rebuild the wall of Jerusalem and end this disgrace!"
Nehemiah 2:17

themselves while carrying on the work. Even when Sanballat and Tobiah made plans to kill him, Nehemiah went on praying.

When the walls were completed and the new gates were hung, all the people met together. The walls of Jerusalem had been rebuilt in 52 days. Even the enemies of God's people knew that God had made this happen, and they began to be afraid.

AUGUST 25 — NEHEMIAH AND THE POOR

NEHEMIAH 5

Remember, O my God, all that I have done for these people, and bless me for it.
Nehemiah 5:19

Some of the people who returned to Jerusalem were very wealthy. Others were poor. The wealthy lent large sums of money to the poor, but when the poor could not repay the money, the wealthy men took away their fields. The poor people came to Nehemiah and told him of their needs and of the unfair ways they were treated by their fellow Jews.

"Once our fields are gone, we have no way of making any money," cried the people to Nehemiah. "Then we are forced to sell our children into slavery."

When Nehemiah heard this, he was very angry. He called the people together.

"What you are doing is against God's law," he cried. "We are all members of the same family. We shouldn't be hurting one another. What will our enemies say? Give back everything that does not belong to you."

The people listened to Nehemiah. He was right. He was their leader, and they respected him. He worked as hard as any of them, and he always used his position for the good of the people.

AUGUST 26—EZRA READS GOD'S LAW TO THE PEOPLE

Once the walls were finished, everyone came together.

Ezra climbed a high wooden platform in the square before the Water Gate, carrying scrolls in his hands. He was a good teacher and knew God's law well. Now he read the scrolls to the people. Everyone listened. One by one, the people understood how disobedient they had been, and they began to weep.

"Do not cry," said Nehemiah. "Today is a special day. Today we must be happy that we have heard and understood God's law. Go and have something good to eat and drink, and share what you have with each other."

Day after day the people listened to Ezra as he read God's law. They remembered how God had looked after his people since they first left Egypt. They saw their disobedience.

"We are sorry for all the things our ancestors did to make you angry," they said to God.

"We are sorry for all our sins."

NEHEMIAH 8–9

Ezra read from the Book of the Law of God on each of the seven days of the festival. Then on the eighth day they held a solemn assembly, as was required by law.
Nehemiah 8:18

AUGUST 27—SINGING NEW SONGS

When it was time to dedicate Jerusalem's new walls to God, the people came together with harps. Nehemiah gave instructions for the singers to form two choirs. Each choir walked around the top of the wall in opposite directions, while the people followed.

The people had wept in Babylon and been too sad to sing songs to God. But now they sang some new songs.

Praise the Lord! I will praise the Lord all my life.
I will sing to God for as long as I live!
Happy are those who trust God,
the maker of heaven and earth

and the sea and all that lives in them.
Happy are those who know that God will help them.
God cares for those who are treated unfairly
and gives food to the hungry.
God sets the prisoners free and gives sight to the blind.
God looks after those who are strangers in foreign lands
and those who have lost parents, wives, or husbands.
Our God rules forever! Praise the Lord!

NEHEMIAH 12:27-47;
PSALMS 146–147

I will praise the
LORD as long
as I live. I will
sing praises to
my God with my
dying breath.
Psalm 146:2

They met together in God's Temple. Every man, woman, and child sang to God. Everyone was happy and filled with joy. They knew that God had kept his promises.

How good it is to sing praises to God!
The Lord builds up Jerusalem.
He gathers up the lost and returns them to Israel.
He heals the brokenhearted and cares for their wounds.
The Lord decides the number of the stars
and calls each of them by name.
Our Lord is great and mighty—
his understanding is without limit.
Sing to the Lord with thanksgiving!
Make music to our God on the harp!
The Lord loves those who look to him for help,
who put their trust in his unfailing love!
Praise the Lord! Praise the Lord!

Some time later, Nehemiah returned to work for King Artaxerxes, as he had agreed to do.

AUGUST 28 — PREPARING THE WAY

When Nehemiah left God's people in Jerusalem, they settled down to rebuild their lives. For a while they remembered how they had hated their time in exile and how much they wanted to come home.

But time passed. Sometimes their lives were a struggle. Things were not always as easy as they had hoped.

"People who don't worship God seem to live happily," they said. "Sometimes it seems pointless following God's laws. Worshipping God all the time is boring."

Malachi brought God's words to his people: "I love you, just as I have always loved you from the beginning. Remember how children obey their fathers. Think about how servants respect their masters. I am your father; I am your master."

"The priests have stopped leading you as they should," said Malachi. "They have stopped obeying the laws God gave them. You have started to marry wives from the people who worship gods of wood and stone. You don't set aside the Sabbath as a special day of rest. You don't trust God to provide for your needs.

"The time is coming when God himself is coming to live with you! Look for his messenger who will prepare the way. This messenger will come to judge, and he will come to save. He will be like a fire that makes gold and silver pure, removing all the flaws that spoil it. The people who serve him and do what is right will be happy on that day!"

Nehemiah returned to Jerusalem and tried to make right the things that God had warned the people about through Malachi. After Malachi, there were no more prophets in the land for 400 years.

MALACHI 1–4

"Look, I am sending you the prophet Elijah before the great and dreadful day of the LORD arrives."
Malachi 4:5

AUGUST 29—THE ANGEL IN THE TEMPLE

Zechariah was a priest living in the hill country of Judea. He and his wife, Elizabeth, had loved and served God all their lives. But God had not blessed them with children.

Now Zechariah had been chosen to burn the incense in the Temple—an honor that a priest might be chosen for only once in his lifetime. Outside the Temple in the morning sunshine, people were praying. Inside the Temple, where it was cool and quiet, Zechariah lit the incense.

Then Zechariah realized he was not alone. Standing on the right side of the altar was an angel.

"Don't be afraid," said the angel. It was clear that Zechariah was terrified. "God has heard your prayers. Elizabeth will have a son named John, and God's Holy Spirit will be with him in a special way. He will help people understand what God wants of them so that they will be ready for him."

"Can this be true?" asked Zechariah. "Surely Elizabeth is now too old to have children."

"My name is Gabriel," said the angel, "and I stand in the presence of God. Because you doubt the truth of the message I have brought to you from God, you will not be able to speak until everything I told you has come true."

Zechariah had been in the Temple for longer than was usual. The people outside began to wonder what had happened. When he came out, he tried to tell them about the angel. But Zechariah could not speak. He waved his arms around. The people could not understand him, but they realized he must have had some sort of vision.

Some time later, just as the angel had said, Elizabeth found she was expecting a baby.

AUGUST 30—ANOTHER VISIT FROM GABRIEL

The angel Gabriel had another surprise announcement to make.

He went to see Mary, who lived in Nazareth in Galilee. Mary was not much more than a girl, but she was engaged to be married to Joseph, a local carpenter.

"Mary," said Gabriel. "God is with you!"

LUKE 1:5-25

The angel said, "Don't be afraid, Zechariah! God has heard your prayer. Your wife, Elizabeth, will give you a son, and you are to name him John."
Luke 1:13

Mary was afraid. She didn't know what to think.

"There is no need to be afraid!" said Gabriel. "You will have a son and give him the name Jesus. He will be known as God's Son, and he will be a king who will rule forever!"

"But I am not yet married," said Mary. "How can I have a baby?"

"The Holy Spirit will make this happen, for God is able to do anything. Another woman in your family, Elizabeth, is now six months pregnant. Everyone said that she couldn't have children, but with God, nothing is impossible."

"I will do anything God wants me to," said Mary. "I am ready to serve him in this way."

Then Gabriel left Mary.

LUKE 1:26-38

Mary responded, "I am the Lord's servant. May everything you have said about me come true."
Luke 1:38

AUGUST 31 — TWO SPECIAL BABIES

LUKE 1:39-56

Mary thought about what the angel had told her. If Elizabeth was expecting a baby, perhaps she should go and visit her and talk to her about what had happened. Elizabeth lived in the hills. Mary prepared for her journey and went to stay with her.

Elizabeth gave a glad cry and exclaimed to Mary, "God has blessed you above all women, and your child is blessed."
Luke 1:42

When she reached Zechariah and Elizabeth's house, Mary hugged Elizabeth. Then the baby inside Elizabeth's belly jumped with joy.

"God has blessed you!" Elizabeth told Mary. "And he will bless your baby, too. You have been willing to do what God has asked of you—and you will be rewarded. But why am I so lucky to have you come to stay with me?"

"God is very great!" said Mary. "I am no one, yet God has made me special by giving me this amazing thing to do. He has always been good to people who try to listen to him and follow his ways. He was good to Abraham and Isaac and Jacob, and he is good to us now. God always chooses people who feel they have nothing to offer—and he makes them great. But he also sends away people who think they are too good or important to need his help. God is good."

Mary stayed in the hills with Elizabeth for three months before returning to her home in Nazareth.

SEPTEMBER 1 — ZECHARIAH SPEAKS AGAIN

Nine months had passed since Zechariah had seen the angel Gabriel in the Temple. Now Elizabeth was ready to give birth to her baby. It was a little boy, just as Gabriel had told Zechariah. Elizabeth was full of joy, and her friends and neighbors shared in her happiness.

Eight days later, it was time for a special ceremony to dedicate the baby boy to God. Some people there were ready to name him Zechariah after his father, but Elizabeth insisted he should be called John.

LUKE 1:57-79

When it was time for Elizabeth's baby to be born, she gave birth to a son.
Luke 1:57

"What does Zechariah say?" they said. Then Zechariah asked for something to write on so he could tell them. He had not spoken since he met the angel.

"His name is John," he wrote.

Right away he was able to speak again. The first words he spoke were in praise of God, who had blessed them with this special child.

Everyone was amazed. They couldn't stop talking about these events.

"God has not forgotten us, his people," Zechariah said. "He is sending his chosen one to save us from our enemies. And he has chosen this child, my son, John, to be the one who will prepare the way and tell us about the one who is to come."

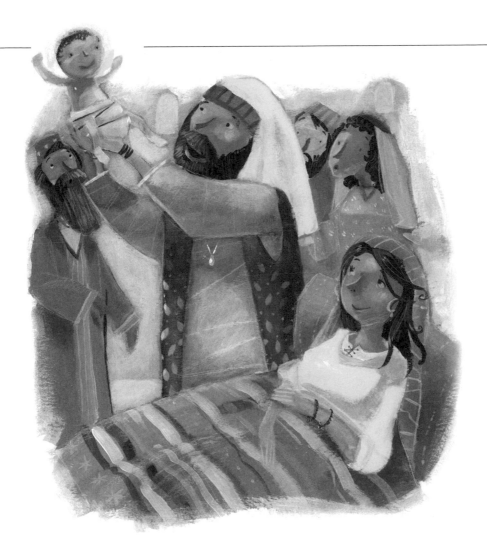

September 2—Joseph, the Carpenter

Mary was happy to serve God and do all that he wanted of her. But Joseph was very sad.

Joseph knew that Mary's baby was not his baby. But he cared about Mary. He didn't want people to be unkind to her. But should he marry her as they had planned?

Then one night Joseph dreamed a strange dream, in which an angel appeared to him.

"You don't need to worry about marrying Mary," the angel said. "The Holy Spirit has caused the baby to grow inside her. She will have a baby boy, and you must call him Jesus, because he will be the Savior of the world."

Joseph didn't need any more encouragement to marry Mary. He did what the angel of the Lord had told him.

MATTHEW 1:18-25

[Jesus'] mother, Mary, was engaged to be married to Joseph. But before the marriage took place, while she was still a virgin, she became pregnant through the power of the Holy Spirit.

Matthew 1.18

SEPTEMBER 3 — THE JOURNEY TO BETHLEHEM

LUKE 2:1-5

At that time the Roman emperor, Augustus, decreed that a census should be taken throughout the Roman Empire.
Luke 2:1

The months passed quickly, and soon the time came for Mary's baby to be born. It looked as though this would not happen in Nazareth but in Bethlehem.

The Roman emperor, Augustus, wanted to tax his people. He ordered everyone to go to the town of their ancestors to be counted. This meant that Joseph had to take Mary with him to Bethlehem, because he belonged to the family of King David.

Mary and Joseph made their way to the village of Bethlehem in Judea. The roads were full of people traveling, all obeying the command of the Roman ruler.

SEPTEMBER 4 — THE BABY BORN IN BETHLEHEM

LUKE 2:6-7

[Mary] gave birth to her first child, a son. She wrapped him snugly in strips of cloth and laid him in a manger.
Luke 2:7

Bethlehem was bustling with people.

Men, women, and children had all come to be counted there. By the time Mary and Joseph arrived, it was already difficult to find somewhere to stay.

Mary felt tired. She was starting to feel the pains that meant her baby would soon be born.

Joseph went from house to house looking for a room because the inn was full. Eventually he found a place for them to stay where the animals were kept.

That night, Mary gave birth to a baby boy, her firstborn child. She wrapped him in strips of cloth and made a bed for him in a feeding box for the animals, because there was no room anywhere else.

SEPTEMBER 5 — SHEPHERDS HEAR THE NEWS

While Jesus was being held by his mother, Mary, shepherds were on the hills outside Bethlehem, looking after their flocks of sheep.

The soft, flickering flames of their fires suddenly gave way to dazzling light as an angel appeared in the night sky. The shepherds were terrified.

"Don't be afraid!" said the angel. "I have come with good news! Tonight,

LUKE 2:8-20

The shepherds went back to their flocks, glorifying and praising God for all they had heard and seen. It was just as the angel had told them.
Luke 2:20

in Bethlehem, a baby has been born, who is the Savior of the world. You will find him wrapped in strips of cloth, lying in a feeding box for animals."

Then the sound of hundreds of angels singing and praising God filled their ears.

"Glory to God in the highest heaven!" the angels sang. "And peace on earth."

The shepherds wasted no time. They ran down the hillside, determined to find the baby who had been born that night.

They found the place where Mary and Joseph were staying, and they knew that this baby lying in the manger was the baby the angels had spoken of.

They went from there to tell everyone what they had seen and heard so that no one would be in any doubt about who the baby was. But Mary, watching Jesus sleeping, thought about all she had heard that night.

SEPTEMBER 6 — GOD'S CHOSEN ONE

LUKE 2:21-40

"I have seen your salvation, which you have prepared for all people."
Luke 2:30-31

When Jesus was still a tiny baby, Mary and Joseph prepared to take him to the Temple in Jerusalem. They went to thank God for his safe birth and give an offering of two pigeons.

As they went into the Temple courts, they met a man named Simeon. Simeon had been waiting for the day when God would send his Messiah— the chosen one who would save his people. Simeon believed that God had promised him that he would see this Savior before he died.

When Simeon saw Mary and Joseph and the baby boy in their arms, he knew that the special day had arrived. He took Jesus from them and praised God.

"Lord, you can now let me die in peace, because I have seen with my own eyes the Savior you have promised your people," he said. "This child will reveal your truth to all people on Earth. He will be everything the Jewish nation has been waiting for."

Mary and Joseph listened with some surprise to his words, but before they had taken it all in, an elderly woman approached them. Anna was a prophet who had lived in the Temple, praying and worshipping God for most of her long life. She also knew that Jesus was God's chosen one. And she thanked God for him.

Mary and Joseph made their offering. They were amazed by all they had learned that day about their baby son.

SEPTEMBER 7 — WISE MEN FROM THE EAST

MATTHEW 2:1-8

About that time some wise men from eastern lands arrived in Jerusalem, asking, "Where is the newborn king of the Jews! We saw his star as it rose, and we have come to worship him."
Matthew 2:1-2

Wise men living in the East had been studying the night skies when Jesus was born. They saw a strange new star and wondered what it could mean.

They set out on a journey, following the star, because they thought it meant the birth of a new king. They wanted to worship him.

When they reached Jerusalem, they stopped at King Herod's palace.

"Where is the child born to be King of the Jewish people?" they asked. "We have come to pay our respects—to welcome and worship him."

Herod was upset by their arrival. What king could there be apart from him?

Quickly, Herod met with the chief priests and teachers of the law. They told him what they knew from the ancient prophecies: The King would be born in Bethlehem.

Herod then talked to his Eastern visitors and tried to find out exactly when they had first seen the star. This way he could know how old the baby might be.

Then he sent them to Bethlehem.

"If you find this King," he said slyly, "let me know. I would like to be able to worship him as well."

SEPTEMBER 8 — THREE SPECIAL GIFTS

MATTHEW 2:9-12

The wise men continued their journey until they reached Bethlehem, where the star seemed to stop over a house. They went inside and found Mary with her young child.

The wise men knew they had found the right place, and they worshipped Jesus, the new King. Then they gave him the gifts they had brought—gold, frankincense, and myrrh.

They stopped for the night before beginning their return journey, but they did not go back the way they had come. In the night they had dreamed that it was not safe to return to King Herod.

They entered the house and saw the child with his mother, Mary, and they bowed down and worshiped him. Then they opened their treasure chests and gave him gifts of gold, frankincense, and myrrh.

Matthew 2:11

SEPTEMBER 9—THE JOURNEY TO EGYPT

After the wise men had left, Joseph also had a strange dream. In it, he was warned by an angel.

"Wake up!" said the angel. "Herod plans to kill Jesus. You must take your family and escape to Egypt!"

It was still night when Joseph woke Mary and took her and her child to safety.

MATTHEW 2:13-23

After the wise men were gone, an angel of the Lord appeared to Joseph in a dream. "Get up! Flee to Egypt with the child and his mother," the angel said. "Stay there until I tell you to return."
Matthew 2:13

Meanwhile, Herod waited for the wise men to return. A day passed. Two days passed. Soon he realized that he had been tricked. The men from the East were not going to return. He was furious. Herod was a cruel man. He thought of another way to get rid of Jesus. He had figured out how old Jesus must be from what the wise men had told him, so he gave orders to kill all boys under two years old in the area.

But Herod did not know that Jesus was safely in Egypt. Joseph kept him there until Herod died.

Then, when Jesus was a little boy, an angel came again to Joseph in a dream and told him it was safe to return. Joseph traveled to Nazareth, where he and his family made their home. Jesus grew up strong and healthy and wise.

SEPTEMBER 10—LOST IN JERUSALEM

Jesus worked alongside Joseph, learning how to be a carpenter in the area of Galilee.

Each year they went to Jerusalem with everyone else to celebrate the Passover festival. So when Jesus was 12, Mary and Joseph expected their journey to be as it had been before. Jesus traveled with Mary and Joseph and a group of other people from Nazareth. Then at the end of the festival, they made their way home.

LUKE 2:41-52

"Why did you need to search?" he asked. "Didn't you know that I must be in my Father's house?"
Luke 2:49

Mary and Joseph had been walking for some time when they realized that Jesus was missing. They assumed he was with friends or relatives, but it became clear that they all thought he was with someone else. They began to panic. Where could he be?

They returned to Jerusalem, where it was always busy and anyone could get

lost. They questioned the market traders, and they asked other children if they had seen Jesus. At the end of three days, Mary was very worried. Then they went to the Temple.

Surrounded by religious experts and teachers, there was Mary's son. Jesus was listening to them and asking questions. Mary watched as he spoke and saw that his elders were surprised by his answers.

But Mary's fear got the better of her.

"Where have you been?" asked Mary. "We have been so worried! We have been searching everywhere for you."

"I have been here in my Father's house," Jesus replied. "Couldn't you guess?"

Jesus was a good son. He went back home with them. And as he grew older, Mary remembered all the special things that had happened to him.

SEPTEMBER 11 — JOHN THE BAPTIST

Jesus was not the only boy to have grown up. Elizabeth's son, John, had not only become a man, he had gone to live alone in the desert.

When he was ready, John started to do the work he knew God wanted him to do. He started to tell people how God wanted them to live. He was not a well-dressed man—in fact, he looked rather wild. He wore clothes made of

LUKE 3:1-18

John went from place to place . . . preaching that people should be baptized to show that they had . . . turned to God.

Luke 3:3

camel's hair and ate strange food. But people listened to him. Somehow they knew that what he said was true. They knew that God spoke through him and that they needed to do the things he said.

"Stop doing things that are wrong. Obey God," John told them. "Be baptized, and show that you are sorry and that God has forgiven you."

The people came to the Jordan River, and John baptized them.

"It is not enough that Abraham is your ancestor," he said. "You must show that you love God by the way you live. If you have two coats, give one away to someone in need. If you have plenty of food, share it with someone who has nothing. If you are a tax collector, live honestly and fairly—don't cheat people. If you are a soldier, don't bully people."

"Who is this man?" the people whispered. "Is John God's Savior?"

But John heard them.

"I baptize you with water," he said. "But soon someone will come who will baptize you with God's own Spirit!"

SEPTEMBER 12—JESUS IS BAPTIZED

MATTHEW 3:13-17

A voice from heaven said, "This is my dearly loved Son, who brings me great joy."

Matthew 3:17

Jesus came to the Jordan River one day. He was now a man of about 30 and had been a carpenter for many years.

Jesus stepped forward as John was calling people to be baptized. John knew right away who he was. He also knew he was not good enough to baptize Jesus!

But Jesus convinced him. He told John it was what God wanted. As Jesus came out of the water, God's Spirit came down from heaven like a dove and rested on Jesus.

A voice from heaven said, "This is my Son. I love him very much. I am pleased with him."

SEPTEMBER 13—JESUS IS TESTED

After his baptism, Jesus was led by God's Spirit into the desert. He went without food for 40 days, and at the end of this time Jesus was weak and very hungry.

God's enemy, the devil, tried to test Jesus.

"You need food," he said. "If you are God's Son, you can make this stone turn into bread."

"Life is more than just food," replied Jesus, quoting God's law.

Then the devil led Jesus to a very high place and showed him all the kingdoms of the world.

"Look at all this!" whispered the devil. "I will give it to you if you bow down and worship me."

"God has said that we must worship him alone," replied Jesus.

Then the devil took Jesus to Jerusalem. They stood on the highest part of the Temple.

LUKE 4:1-13

Jesus responded, "The Scriptures also say, 'You must not test the LORD your God.'"
Luke 4:12

"God has promised to send his angels to protect you," continued the devil. "Throw yourself off the Temple so we can see his power!"

"God's law says that we must not put him to the test," Jesus replied.

The devil had tried to tempt Jesus to break God's laws and do something wrong, but Jesus would not give in. Finally, the devil left him alone.

SEPTEMBER 14 — THE FOUR FISHERMEN

Jesus returned to Galilee and began to travel around, telling the people the good news of salvation.

"Stop doing things that are wrong. Live your lives the way God wants you to. Love God and learn to love the people around you as much as you love yourself."

Jesus watched Simon (also called Peter) and Andrew throwing their fishing nets into the waters of Lake Galilee.

"Come and follow me!" Jesus said to the two brothers. "You can catch people for God instead of catching fish."

Simon and Andrew dropped their nets and joined Jesus right away.

Farther up the shore, they saw James and his brother, John, fixing their nets. Their father, Zebedee, was in the boat with them.

"Come and follow me!" called Jesus.

James and John got out of the boat and went with him.

These four fishermen became Jesus' first followers, or disciples. Jesus went with them to their homes in Capernaum. There Jesus taught in the Jewish place of worship. Crowds of people came to him for help, and he healed those who were sick.

MARK 1:14-34

Jesus called out to them, "Come, follow me, and I will show you how to fish for people!"
Mark 1:17

SEPTEMBER 15 — THE BEST WINE OF ALL

One day there was a wedding in the village of Cana. Jesus' mother, Mary, had been invited. Jesus and some of his disciples went too.

While everyone was celebrating and enjoying themselves, the wine ran out. Mary went to Jesus and told him what had happened.

"It is not yet the right time for me," Jesus replied.

JOHN 2:1-11

This miraculous sign at Cana in Galilee was the first time Jesus revealed his glory.
John 2:11

Mary knew her son was special. She knew he would help in some way.

"Do whatever he asks," she whispered to the servants.

"Fill these six jars with water," Jesus said. The jars were used for washing. They were very large, each holding many gallons of water.

The servants filled them with water, and when they had finished, Jesus asked them to pour some out and offer it to the man in charge of the feast. The servants were nervous, but when they poured it, they saw that the water had become wine.

The man tasted it and then went to speak to the groom.

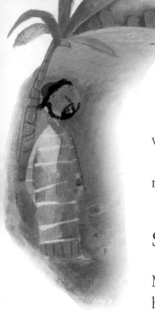

"This wine is wonderful," he said. "Most people serve the cheap wine last when no one notices. But you have saved the best until the end."

The disciples saw what Jesus had done and were amazed. They began to realize that he was no ordinary man.

SEPTEMBER 16 — THE GOOD NEWS

Many people throughout Galilee had seen the way Jesus healed people. They had heard him talk about the way God loves and cares for everyone.

It was time for Jesus to visit Nazareth, his hometown. He went as usual to the worship place on the Sabbath day. He stood up, ready to read from the Scriptures. Someone handed him a scroll containing the words of the prophet Isaiah.

"God's Spirit is on me," read Jesus. "He has chosen me to bring good news to the poor, to free those who are in chains, to give sight to the blind, to help those who are suffering, and to tell everyone that God's blessing has come." Jesus rolled up the scroll and sat down. "That was written hundreds of years ago. Today, here, you have seen it come true."

The people stared at him. They began to whisper among themselves.

"But this is Joseph's boy," they said. "He's no one special."

"I know what you think. And because you do not believe, you will see no miracles here," replied Jesus.

The people of Nazareth were angry. They would not let Jesus stay in the town but sent him away.

LUKE 4:14-30

He began to speak to them. "The Scripture you've just heard has been fulfilled this very day!"
Luke 4:21

SEPTEMBER 17 — THE MAN ON THE MAT

Jesus received a very different reaction in Capernaum. Crowds of people gathered to hear him speak about God wherever he went. They were hungry for the truth.

Four men were particularly eager to find Jesus. They were carrying their friend, who was lying on a mat. They wanted Jesus to heal this friend because he could not walk.

When they reached the house where Jesus was speaking, they found it was too crowded. People were packed all around him and spilling out of the doorway.

Outside the house, steps led up to the roof. The men climbed up, desperate for Jesus to help their friend. They dug through the roof, which was made of mud and branches, until there was a hole large enough to lower the man and his mat down in front of Jesus and the amazed crowd.

Jesus saw how sure the friends were that he could help them. He spoke to the paralyzed man.

"Go," he said. "Your sins are forgiven."

The Pharisees and other religious experts were shocked. Surely only God could forgive sins! Jesus may have had interesting things to say—but this was too much!

MARK 2:1-12

"Is it easier to say to the paralyzed man 'Your sins are forgiven,' or 'Stand up, pick up your mat, and walk'?"

Mark 2:9

Jesus knew what they were thinking.

"Which is easier?" Jesus asked. "To forgive this man's sins or to make him walk? Nothing is impossible for God." Then he looked again at the paralyzed man and spoke. "Stand up, take your mat, and go home."

The man stood up. His friends were overjoyed. Everyone else was amazed! They praised God for the miracle they had seen.

SEPTEMBER 18 — MATTHEW JOINS JESUS

MARK 2:13-17

When Jesus heard this, he told them, "Healthy people don't need a doctor—sick people do. I have come to call not those who think they are righteous, but those who know they are sinners."
Mark 2:17

Jesus and Matthew first met when Jesus was walking beside the lake, teaching the crowds of people who followed him.

Matthew was a tax collector. He had set up his booth, where day after day he collected money for the Romans.

"Come, follow me," Jesus said to him.

Matthew stopped what he was doing right away. He joined the others who were following Jesus and walked with them.

Later that day, Matthew invited Jesus to his house for dinner with many of his friends. When the religious leaders saw that Jesus was Matthew's guest, they were shocked and angry.

"Why does Jesus spend time with such terrible people?" they asked Jesus' followers.

But Jesus heard them.

"Healthy people don't need a doctor," he said. "I am here with the people who most need to hear God's message."

SEPTEMBER 19—LIVING GOD'S WAY

The people who heard Jesus speak told others about him. Soon there were people following Jesus wherever he went.

One day Jesus walked up to the top of a hillside. He sat down and began to talk to the people about the way God wanted them to live their lives.

"The people who are happy are not the proud ones who think highly of themselves, but those who know how much they need God's help and forgiveness," Jesus said. "If you follow God's ways, you will be like a little salt in the cooking pot, making the whole meal taste good. You will be like a lamp shining brightly in a dark place, bringing light so that all can see."

MATTHEW 5

"God blesses those who are persecuted for doing right, for the Kingdom of Heaven is theirs."
Matthew 5:10

Then Jesus began to talk about God's law. It was the law the Pharisees thought they knew all about, but Jesus spoke about it in a way that no one had understood before.

"If someone hurts you, don't try to get back at them on your own," said Jesus. "Instead, be kind to those who hurt you. Go out of your way to help everyone. God's law says that we must love not only our friends, family, and neighbors, but our enemies as well. It's easy to love people who already love us. God wants us to be different. God is perfect. We must try to be like him."

SEPTEMBER 20—LESSONS ON PRAYER

Jesus went on to teach the people how they should talk to God in prayer.

"Be careful," said Jesus, "not to pray with words you don't mean just so others will notice you. Make sure your prayers are honest talks between you and God. God sees everything. He knows what you want to tell him before you begin to speak. So talk to God simply and quietly, without drawing attention to yourself."

Then Jesus gave his followers an example of how to pray:

MATTHEW 6:5-15

"When you pray, go away by yourself, shut the door behind you, and pray to your Father in private. Then your Father, who sees everything, will reward you."
Matthew 6:6

Our Father in heaven,
your name is holy.
May your Kingdom come
and your will be done,
on earth as it is in heaven.
Give us today the food we need.
Forgive us our sins,
as we also have forgiven those who sin against us.
Don't let us fall into doing what's wrong,
but rescue us from the evil one.

"Speak to God as your Father in heaven," explained Jesus. "God is holy, so ask that God's name be treated as holy, and ask that God's Kingdom will arrive quickly. Ask God for the things that you need for today, like food. Then ask for his forgiveness, and at the same time forgive anyone who may have hurt you. And ask God for help, to keep you from doing anything wrong."

SEPTEMBER 21 — DON'T WORRY

Jesus looked at the people around him. Some were poor; others were sad or anxious; some could not walk or see.

MATTHEW 6:25-34

"Don't worry about tomorrow, for tomorrow will bring its own worries. Today's trouble is enough for today."
Matthew 6:34

"Don't worry about the everyday matters of living," Jesus said. "Don't worry about what you will eat or drink or about what clothes you're going to wear. Look around you at the wild birds. They don't have huge storage places filled with food. They rely on God to feed them. God cares about them, but he cares about you even more than he cares about the birds. You will not live longer by worrying about your life.

"As for worrying about clothes, look at the lilies that grow in the fields. They do not work or dress themselves, but God has made them beautiful.

"If you put God first, he will make sure that you have everything you need—and much more besides."

SEPTEMBER 22 — A STORY ABOUT TWO HOUSES

MATTHEW 7:24-27

As the people listened to what Jesus had to say, they divided into groups. Many were eager to hear more. They wanted to know how to please God. Some were doubtful or angry about this way of teaching. It was different from the teaching of the religious leaders and Pharisees. So Jesus told a story.

"If you listen to me and do what I say, you will be like a wise person who

"Anyone who listens to my teaching and follows it is wise, like a person who builds a house on solid rock."

Matthew 7:24

built his house on a rock. Before he started work, the man made sure that his house had a firm foundation on the rock. Then when the rain beat against the house and the wind blew around it, it did not fall down. It remained firm and solid.

"If you don't pay attention to what I have said, you will be like a foolish person who built his house on sand. When the wind blew and the rain beat against his house, it had no foundation, so it fell down. The walls, the roof, the door, and all his belongings were swept away.

"Don't be like the foolish person, sorry for his mistake when it was too late to change things. Be like the wise person. Listen well and act on what you hear."

SEPTEMBER 23—JESUS AND THE ROMAN OFFICER

MATTHEW 8:5-13

When Jesus heard this, he was amazed. Turning to those who were following him, he said, "I tell you the truth, I haven't seen faith like this in all Israel!"
Matthew 8:10

The crowd stayed with Jesus as he walked back to Capernaum. But the people fell back as a Roman officer rushed toward him.

The officer was clearly upset.

"Will you help me?" he asked Jesus. "One of my servants is very ill. He is in terrible pain and cannot move at all."

"I can come to your house," said Jesus. "Then I will heal him."

But the officer stopped Jesus.

"Lord, I don't deserve to have you under my roof. I know that if you just say that my servant is healed, he will be healed. In my position, I know about power and authority. Those above me expect me to do what they tell me. I tell people below me to come and go, and they obey me."

Jesus was amazed at the man's faith.

"I have not found anyone here with such faith," he said. "Return to your home, and you will find that your servant is well again."

The officer went home. His servant had recovered, just as Jesus had promised he would.

September 24 — The Widow's Only Son

Soon afterward Jesus and his disciples visited the town of Nain. Although it was about 20 miles away, a large crowd followed them there.

As they approached the gates of the town, another group of people was making its way to the little cemetery on the hillside.

Jesus watched as the group went by and saw that the people were carrying the body of a young man on a stretcher. The dead man's mother was weeping as she followed behind. He was her only son, and her husband had already died. She was now all alone.

Jesus felt sad for the woman. He went to comfort her.

"There's no need to cry," Jesus said.

Then Jesus went up to the stretcher and touched it. The men carrying it stopped and waited.

"Young man," Jesus said to the dead man lying there, "sit up!"

As soon as Jesus spoke, the young man moved and sat up on the stretcher. He began talking right away! His mother cried tears of joy at the miracle that had happened. Jesus took the young man by the hand and helped him to his mother.

Everyone was amazed, and there was much joy among the people. They could hardly believe what they saw. But some of them remembered the stories of Elisha, who had lived nearby long ago. He had also brought a boy back from the dead and had restored him to his mother in much the same way.

LUKE 7:11-17

[Jesus] walked over to the coffin and touched it, and the bearers stopped. "Young man," he said, "I tell you, get up." Then the dead boy sat up and began to talk! And Jesus gave him back to his mother.

Luke 7:14-15

"Praise God!" they said. "God has sent a prophet to help his people!"

After this, the news spread all over the country about what Jesus had done.

SEPTEMBER 25 — THE FARMER AND THE SEED

MARK 4:1-20

"The seed that fell on good soil represents those who hear and accept God's word and produce a harvest of thirty, sixty, or even a hundred times as much as had been planted!"
Mark 4:20

Jesus went from village to village and from town to town, telling people about how much God loved them and healing people who were ill.

When he returned to the lake, he talked to the crowds of people on the shore while he sat on a boat on the water. Jesus taught the people using parables, stories about things they understood but with special meanings.

"A farmer went out to plant some seed," began Jesus. "He took handfuls of seed and scattered it from side to side as he walked along.

"Some seed fell on the path. Birds came and quickly ate it up.

"Some seed fell on soil that was full of stones. The seed began to grow quickly, but it did not last long. Its roots had not reached down deep into the soil so that when the sun beat down on it, the plants shriveled up and died.

"Some seed landed among thorns, and as it grew, it was choked by the thorns so it could not produce fruit.

"But some seed fell on good, rich soil. There it began to grow strong and healthy until eventually it produced a good harvest.

"Listen well, and try to understand the message of the story."

Later, when the disciples were alone with Jesus, they asked him what the story about the farmer and the seed meant.

"The farmer who plants the seed is like God planting his message of truth in those who hear it," Jesus said.

"Some people who hear the message are like the soil on the path. They hear the message about God, but they quickly forget about him.

"Some people are like the stony soil. They try to obey God, but they give up when things get difficult or when people make fun of their faith.

"Some are like the seed that fell among thorns. They try to follow God, but they become distracted by money or other worries, and their faith is choked.

"But others are like the good, rich soil. They hear the word and grow up like strong, healthy plants, living fruitful lives that God can use. They are not swayed by the worries of the world, and they share their faith with others."

SEPTEMBER 26—SECRETS OF GOD'S KINGDOM

MATTHEW 13:44-46

Jesus told other stories to explain what God's Kingdom is like.

"Imagine that there is some treasure hidden in a field. One day a man accidentally finds the treasure. He buries it again quickly, then goes back home. He sells his home, his furniture, his cooking pots—even his donkey—so that he can buy the field. Then the treasure is his, and nothing could be worth more than that."

The people listened. Some of them understood. Jesus meant that God's Kingdom is more valuable than anything they owned. It is worth doing anything to be part of it.

Then Jesus told another story.

"God's Kingdom is like a man who buys and sells pearls. One day he finds an extremely beautiful pearl that is more valuable than any other. What does the man do? He goes home and sells everything he has so that he can buy it and have the beautiful pearl for himself."

"The Kingdom of Heaven is like a treasure that a man discovered hidden in a field. In his excitement, he hid it again and sold everything he owned to get enough money to buy the field."
Matthew 13:44

SEPTEMBER 27 — THE STORM ON THE LAKE

MARK 4:35-41

"Who is this man?" they asked each other. "Even the wind and waves obey him!"
Mark 4:41

It was evening, and Jesus was tired after teaching the crowds of people all day.

"Let's cross to the other side of the lake," Jesus said to his friends. So they prepared the boat and set sail.

Jesus went to the back of the boat and lay down, a cushion under his head. He was soon fast asleep.

At first the boat bobbed up and down gently and steadily. Jesus' friends thought about all they had seen and heard during the day as the boat moved across the lake. But then, as so often happened on that stretch of water, the wind suddenly changed direction. The waves began to crash over the side, and the boat rocked dangerously up and down.

The men clung to the long pole at the front of the boat. Even the fishermen among them knew they were in danger. They felt sure they were going to drown. But Jesus was still fast asleep.

"Master, help us!" they shouted, waking him. "Don't you care if we die?"

Jesus stood up. He spoke to the wind and to the waves.

"Be calm!" he said. The wind stopped and the lake was still.

Then Jesus turned to look at his frightened followers.

"Why are you afraid?" he asked. "Don't you trust me?"

Jesus' friends were amazed. They had no idea he had so much power.

"Who is he?" they asked one another. "Even the wind and the waves do what he says!"

SEPTEMBER 28 — ANOTHER VISIT TO CAPERNAUM

When Jesus arrived in Capernaum, the crowds came out to greet him.

But Jairus, the leader of the local place of worship, hurried to speak to Jesus. Everybody knew him. They watched as he knelt at Jesus' feet.

"Please help us," he cried. "My daughter is dying. She is only 12 years old. Will you come and help her?"

Jesus followed Jairus at once, and they made their way through the crowds to his home.

While they were on their way, Jesus stopped suddenly.

"Who touched me?" he asked those around him.

As the people in the crowd all denied it, Peter spoke to Jesus.

"Master," he said, "there are crowds all around, pressing close to you. Any one of these people could have touched you."

But Jesus knew that someone in the crowd had needed his help.

"I have felt power go from me," Jesus said. "Someone touched me, and now that person is healed."

Then a woman stepped forward, seeing that she could not hide from Jesus.

"It was me. I touched your coat," she said, falling to her knees. "I have been suffering for many years. No doctor has been able to help me. I didn't want to bother you, but I thought that if only I could touch the bottom of your coat, it would be enough, and I would be well again."

Jesus spoke gently to the woman.

LUKE 8:40-56

"Daughter," [Jesus] said to her, "your faith has made you well. Go in peace."
Luke 8:48

"There's no need to be afraid anymore," he said. "Your faith has healed you."

Just then, someone came quickly through the crowd. He had come from Jairus's house with news.

"Sir," he said, "it's too late. Don't bother Jesus anymore. Your daughter has died."

Jesus looked at Jairus. He saw that Jairus was close to tears.

"Don't be afraid," Jesus said. "Keep on believing. Your daughter will be well."

Jesus knew when he had arrived at Jairus's house, because mourners were already weeping loudly outside.

"Stop crying," said Jesus firmly. "The little girl isn't dead. She's only asleep."

Jesus went inside with the girl's father and mother and with Peter, James, and John. Then Jesus took the little girl's hand in his.

"Get up, little girl," he said.

The girl's eyes opened immediately, and she began to breathe again. She sat up.

"She is hungry," said Jesus. "Give her something to eat."

Jairus and his wife were astonished by what they had seen, but Jesus told them not to tell anyone what had happened.

SEPTEMBER 29—THE SECRET VISIT

Many people heard about the amazing things Jesus was doing and the incredible things he was saying.

Among them was Nicodemus, who was a Pharisee, a member of an important religious group. Nicodemus was eager to hear what Jesus had to say. But he was also afraid of what others might think. He knew that Jesus was already making enemies among the religious leaders.

So Nicodemus visited Jesus at night.

"Teacher," said Nicodemus respectfully, "I have seen you do many amazing things. God is obviously with you."

Jesus looked at Nicodemus. He could see that Nicodemus wanted to know more about God.

"To see God's Kingdom, you need to start all over again," said Jesus. "You need to be born again."

"But that's impossible!" said Nicodemus. "No one can do that!"

"Your mother cannot give birth to you again," said Jesus. "But God can give you a completely new start, a new life with God by the power of his Holy Spirit."

"How can I do this?" asked Nicodemus.

"You must believe in the Savior God has sent into the world. God has love enough for all the people he has made, but people love the darkness rather than light. They want to hide the evil things they do and are afraid that the light will show their sins. God has sent his Son so that all who sin can be forgiven and then have eternal life. They only need to put their trust in God's Son to know that forgiveness.

"Anyone who believes in God's Son will not die but will live forever!"

JOHN 3:1-21

Jesus replied, "I tell you the truth, unless you are born again, you cannot see the Kingdom of God."

John 3:3

SEPTEMBER 30—THE WOMAN WITH FIVE HUSBANDS

Jesus once traveled through a village called Sychar in Samaria on his way back to Galilee.

His friends went to buy food in the village and left him sitting by the well—the well that Jacob had drunk from many generations before. It was about noon, and the sun beat down on him. Jesus felt tired and thirsty.

Just then a Samaritan woman walked toward him. Although it was the time of day when people would usually be resting in the shade, she had brought her jar to fill with water.

"Please, will you give me a drink?" asked Jesus.

The woman looked at him.

"You're a Jew, aren't you?" she said. "And I'm a Samaritan. Don't you know our people are enemies? How can you ask me for a drink?"

"If you knew who I am, you would be asking me for water!" said Jesus. "I would not give you water from this well, but God's living water, so that you would never be thirsty again."

"I want that water!" replied the woman. "It would save me from having to come here every day."

"Go and tell your husband what I have said, then come back," said Jesus.

"I have no husband," the woman replied.

"That's true," said Jesus. "But you have been married five times, and now you live with someone you are not even married to."

The woman was amazed. How could Jesus know these things about her? She forgot about her water jar and ran to the town.

"Quick!" she said to as many people as possible. "Come and meet a very special man. He knows all about me! Could he be the Savior God promised to send?"

JOHN 4:1-29

"Anyone who drinks this water will soon become thirsty again. But those who drink the water I give will never be thirsty again."

John 4:13-14

OCTOBER 1 — THE END OF JOHN'S WORK

God had chosen John the Baptist to prepare the way for Jesus, to teach people that he was the Savior they were waiting for.

But John's message was a hard one. By speaking the truth and telling people to stop doing the things that were against God's laws, he made enemies.

One of the people he had upset was Herodias, the woman married to King Herod Antipas. She had been married before to Herod's brother Philip, and Philip was still alive. This was not allowed by Jewish law.

Herod had put John in prison, but he was afraid to punish him further. He knew John was a man of God, and he knew it would greatly upset the people.

One day, Herod held a birthday party for himself. Herodias's beautiful daughter got up and danced. Herod was very pleased and told her she could ask anything of him, and he would give it to her.

The girl asked her mother what she should ask for, and Herod regretted his promise immediately. She asked for the head of John the Baptist on a plate.

Herod knew that all his guests had heard his promise. He could not refuse her request. John was killed—and his head was brought to Herod.

John's work was over. Some of his friends buried his body. Then they made sure Jesus knew what had happened.

Jesus was very sad. He wanted to be alone to think, grieve, and pray. But wherever he went, people followed him.

MARK 6:14-29

The king deeply regretted what he had said; but because of the vows he had made in front of his guests, he couldn't refuse her.
Mark 6:26

OCTOBER 2—FIVE ROLLS AND TWO LITTLE FISH

Jesus went by boat into the hills on the far side of Lake Galilee. When he found people waiting for him even there, he could not turn them away. He healed those who were sick until late in the day.

Then Jesus looked at how many people had come. There were more than 5,000 men, plus women and children. Jesus turned to Philip, who came from nearby Bethsaida.

"Do you know where we could buy bread for all these people?" Jesus asked.

"It would cost far too much to buy bread for this number!" answered Philip.

Then Andrew, another of Jesus' friends, noticed a boy in the crowd who had with him a picnic lunch of five small barley rolls and two little fish. He brought the boy to Jesus.

"This boy has some food," he said, "but it won't go very far!"

Jesus took the food he was offered.

"Ask the people to sit down," he said to his friends.

The people sat down on the grass and watched as Jesus took the food and asked God to bless it. Then he began to break the bread and fish into pieces. He passed it to his friends, who then shared it with the people.

The people shared the food among themselves and ate until they were no longer hungry. Then Jesus' friends went among the people picking up anything that was left. They collected 12 basketfuls of leftover pieces.

More than 5,000 people ate that day and had more than enough to eat.

JOHN 6:1-13

"There's a young boy here with five barley loaves and two fish. But what good is that with this huge crowd?"
John 6:9

OCTOBER 3 — WALKING ON WATER

In the evening, Jesus said good-bye to the crowd and told his disciples to go back across the lake without him.

Then Jesus went farther into the hills to pray. He needed to spend time talking to God, his Father.

It was a windy night, and the disciples were working hard, fighting against the waves. Just before dawn, they saw a figure out on the water. They didn't realize it was Jesus, and they were frightened.

"Don't be afraid!" Jesus said to them, as he walked toward them across the water. "It's me."

Peter heard Jesus' voice.

"If it's really you," he shouted, "tell me to come to you on the water."

"Come on, then," said Jesus.

Peter stepped out of the boat in the darkness and onto the choppy waves. He walked toward Jesus until a gust of wind blew around him. Then Peter panicked.

"Lord, save me!" he called out to Jesus as he began to sink.

Jesus reached out and took Peter's hand.

"Why didn't you trust me?" he asked, as he helped Peter back into the boat. The wind stopped and the lake became calm.

The other disciples who had seen it all knelt before Jesus.

"You really must be God's Son," they said.

MATTHEW 14:22-33

About three o'clock in the morning Jesus came toward them, walking on the water. When the disciples saw him walking on the water, they were terrified.
Matthew 14:25-26

OCTOBER 4—THE MAN WHO COULD NOT HEAR

When Jesus was traveling through the area of the Ten Towns, a group of people came out to meet him. They brought to him a deaf man who could hardly talk.

"Please help him," they said. "Make him well."

Jesus took the man away from his friends and all those who were there so he could be alone with him. Jesus put his fingers in the man's ears, then he put some of his own spit on the man's tongue. He prayed for the man, asking for God's help.

"Open up!" Jesus said.

The man could hear. The man could talk! Suddenly the man couldn't stop talking! His friends and the others in the crowd were amazed and excited.

Jesus tried to keep them from telling anyone else about it, but they wouldn't listen. They could talk of nothing else—they wanted to tell everyone about how Jesus had given speech and hearing to a man who couldn't talk or hear.

MARK 7:31-37

They were completely amazed and said again and again, "Everything he does is wonderful. He even makes the deaf to hear and gives speech to those who cannot speak."
Mark 7:37

OCTOBER 5 — ON THE MOUNTAIN

One day Jesus took his closest friends, Peter, James, and John, to a high mountain.

While they were there, something amazing happened to Jesus. As they watched, Jesus' face and clothing became like a bright, shining light. Then two men appeared, standing beside Jesus and talking to him. Jesus' friends recognized the men as Moses and Elijah.

Peter could not keep quiet.

"Let us build three shelters, one for each of you," he called out. But before Peter could finish speaking, a bright cloud covered them, and they heard a voice speaking from heaven.

"This is my Son," said the voice. "I love him. I am pleased with him. Listen to him."

At the sound of God's voice, Jesus' friends were terrified. They fell to the ground.

While they were lying there, Jesus came and touched them.

"Don't be frightened," he said. "And don't tell anyone what you saw until you have seen God's Son risen from the dead."

When they looked up, Jesus was there, but the two other men had gone.

MATTHEW 17:1-9

Peter exclaimed, "Lord, it's wonderful for us to be here!"
Matthew 17:4

October 6—The Story of the Good Samaritan

One day a man came to Jesus to see how he would answer questions about God's laws. He had heard that people followed Jesus because what he said about God was different from what the religious leaders taught.

"Teacher," the man said. "What must I do to live with God forever?"

"What does God's law say?" Jesus asked the man.

"Love God with all your heart, your soul, your strength, and your mind. Love your neighbor as you love yourself," replied the man.

"Then you know the answer," said Jesus. "Do it and you will live with God forever."

"But who is my neighbor?" asked the man.

"I will tell you a story," said Jesus. "There was once a man who was walking on the lonely road from Jerusalem to Jericho. He was attacked by some robbers, who stole his money and took his clothes and left him half dead by the side of the road.

"Later on, a priest came along the same road. He saw the injured man but decided not to help him. He walked by on the other side.

"Some time later, a Temple helper came along the road. He also saw the wounded man but did not stop to help.

"Finally, a Samaritan came along the road. As soon as he saw the man lying there, he stopped. He cared for his wounds, helped him onto his own donkey, and took him to an inn. He gave the innkeeper some money and asked him to look after the injured man until he was well again. 'When I return, I will give you more money if you need it,' he said."

Then Jesus asked the man who was listening to the story, "Who was a good neighbor to the wounded man?"

"The one who helped him," said the man.

"You must do the same," said Jesus.

LUKE 10:25-37

"Which of these three would you say was a neighbor to the man who was attacked by bandits?" Jesus asked. The man replied, "The one who showed him mercy."
Luke 10:36-37

October 7—Mary and Martha

Jesus and his followers passed through the little village of Bethany on their way to Jerusalem. A woman named Martha welcomed them and invited them to eat with her.

Martha made herself busy in the kitchen, preparing all the food. She wanted everything to be just right for her visitors. Her sister, Mary, sat on the floor in the other room, listening to Jesus as he talked.

When Martha saw how Mary was doing nothing to help her, she was upset.

"Lord," she said to Jesus, "Mary is just sitting there, doing nothing, while I am having to do all the work. Tell her to help me!"

Jesus looked at Martha.

"Martha," he said, "there is always something that has to be done. Sometimes it's good to stop and listen and spend time with me. Mary has chosen to do that now. Let her stay and listen."

LUKE 10:38-42

"My dear Martha, you are worried and upset over all these details! There is only one thing worth being concerned about."
Luke 10:41-42

OCTOBER 8 — THE GOOD SHEPHERD

Many of the Pharisees and religious teachers criticized Jesus because he spent time with ordinary people, many of whom they thought were sinners.

"If you owned 100 sheep," Jesus said to them, "and one of them was lost, what would you do? Leave it to die and be happy with the 99 that are safe in the sheep pen? No, you would go in search of the one that was lost. You would look everywhere until it was found, then you would be happier over that one lost sheep than all the others. So it is with God. He cares about all his children, and he will not be happy until he has saved the one who has wandered away from the right path."

JOHN 10:1-21;
LUKE 15:1-7

"I am the good shepherd. The good shepherd sacrifices his life for the sheep."
John 10:11

"I am like a good shepherd," Jesus said. "I know all my sheep by name and care about them. They know my voice and know they can come to me. I will lead them to good pasture. I will give my sheep everything they need and much more besides.

"Like a good shepherd, I love my sheep and will let no harm come to them. When someone who is not a real shepherd looks after the sheep, he runs away if a wolf comes and attacks the flock. He doesn't really care about them. But I am willing to die for my sheep.

"I am the good shepherd. I know my sheep, and my sheep know me. I have other sheep, too, that are not in the same flock. One day there will be one great flock, all led by one shepherd. I will lay down my life for the sheep—no one will take my life from me. Then I will take up my life again."

"What is he talking about?" some of the people said. "Is Jesus crazy?"

But others in the crowd tried to understand. "Can a crazy person help a blind person see or a deaf person hear?"

October 9 — The Loving Father

Jesus told another story about God's love.

"There was once a man with two sons. One day the younger son said to his father, 'Let me have my share of the money I will get when you die. I'd like to travel and enjoy myself now.' So the father divided everything he had between his two sons.

"The younger son took his money and went far away. He used all his money enjoying himself and making lots of friends, but after a time he had spent it all.

"Then there was a terrible time without food in the land. There was nothing to eat. The younger son took the only job he could find: feeding pigs. He was so hungry, he could have eaten the pigs' food. Then the young man realized how foolish he was.

"'The people who work for my father have far more than I have now. I'll go home and tell him I am sorry. I will ask if I can have a job on the farm.'

"But the young man's father had been watching and waiting, hoping his son would come back. He saw his son coming and ran to meet him. He threw his arms around him and hugged him.

Luke 15:11-24

"'This son of mine was dead and has now returned to life. He was lost, but now he is found.' So the party began."
Luke 15:24

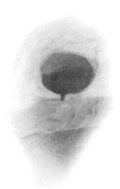

"'I have let you down and done things I am ashamed of,' the son said. 'I'm so sorry. I don't deserve to be treated as your son. Let me work for you instead.'

But his father shook his head.

"'Get the best clothes for my son,' the father called to one of his servants. 'Find new sandals and a ring for his finger. Prepare the best food! I thought my son was dead. He was lost, but now he's found. Let's have a party to celebrate his return!'"

OCTOBER 10—THE MAN WHO HAD EVERYTHING

One day a man in the crowd listening to Jesus shouted out to him. "Teacher, tell my brother to share his family money with me!"

"I am not here to settle family arguments," Jesus replied. "But I am here to warn you about greed. Make sure you don't fall into the trap of thinking that your life is made up of the things you own. Life is worth so much more than that!

LUKE 12:13-21

He said, "Beware! Guard against every kind of greed. Life is not measured by how much you own."
Luke 12:15

"Let me tell you a story. Once there was a rich farmer. His land produced an excellent harvest. He had so many crops he couldn't store them all. So he thought he would pull down his barns and build new, bigger barns. Then he could store everything he owned and rest and enjoy life. He could eat all he wanted, drink all he wanted, and be happy.

"But that night God said to him, 'Tonight will be your last. It is your time to die. You have stored up many things on earth, but now you must leave them all behind.'

"What good was all the rich farmer's money to him after his death?" asked Jesus after the story was finished. "None at all. This is what happens when people live their lives for themselves alone, thinking only of how many things they own. Live your lives for others, thinking of their needs before your own. God will look after you, and your great treasure will be in heaven—a rich relationship with God."

October 11 — The Outcasts

As Jesus passed near the border of Samaria and Galilee, he saw 10 men standing together in a huddle. They were dressed in rags and had covered their faces and their damaged hands and feet. Jesus knew that they had a skin disease called leprosy, which made them outcasts. No one would come close to them.

Luke 17:11-19

Jesus asked, "Didn't I heal ten men? Where are the other nine?"
Luke 17:17

They called to Jesus from a distance. "Jesus! Please heal us!"

Jesus knew how much they suffered and wanted to help them.

"Go to the priest," Jesus told them. "Show him your skin."

The 10 men turned to walk away, but as they did so, they realized that they had been healed. Their skin was healthy! The leprosy was gone.

One of the men was a Samaritan. He turned back to Jesus, praising God, and knelt at Jesus' feet.

"Thank you, Master! Thank you!" he said.

Jesus looked at the man on his knees, then he looked into the distance at those who were still walking away.

"Were there not 10 men who needed help?" said Jesus. "Are you the only one who came back to thank God? Go home now. You are well because you believed that God could heal you."

October 12 — Life after Death

John 11:1-44

*Jesus shouted,
"Lazarus, come
out!"*
John 11:43

Mary and Martha had a brother named Lazarus, who was also one of Jesus' close friends. When Lazarus became sick, the two sisters sent a message to Jesus, asking him for help.

Jesus was some distance away, but when he heard the message, he knew exactly what he had to do. Instead of going straight to the sisters, he told those around him that God's purposes would be seen more clearly if he waited awhile. So after two days, Jesus told his disciples that they should set out for Bethany.

"But they tried to kill you when you were last there, Master! Shouldn't you stay away?" one asked.

Jesus explained that there was a right time for everything. This was the right time for going to help Lazarus.

"Our friend has died. We need to go so I can bring him back to life."

Thomas looked at the other disciples.

"Come on," he said. "Let us die with him, if that's what's needed."

By the time Jesus arrived, Lazarus was dead and had been buried for four days. There were many friends there, mourning his death and weeping with his sisters.

"If you had been here earlier, Lord, Lazarus would still be alive!" said Martha, going to meet him. "But even now, I know that God will give you whatever you ask for."

"Lazarus will live again," said Jesus. "I am the resurrection and the life. If you believe in me, you will live forever. Do you believe, Martha?"

"Yes, I do!" said Martha, and she ran to get her sister.

When Mary saw Jesus, she fell at his feet, weeping. Jesus knew how sad she was, and he cried with her. Then they took Jesus to the place where Lazarus was buried.

"Open the tomb!" he ordered.

"But he's been dead for days!" cried Martha.

"Trust me, Martha," Jesus said to her. Then Jesus prayed to God before calling to Lazarus.

Lazarus walked out of the tomb, still wrapped up in the clothes he'd been buried in.

"Take off his burial clothes and take him home," said Jesus.

Mary and Martha were overjoyed to have their brother back. Many of their friends believed in Jesus because they had seen what had happened.

OCTOBER 13 — SEVENTY TIMES SEVEN

Peter came to Jesus and asked him about forgiveness.

"How many times should I forgive someone who wrongs me?" he asked. "Will seven times be enough?"

"No," Jesus replied. "Not seven but 70 times seven—you must always be ready to forgive."

Then Jesus told this story to explain.

"A king asked his servants to repay the money thay had borrowed from him. The first man came before him owing millions of dollars. But he could not pay any of it. The king was ready to sell the man, his wife, and his children into slavery and sell everything he owned so the debt could be paid. But the man begged him to let him have more time to pay. The king was more kind than the servant could have imagined. He canceled the debt completely.

"The servant left the king, unable to believe how lucky he was—until he bumped into a man he knew who owed him a few thousand dollars. He grabbed the man by the throat and shouted at him.

"'Give me back what you owe me now!' he said.

MATTHEW 18:21-35

Peter came to him and asked, "Lord, how often should I forgive someone who sins against me? Seven times?"
Matthew 18:21

"The man begged him to be patient—he needed more time to pay. But the servant would not listen. He had the man thrown into prison until he could pay back his debt.

"The other servants who had seen what had happened felt the servant had been wrong and acted unfairly. They went and told the king.

"Then the king called for the servant.

"'What you have done is wicked. I forgave you and canceled your large debt because you begged me to. How could you not show the same kindness to the man who owed you a much smaller amount? Now you must go to prison and stay there until you can pay me back.'

"This is why you must forgive from your heart, no matter what others have done," said Jesus. "You need God's forgiveness for all you have done wrong."

OCTOBER 14—THE PRAYERS GOD HEARS

LUKE 18:9-14

"Those who exalt themselves will be humbled, and those who humble themselves will be exalted."
Luke 18:14

Jesus once told this story to teach people how to pray.

"Two men went to the Temple to pray to God. One was a Pharisee—a religious leader—and the other was a tax collector.

"'Thank you, God, for making me what I am,' said the Pharisee in a loud voice. 'I don't steal or break any of your laws. I am much better than this man here, one of the hated tax collectors! I give you a tenth of all I have, and I pray on an empty stomach twice a week to show you how good I am.'

"The Pharisee was very pleased with himself. But the tax collector bowed his head and mumbled his prayers in his shame. 'God, please forgive me and be kind to me. I am a sinner, and I deserve nothing from you.'

"God heard the prayers of both men," said Jesus. "But only the prayers of the tax collector were acceptable to him."

OCTOBER 15—JESUS BLESSES THE CHILDREN

Not all the people who came to Jesus were blind or deaf. Not all of them were in need of his healing touch. Some came to Jesus just for his blessing.

When some parents brought their babies and small children to Jesus to be blessed, the disciples tried to send them away.

LUKE 18:15-17

"I tell you the truth, anyone who doesn't receive the Kingdom of God like a child will never enter it."
Luke 18:17

"Jesus is too busy," they said. "Take the children home."

Jesus got down to the level of a small child and smiled.

"Come here," he called to one. "Let them all come."

Then Jesus spoke to the disciples. "God's Kingdom belongs to people like these children. Learn from them. They trust me and love me without question. No one can be part of God's Kingdom without such simple trust."

OCTOBER 16 — THE RICH YOUNG MAN

A young man who had lots of money came to Jesus and went down on his knees.

"Good Teacher, tell me, please—how can I live forever?"

"You must keep God's laws," replied Jesus.

"I have done that since I was a boy," said the man.

Jesus smiled kindly at the man. He saw what the problem was.

"There is one more thing you can do," said Jesus. "Sell everything you have, give your money to the poor, and follow me."

The rich man suddenly looked sad. He got up and walked away. He was very wealthy. He could not do what Jesus asked—his money meant more to him than God.

Jesus looked at his friends.

"It is very hard for a rich man to enter God's Kingdom—it is easier for a camel to go through the opening of a needle."

MARK 10:17-25

"It is easier for a camel to go through the eye of a needle than for a rich person to enter the Kingdom of God!"
Mark 10:25

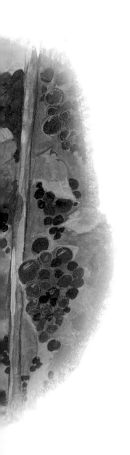

MATTHEW 20:1-16

OCTOBER 17—THE GENEROUS MASTER

"Those who are last now will be first then, and those who are first will be last."
Matthew 20:16

Jesus told the disciples a story about what God's Kingdom is like.

"There was once a man who owned a vineyard. He had many rows of vines and plenty of work to be done, so he went down to the marketplace early in the morning to hire some workers.

"He agreed to pay them a fair amount of money for the day, and the men came to work for him.

"At 9:00 in the morning, the owner went again to the marketplace. He found there were more men there looking for work, so he hired them, too.

"At noon, the owner went a third time and hired more workers. He went again at 3:00 and then at 5:00. Each time he found more men who were looking for work, and he hired them.

"When evening came and the day's work was ended, the men all came to be paid. The owner told his manager to start paying the men who had been hired last first of all, and to end with those who had been working in his vineyard all day long.

"Each of the men was paid the same amount—whether he had been there a few hours or all day.

"'But this is not fair!' grumbled one of the men who had started early in the morning. 'I have been here all day, and I worked in the hot sun—but I have no more for my trouble than those who came a short while ago!' Others agreed with him. They were so unhappy that they complained to the owner.

"'But what is your problem?' the owner asked. 'I have been fair to you. I paid you what we agreed on. You received what you expected at the end of the day. The only difference is that you saw that I was generous to the other men here. The vineyard is mine, and I chose to give all who came here the same payment. Surely I have the right to share all I have in whatever way I choose!'

"This is the way God is," said Jesus. "He will not just be fair—he will be generous. Those who come last will still be rewarded."

OCTOBER 18—BLIND BARTIMAEUS

Bartimaeus was begging at the side of the road when Jesus and his friends arrived in Jericho. Bartimaeus was blind, but he heard the crowd following Jesus. He knew something unusual was happening.

"Who's passing by?" he shouted out. "What's happening?"

"It's Jesus," someone answered him. "The teacher from Nazareth is here in Jericho!"

Bartimaeus had heard all about Jesus. He knew that he had made a paralyzed man walk and helped a deaf man hear.

"Help me!" he shouted out. "Jesus, have pity on me!"

"Be quiet!" said someone else in the crowd.

"Stop shouting!" said another.

But Bartimaeus would not stop. He shouted even louder.

"Jesus! Help me!"

Jesus heard Bartimaeus and stopped.

"Tell him to come to me," he said.

"It's okay!" someone told Bartimaeus. "Jesus has heard you. He's asking for you!"

Bartimaeus threw off his coat and jumped to his feet. He felt his way through the crowd until he came to Jesus.

"How can I help you?" asked Jesus.

"I want to see again," said Bartimaeus.

"Then you will see," replied Jesus. "Go now. You believed I could make you well. You can have what you asked for."

MARK 10:46-52

"My rabbi," the blind man said, "I want to see!" And Jesus said to him, "Go, for your faith has healed you."

Mark 10:51-52

Bartimaeus was no longer blind! He could see! He didn't return to his place along the road to beg. Now Bartimaeus joined the crowd of people following Jesus.

OCTOBER 19 — THE LITTLE TAX COLLECTOR

LUKE 19:1-10

"The Son of Man came to seek and save those who are lost."
Luke 19:10

Farther up the road, a crowd was gathering to hear Jesus speak. Zacchaeus, a tax collector, was among them.

Zacchaeus was not a very tall man, and because he cheated people when he collected their taxes, he was also unpopular. He wanted desperately to see Jesus, but because he was short and because no one would let him come to the front, he could see nothing over the heads of everyone else.

He saw the low branches of a fig tree up ahead. Then he had an idea. He went ahead of the crowd and climbed the tree so that he could see Jesus coming down the road.

When Jesus reached the tree, he stopped.

"Zacchaeus!" said Jesus, looking up at him. "Come down from the tree! I want to come to your house today."

Zacchaeus couldn't believe what he was hearing. He couldn't wait to get down from the tree.

"You are welcome to stay with me, Jesus!" he said.

But the people in the crowd were angry.

"Why stay with that sinner? Why even speak to him?" they muttered to each other.

Zacchaeus knew what the people were saying. He wanted to make things right.

"Jesus!" he said in a loud voice. "I'm going to give half of all I own to the poor. And if I have cheated people, I will pay them back four times the amount."

Jesus smiled at Zacchaeus.

"Today is a wonderful day!" he said. "It is for this that I have come— to save people who had forgotten how to live God's way."

October 20—The End of the World

Jesus talked to his disciples about how to love and serve God and other people. But he also told them about a time in the future when God would send his angels to the whole earth to gather together all the people who loved him.

"No one knows when that time will come," said Jesus, "except God himself. People will be working right up to that time. They will be getting married and having children. When this time comes, one person will be taken to be with God and another will be left behind. Make sure you are one of those who loves God. Be ready for that day to come.

"Let me tell you a story about 10 bridesmaids," said Jesus. "Each one had a little oil lamp so she could welcome the groom to the house that night. Five of the bridesmaids were prepared. They had brought some spare oil. But the other five were not prepared.

"Hours passed, and the groom did not come. The bridesmaids grew tired of waiting and fell asleep.

"Then in the middle of the night, they heard a noise. 'The bridegroom is coming! Wake up!' someone shouted.

MATTHEW 24:30-44; 25:1-13

"You, too, must keep watch! For you do not know the day or hour of my return."
Matthew 25:13

"The bridesmaids picked up their lamps. The five who had brought the spare oil could light them, but the lamps of the others had gone out. They had to go and get some more.

"While they were away, the groom arrived. The five bridesmaids with oil held up their lamps and walked with him into the wedding feast. Then the door was shut. The other five were too late. They missed the wedding feast."

OCTOBER 21 — THE FINAL JUDGMENT

MATTHEW 25:31-46

"The King will say, 'I tell you the truth, when you did it to one of the least of these my brothers and sisters, you were doing it to me!'"

Matthew 25:40

Jesus told the disciples what would happen at the end of the world. He described it in this way:

"The King will sit on his throne, surrounded by angels. He will divide all the people of the earth into two groups.

"'Come to me and enjoy all the good things I have prepared for you,' the King will say to one group. 'For you lived the way God wanted you to live. When I was hungry, you shared your food with me. When I was thirsty, you gave me a drink. You welcomed me into your home when you didn't know me, and you gave me clothes when I had none. You cared for me when I was sick, and you even came to visit me in prison.'

"Then those people will say to the King, 'But when did we ever do these things? When did we see you hungry and feed you or thirsty and give you a drink? When did we give you clothes or welcome you into our homes? When did we look after you in illness or visit you in prison?'

"Then the King will answer, 'Whenever you helped someone in need, you did this for me.'

"The King will turn to the other group and send them away. 'You gave me no food when I was hungry, and you let me die of thirst. You shut your door on me and wouldn't let me in. You saw that I needed clothes, but you wouldn't help me. And when I was sick and in prison, you had no time to take care of me.'

"'But when did we do these things?' the other group will say. 'When did we ever see you in need—hungry, thirsty, without a home or good clothes, sick, or in prison?'

"The King will reply, 'Whenever you saw someone in need and you walked by without helping them, you refused to help me.'"

OCTOBER 22 — THE JAR OF PERFUME

A few days before the Passover, Lazarus invited Jesus to his home in Bethany.

Lazarus and the disciples sat with Jesus at the table while Martha served the food. Mary went to wash Jesus' feet—but instead of using water, as she would for any other guest, Mary poured out some expensive perfume. Then she wiped Jesus' feet with her long hair.

The room was filled with the beautiful smell of the perfume. Judas Iscariot watched and judged her harshly.

"What a waste!" he said. "That perfume could have been sold, and the money could have been given to the poor."

Judas wasn't being completely honest. He was in charge of the money that was given to support Jesus, but he often stole from that and spent it on himself. Jesus was sad at Judas's reaction.

"Leave Mary alone," said Jesus. "What she has done has prepared me for my burial. There will always be people in need of your help, but I will not be here with you for much longer."

JOHN 12:1-8

"You will always have the poor among you, but you will not always have me."
John 12:8

OCTOBER 23—JESUS GOES TO JERUSALEM

On their way to Jerusalem, Jesus and his friends passed through Bethphage on the Mount of Olives. Jesus asked two of his disciples to go ahead and bring back a young donkey that would be waiting for them.

LUKE 19:28-40

"Blessings on the King who comes in the name of the LORD! Peace in heaven, and glory in highest heaven!"
Luke 19:38

"If anyone asks what you are doing, say that I need it, and then no one will stop you."

The two friends did as Jesus asked. They found the young donkey and brought it to Jesus. They put a coat on the back of the animal, which had never been ridden before. Then Jesus sat on its back and started to ride toward Jerusalem.

A large crowd gathered along the sides of the road. Some people spread their coats on the ground for the donkey to walk on. Some cut huge palm branches from the trees. They spread some branches across the road and waved some too.

Everyone was shouting.

"Hosanna!" they cried. "God bless the King!"

There were some religious leaders there watching, and they spoke to Jesus.

"What nonsense is this?" they said to him. "Stop these people. Make them be quiet!"

But Jesus knew that this would be the last time he received such a welcome. Next time the crowd would be shouting something very different.

October 24 — A Den for Thieves and Robbers

Once inside the city, Jesus went into the Temple courtyard. He saw the money exchangers and dove sellers busy making money for themselves, and he was angry.

Jesus took hold of one table after another and turned them upside down. Money scattered everywhere.

"This is God's house!" he said. "It is a place for people to pray and worship God, but you have made it into a dishonest marketplace, a den for thieves and robbers!"

Every day Jesus taught in the Temple, surrounded by crowds of people who didn't want to miss anything he said. Others came to him to be healed: the blind, the deaf, those who couldn't walk, those who suffered from various illnesses—anyone who needed Jesus came, and he healed them.

The chief priests and religious leaders watched Jesus. They hated what he was saying. They hated what he was doing. They hated Jesus himself. But because the people loved him, there was nothing they could do.

But little children danced around the Temple courts singing, "Hosanna! Praise Jesus! God has come to save us!"

LUKE 19:45-48

[Jesus] said to them, "The Scriptures declare, 'My Temple will be a house of prayer,' but you have turned it into a den of thieves."
Luke 19:46

October 25 — The Greatest Commandment

The religious leaders kept asking Jesus questions to see if they could trick him.

"Tell me, which is the most important of all the commandments?" asked one of the teachers of the law.

"The most important of all is this," said Jesus. "The Lord our God is the only Lord. Love the Lord your God with all your heart, with all your soul, with all your mind, and with all your strength. The second is this: Love your neighbor as yourself."

"You are right," said the teacher. "To do these things is better than to offer sacrifices to God."

Jesus looked at the man. He was pleased with the wisdom of his answer.

"If you understand this much, you are close to God's Kingdom," Jesus said to him.

Then no one else dared to ask him anything else.

MARK 12:28-34

"You must love the LORD your God with all your heart, all your soul, all your mind, and all your strength."
Mark 12:30

OCTOBER 26—THE GREATEST GIFT

LUKE 21:1-4

"They have given a tiny part of their surplus, but she, poor as she is, has given everything she has."
Luke 21:4

While he was in the Temple, Jesus saw some rich men putting money into the collection box. As he watched, a poor woman whose husband had died came and slipped two small coins into the box. Jesus turned to the people around him.

"That woman has given far more than anyone else," he said. "These men gave large gifts, but they were a small piece of what they had. They could easily afford to give them—it didn't cost them much. But that woman gave everything she had to God."

OCTOBER 27—THE PLAN TO KILL JESUS

MATTHEW 26:3-5,14-16

From that time on, Judas began looking for an opportunity to betray Jesus.
Matthew 26:16

The chief priests and the elders met together secretly.

"We can't let this go on any longer," they said. "We must find a way to kill Jesus."

"But the people are on his side," said one. "Passover is only two days away, and Jerusalem is too busy. If we have Jesus arrested now, there will be a riot!"

Meanwhile, Judas Iscariot was also making plans. He went looking for some of the chief priests. "What will you give me if I turn Jesus over to you?" he asked.

"We will give you 30 silver coins," they answered. This was the opportunity they needed—someone who could help them trap Jesus when he was alone.

Judas took their money. Now all he had to do was wait for the right moment.

OCTOBER 28—THE UPSTAIRS ROOM

LUKE 22:7-13

They went off to the city and found everything just as Jesus had said, and they prepared the Passover meal there.
Luke 22:13

The people in Jerusalem were getting ready for the Passover feast. Jesus sent Peter and John to make arrangements for him and the disciples.

"You'll meet a man carrying a water jar as you go into the city," Jesus told them. "Follow him. He will enter the house where we will celebrate the feast. Find the owner and ask him which room he has prepared for the Teacher and his disciples. He will show you a large room upstairs that is already set up for the meal. Then you can get everything ready."

The two men went into the city and saw the man with the water jar. They went into the house with him, and the owner took them to the upstairs room.

Everything was just as Jesus had told them. Then Peter and John started to get things ready for the special feast.

October 29 — Jesus, the Servant

The night before Passover, Jesus and his disciples met in the upstairs room to have supper together. Jesus knew that his time with his friends was coming to an end. There was still so much he wanted to teach them.

Jesus wrapped a towel around his waist and filled a jar with water. Then he started to wash his friends' feet. Normally a servant would wash the dust from their feet before they sat down to a meal. Jesus knew how strange it would seem to his friends that he was doing it now.

"I won't let you wash my feet," said Peter, as Jesus prepared to do just that.

"Peter, if I don't wash your feet, you cannot be my friend."

"Then don't just wash my feet—wash all of me!" said Peter.

"There's no need," said Jesus. "Only your feet are dirty." His thoughts turned to Judas. "But that's not true of everyone here," he added.

When Jesus had finished, he returned to the table with his disciples.

"Do you understand what I have just done?" Jesus asked them. "I am your teacher, but I have just done the job of a servant. I want you to treat each other with that same love and respect. Follow my example."

JOHN 13:1-17

Simon Peter exclaimed, "Then wash my hands and head as well, Lord, not just my feet!"
John 13:9

OCTOBER 30—THE BETRAYER

Jesus ate with his friends but they could see that he was thoughtful—and even unhappy. Then he spoke.

"One of you here is going to turn against me," he said.

The disciples looked at him in amazement. Then they looked at one another.

"Ask him who it is," said Peter to John, who was next to Jesus.

John whispered to him, "Who is it, Lord?"

JOHN 13:21-30;
MATTHEW 26:26-28

"Take this and eat it, for this is my body."
Matthew 26:26

"I will dip some bread in the bowl and give it to him," Jesus told John. Then Jesus gave the bread to Judas.

"Go now," Jesus said to Judas. "Do what you have to do."

Judas took the bread, stood up, and made his way out of the room quietly into the darkness.

Then Jesus held up the loaf of bread and thanked God for it. He broke it into pieces and shared it with his friends.

"Eat this. This is my body, which is given for you," he said. "Remember me whenever you eat bread together." Then Jesus picked up a cup of wine. "Drink this. This wine is my blood, poured out for you so that your sins may be forgiven."

Jesus' friends ate and drank with him, but they did not understand what Jesus was telling them until after he had died.

OCTOBER 31 — SLEEPING FRIENDS

Jesus and his disciples left the upstairs room and walked to a nearby olive grove, where Jesus wanted to pray.

"All of you will run away and leave me tonight," Jesus said to them. "But after I am raised from the dead, I will go to Galilee. I will meet you there."

"I will never leave you," said Peter, "even if all the others do!"

"Peter," Jesus replied sadly, "before the rooster crows at first light, you will have said three times that you don't even know me."

"No! I would rather die than say that!" Peter told him bravely. And all the other disciples agreed with him.

They arrived at a garden called Gethsemane, and Jesus told them to wait for him while he went to pray. He asked Peter, James, and John to go farther and wait with him, but he walked away from them to pray. They saw that he was very sad.

"My Father," Jesus said, "don't make me go through all the pain and suffering ahead of me! Take it away if that's possible. But let me do what you want me to—not what I want."

Then Jesus got up and walked back to his waiting friends, but he found they had all fallen asleep.

"Can't you even stay awake with me for one hour?" he asked. "I know you want to help me, but you have no strength."

Jesus went to pray again. "Father, if I must go through this suffering, then I am ready to obey you."

When he went to his friends a second time, they were sleeping again. Jesus prayed for a third time, alone in the garden, and when he returned to his disciples, they were asleep once more. They could not keep their eyes open.

"Wake up!" said Jesus. "It is time. Here is the man who has turned against me."

MARK 14:26-42

"The spirit is willing, but the body is weak."
Mark 14:38

NOVEMBER 1 — JESUS IS ARRESTED

The quiet of the dark olive grove gave way to the sound of people—a large crowd with swords and other weapons in their hands. Leading them all was Judas Iscariot.

Luke 22:47-54

Jesus said, "Judas, would you betray the Son of Man with a kiss?"
Luke 22:48

Judas walked right up to Jesus and gave him the usual greeting of a friend—a kiss on the cheek.

It was the signal the crowd needed. They closed in around Jesus and held him so he could not move.

The disciples were afraid. One of them pulled out a sword and cut off the ear of the high priest's servant.

"Put down that sword!" said Jesus, touching the man's ear and healing him. "There's no need for violence. If I wanted help, I could ask God to send angels to rescue me! But why do you people need to use force to take me away? You could have come any day when I was teaching the crowds."

They marched Jesus away to see Caiaphas, the high priest. His friends ran away, leaving him alone. Only Peter followed some distance away.

November 2—The Next Morning

There was a crowd seated around a fire in the courtyard of the high priest's house. Peter went in the darkness to sit with them.

Inside the house, the elders and religious teachers had gathered to wait for Jesus' arrival. They talked among themselves, trying to find some reason to put Jesus to death. They needed some crime to accuse him of, but they could find none. Finally, the high priest asked Jesus if he was the Christ, the Son of God, whom everyone had been waiting for—the one the prophets had said God would send them.

"I am," said Jesus, "and I will soon be seated at God's right hand."

"That's it! He claims to be God!" shouted Caiaphas. They had the reason they needed to ask the Romans to kill him.

Outside, a servant girl had been watching Peter in the firelight.

"I know you!" she said. "You're one of Jesus' friends!"

"No, I'm not!" said Peter, getting to his feet. "I don't even know him!"

Some time later a man noticed Peter there.

"I'm sure you were with Jesus," he said.

"You're wrong!" Peter replied angrily. "I'm not his friend."

Just before dawn, another man accused Peter.

"You come from Galilee too!" he said. "I can tell by the way you talk! You must know Jesus!"

Matthew 26:57-75

"Before the rooster crows, you will deny three times that you even know me."
Matthew 26:75

"I don't know what you're talking about!" Peter answered.

At that moment, a rooster crowed. It was dawn, and Peter suddenly remembered what Jesus had said to him.

Peter rushed away and cried in shame at what he had done.

November 3 — A Murderer Goes Free

Pilate, the Roman governor, stared thoughtfully at the man who stood in front of him with his hands tied and his head bowed.

"You know that the chief priests want you dead," Pilate said to Jesus. "Don't you have anything to say for yourself?"

Jesus stood silently. Pilate was worried. He could find nothing under Roman law that would allow for Jesus to be punished by death, but he could see that the Jewish leaders wanted some excuse for trouble. He decided to ask the people outside, who were waiting for his judgment.

"You know it is the tradition at Passover to set a prisoner free," he said. "Should I let Barabbas go, or Jesus, who some believe is the Messiah, the chosen one?"

The chief priests and the elders had made sure their supporters were in the crowd.

"Barabbas!" they shouted. "Set Barabbas free!"

"Then what should I do with Jesus?" asked Pilate. "He has done nothing wrong! Should I have him whipped and then set him free?"

MATTHEW 27:11-26

[Pilate] sent for a bowl of water and washed his hands before the crowd, saying, "I am innocent of this man's blood. The responsibility is yours!"
Matthew 27:24

"Kill him!" the men in the crowd shouted.

"But why?" asked Pilate. "I can find no crime to punish him for!"

"Kill him!" they shouted even more loudly. Pilate looked down at their angry faces as they shouted and waved their fists. He shook his head sadly and called for water to wash his hands in front of the crowd.

"This man's death has nothing to do with me," he told them.

But Pilate had Jesus taken away by soldiers to be killed on a cross. And he released Barabbas, the murderer.

NOVEMBER 4 — THE KING OF THE JEWS

MATTHEW 27:27-32

They led [Jesus] away to be crucified.
Matthew 27:31

The Roman soldiers took away Jesus' clothes and dressed him in the red coat of a Roman soldier. They twisted together branches of sharp thorns into a crown and forced it down on his head so that blood trickled down his face. They put a stick in his right hand and knelt in front of him, laughing.

"Look! Here is the King of the Jews!" they sneered, spitting in his face. Then they took away the stick and beat him again and again.

When they were bored with making fun of Jesus, the soldiers gave him back his own clothes and took him away to be hung on a cross.

Jesus was bruised and bleeding. He was exhausted from the beating. As he tried to carry the wooden beam on which he would be killed, he stumbled and fell.

"You! Here!" the soldiers said to a man in the crowd. "Carry this!"

The man, Simon from Cyrene, put the long piece of wood on his shoulder and followed Jesus outside the city walls, to the place where he would be killed.

NOVEMBER 5 — THE PLACE OF THE SKULL

The road was lined with people. Some shouted and made fun of Jesus. Others watched sadly. And more wept to see Jesus taken away to a place called The Skull.

Two other men were led out to be killed that day, both of them thieves. Jesus was nailed to the wooden beam and raised up between them.

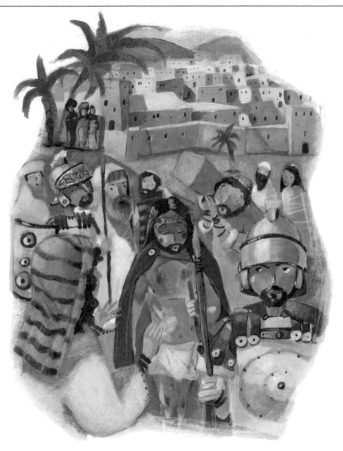

LUKE 23:27-46;
JOHN 19:25-30

Jesus replied, "I assure you, today you will be with me in paradise."
Luke 23:43

"Forgive them, Father!" said Jesus. "They don't know what they are doing!"

The crowds watched and waited. The soldiers jeered.

"You saved other people, but you can't help yourself!" they said.

Some of the soldiers gambled for Jesus' clothes. Others made a sign to hang over his head.

"This is the King of the Jews," it read.

One of the thieves who hung beside Jesus shouted to him, "If you really are God's Son, then save us all!"

"Be quiet!" said the other thief. "We deserve our punishment, but this man has done nothing wrong." Then he spoke to Jesus. "Remember me," he said.

"Today you will be with me in heaven," Jesus replied.

John, one of Jesus' disciples, was standing near the foot of the cross. A group of women, including Jesus' mother, was also there.

"Dear woman," Jesus said to Mary, "treat this man as your son. John," he then said to his friend, "treat this woman as if she were your mother."

At noon the sky turned black. At around 3:00 in the afternoon, Jesus called out loud, "It is finished!" And then he breathed his last breath.

NOVEMBER 6 — SECRET FOLLOWERS

MATTHEW 27:57-61;
MARK 15:42-47;
JOHN 19:32-42

As evening approached, Joseph, a rich man from Arimathea who had become a follower of Jesus, went to Pilate and asked for Jesus' body. And Pilate issued an order to release it to him.
Matthew 27:57-58

Joseph from Arimathea was a member of the Jewish high council. Like Nicodemus, he was a secret follower of Jesus, and neither man had been part of the plan to kill him.

As it was almost the Sabbath, Joseph went to Pilate and asked if Jesus' body could be taken down from the cross and buried.

Pilate was surprised that Jesus was already dead, and he checked first with the guards. Then, with Pilate's permission, Joseph went with Nicodemus and took Jesus' body from the cross. There were wounds in his hands and feet and in his side, where a soldier had stabbed him with a sword to make sure he was dead.

The men wrapped Jesus in strips of cloth with spices, and they placed his body in the newly made tomb. Then they rolled a big stone across the entrance to seal it.

Mary Magdalene and her friend sat nearby and watched where they put Jesus' body.

NOVEMBER 7 — THE EMPTY TOMB

Mary Magdalene wanted to put spices on Jesus' body. She hadn't been able to do it on Friday night or on Saturday because it was not allowed on the Sabbath day. So she went early on Sunday morning so she could be there at sunrise.

When she arrived in the garden, she saw that the huge stone that had been placed in front of the tomb had been rolled away. The tomb was empty.

Mary ran back to find Peter and John.

"They've taken Jesus away!" she cried. "I don't know where his body is!"

Peter and John ran to the tomb to see if there was some mistake. They saw the strips of cloth, but Jesus was not there. The two men ran home, leaving Mary alone in the garden.

Mary was still weeping when she went to look inside the tomb again. But this time she saw two angels, sitting where Jesus' body should have been.

"Why are you crying?" asked one of the angels.

"They have taken my Master away," Mary sobbed. "I don't know where they have put him!"

Mary turned as she heard someone else behind her. She thought it was the gardener.

"Who are you looking for?" the man asked.

"Please, just tell me where his body is," she said.

The man answered with just one word.

"Mary!" he said. Mary knew right away who the man was. It was Jesus!

"Master!" she said, overjoyed to see him.

"Don't touch me," he said to her gently, "but go and tell the others what you have seen."

Mary ran all the way.

"I have seen Jesus!" she said. "He's no longer dead. He's alive!"

JOHN 20:1-18

Mary Magdalene found the disciples and told them, "I have seen the Lord!"
John 20:18

NOVEMBER 8 — THE ROAD TO EMMAUS

Later that same day, two of Jesus' followers were walking along the road from Jerusalem to the village of Emmaus. They were talking together about all the events of the last few days.

As they walked, another man came alongside them. "What are you talking about?" he asked them.

Cleopas looked at the stranger, surprised.

"Surely you must have heard what has happened!" he said. "We were talking about Jesus of Nazareth. We thought he was the Savior God had promised to us. But three days ago, our chief priests and elders had him killed.

Then today we heard that his tomb is empty—they say he has risen from the dead!"

The stranger then began to explain all that the prophets had told the people about God's Savior, about how he had to suffer and die.

It was almost dark when they reached Emmaus.

"Come," said Cleopas to the stranger. "Stay here with us and have something to eat."

As they sat down to share a meal together, the stranger picked up the bread, thanked God for it, and broke it into pieces.

Suddenly the two friends knew who the stranger was. They had been walking and talking with Jesus! But as soon as they recognized him, Jesus disappeared. The men left everything and rushed back to Jerusalem to tell the others that Jesus was alive.

LUKE 24:13-33

They said to each other, "Didn't our hearts burn within us as he talked with us on the road and explained the Scriptures to us!"
Luke 24:32

NOVEMBER 9—BEHIND LOCKED DOORS

When the men arrived with their news, they found that the other disciples were together behind locked doors, talking about Jesus.

"Jesus is alive!" they said. "He appeared today and spoke to Peter!"

"We've seen him too!" Cleopas told them. "He walked with us to Emmaus and told us how he had to suffer and die before he could be raised. We didn't recognize him—until he broke the bread!"

At that moment, Jesus stood with them in the room.

"Peace be with you," he said.

At first they were afraid, but Jesus held out his hands and showed them the wounds where the nails had been.

"It really is you!" cried his disciples. "You're alive!"

Then, to prove he was really alive, he ate some cooked fish in front of them.

Jesus reminded the disciples what they must do next.

"Start in Jerusalem," he said. "Tell people that I died and rose again. Tell them they must turn away from their sins and that now they can be forgiven. Then go out to all the other countries and tell the people there, too!"

LUKE 24:34-49

"Now I will send the Holy Spirit, just as my Father promised."
Luke 24:49

November 10 — Thomas Doubts His Friends

Thomas had not been there when Jesus appeared to his disciples.

"I don't believe it!" said Thomas. "I won't believe that Jesus is alive unless I see him for myself and touch his wounds."

A week later, Thomas and the others met together. As before, the doors were locked to protect them from Jesus' enemies. And as before, Jesus appeared as if from nowhere and stood among them.

"Peace be with you," he said. Then he turned to Thomas. "Look at my hands, Thomas. Touch them. Look at the place where the sword cut my side. Touch that, too. Now stop doubting and believe!"

Thomas sank to his knees. He knew that this was no ghost. Jesus was real, and he was alive.

"My Lord and my God!" he said.

JOHN 20:24-28

[Jesus] said to Thomas, "Put your finger here, and look at my hands. Put your hand into the wound in my side. Don't be faithless any longer. Believe!" "My Lord and my God!" Thomas exclaimed.
John 20:27-28

November 11 — Fishing on Lake Galilee

For a few weeks after Jesus' death, the disciples did not know what to do. One evening Peter was back at Lake Galilee, and he decided to go fishing with some of his friends. He still could not forget that he had let Jesus down and pretended he didn't even know him.

They fished all night but caught nothing. As dawn came, they sailed back to the shore.

JOHN 21:1-12

Jesus appeared again to the disciples beside the Sea of Galilee.
John 21:1

A man was standing on the beach watching them.

"Have you caught anything?" he called out.

"No!" they replied.

"Try throwing your nets on the right side of the boat."

The fishermen did as the man suggested. Immediately, they felt the tug of the net as it filled with fish.

Peter looked at the man on the beach.

"It's Jesus!" he shouted. He jumped into the water and waded to the shore.

Jesus had made a small fire and had some bread there. "Bring some of the fish you caught," he said.

So the disciples dragged the net onto the shore and sat down with Jesus on the beach.

"Come," said Jesus. "Let's have breakfast together."

JOHN 21:15-17

Jesus repeated the question: "Simon son of John, do you love me!"
"Yes, Lord," Peter said, "you know I love you."
"Then take care of my sheep," Jesus said.
John 21:16

NOVEMBER 12 — PETER'S JOB

When breakfast was over, Jesus took Peter to the side to talk to him alone.

"Simon Peter," he said, "do you really love me?"

"You know I do," said Peter.

"Then take care of my lambs," Jesus replied.

Then Jesus spoke again.

"Peter," he said, "do you truly love me?"

"Yes!" said Peter. "You know I do!"

"Then take care of my sheep," said Jesus.

After a little while, Jesus spoke for a third time.

"Peter," he said, "do you love me?"

Peter was hurt. He remembered how he had failed to stand up for Jesus, how he had let him down. But he loved Jesus so much.

"You know everything," he said to Jesus. "You know that I love you."

"I have a special job for you to do," said Jesus. "When I have gone away, I want you to look after my followers."

NOVEMBER 13—JESUS RETURNS TO HEAVEN

After Jesus rose from the dead, his disciples saw him many times and in different places. Jesus taught them more about God. They had no doubt that he was the Jesus they had known before his death. They knew that he was alive.

"Stay in Jerusalem," he told them. "Wait there, because I will send the Holy Spirit to you. Then go and tell people everywhere about me. Teach them everything I have done and said. I promise that I will always be there to help you."

The disciples had often heard Jesus talk about the Holy Spirit and how he would come to be with them after Jesus had gone.

About six weeks after Jesus rose from the dead, the disciples were with him on the Mount of Olives.

"When the Holy Spirit comes, you will have power," Jesus said. "The whole world will hear about me, because you will tell them. You will be my messengers."

Then Jesus was covered by a cloud and seemed to rise up and disappear while they stood and stared.

Jesus was gone.

"What are you looking for?" asked two angels, who were suddenly standing among them. "Jesus has gone back to heaven, but one day he will return."

ACTS 1:1-11

"Jesus has been taken from you into heaven, but someday he will return from heaven in the same way you saw him go!"
Acts 1:11

NOVEMBER 14 — THE NEW DISCIPLE

The 11 friends returned to Jerusalem. They usually met to pray with some of the other believers. Now they called everyone together. There were about 120 people there.

"My friends," Peter said to them, "we have lost a member of our group. Judas was with us from the beginning. He was chosen to learn with us and work with us. But he led the leaders to Jesus and turned his back on him. Now he is dead."

MATTHEW 27:3-10;
ACTS 1:12-26

They cast lots, and Matthias was selected to become an apostle with the other eleven.
Acts 1:26

All the people there knew that Judas Iscariot had realized he had done a terrible thing by turning Jesus in. Judas had taken his own life and had been buried in the field that God had told the prophet Jeremiah to buy.

"We must find someone to replace Judas. This person must be someone who has seen all we have seen and been with us from the start."

Two men from the group were suggested. Then they all prayed, asking God to help them choose the right person. Matthias then became the 12th person in their group, now known as apostles rather than disciples. They were not just those who followed and learned from their Master. They had been sent out with his authority to speak and act in the name of Jesus.

NOVEMBER 15 — THE POWER OF THE HOLY SPIRIT

Jerusalem was full of visitors from all over the world. They had come for the festival of Pentecost.

The believers were together in one room, when suddenly a sound like a strong wind blew through the house, filling it with noise. Something like flames seemed to burn in the air and touch each person there. As the Holy Spirit touched them, they all began to speak in other languages.

The noise from the house attracted a crowd.

"What's happening?" some of them said. "I can understand what these men are saying. They are speaking in my language, talking about God. How is this possible?"

"They're drunk!" others said, laughing.

"No, we're not!" said Peter, coming out to speak to the crowd. "It's only

9:00 in the morning." Then Peter stood up to teach all those who would
listen.

First, Peter reminded them of what the prophets had told them would
happen. Then he told them about Jesus, God's chosen one, the Messiah.
When Peter described how Jesus had been arrested and beaten and then put to
death, the people were horrified.

"What should we do?" they asked.

"You must turn away from your sins and be baptized," Peter told them.
"Then you can be forgiven, and you will receive the Holy Spirit, as we have."

That day 3,000 people became followers of Jesus. The apostles performed
many miracles in the name of Jesus, and they met together with the other
believers to worship God, to pray, and to share what they had with each
other.

ACTS 2:1-47

*Everyone present
was filled with the
Holy Spirit and
began speaking in
other languages, as
the Holy Spirit gave
them this ability.*
Acts 2:4

NOVEMBER 16 — THE MAN BY THE BEAUTIFUL GATE

One afternoon, as Peter and John went to the Temple to pray, they passed a
man begging at the Beautiful Gate. He held out his hands.

"Do you have any money to spare?" he asked them hopefully.

Peter stopped and looked at him. The man had not been able to walk for

ACTS 3:1-11

Peter said, "I don't have any silver or gold for you. But I'll give you what I have. In the name of Jesus Christ the Nazarene, get up and walk!"

Acts 3:6

his whole life. He was carried there, to where he sat, day after day, hoping to be given enough money so he could feed himself.

"I have no silver or gold," said Peter, taking the man by his hand, "but I can give you something much more. In the name of Jesus, stand up and walk!"

The man stood up with Peter's help. Once on his feet, he took some steps—then jumped in the air with joy.

"Praise God!" he shouted. "I am healed! I can walk!"

Peter and John kept walking toward the Temple, smiling. The man went with them and held tightly to them.

The people all around stared, amazed.

"Isn't that the beggar who sat by the gate?" they asked each other. "How is it that he can walk?"

NOVEMBER 17—PETER AND JOHN IN PRISON

Peter gave the people the answer they needed: It was faith in Jesus that had given them the power to help the beggar. He told them that the same Jesus they had killed had risen from death. He was waiting in heaven until the time when there would be a new heaven and a new earth.

The people listened eagerly to all he had to say—until the Temple guards

and religious leaders came to see what was happening. Once they heard that Peter was telling everyone that Jesus had risen from death, they stopped him and put both Peter and John in prison. Some of the leaders taught that there was no resurrection of the dead!

ACTS 4:1-31

"There is salvation in no one else! God has given no other name under heaven by which we must be saved."

Acts 4:12

But many who were there believed what Peter had said and joined the growing number of people who called themselves Christians.

The next morning, Peter and John stood before the high priest and the other elders.

"How did you do this?" they demanded. "How was the man healed?"

The Holy Spirit gave Peter power to answer him.

"He was healed in the name of Jesus," he said. "Jesus is the man you killed and God brought back to life. God has given us Jesus so that we can be saved."

The high priest and elders could not understand what was happening—this man had been healed, and now Peter, an uneducated fisherman, could speak to them with such authority. But they would not be convinced that what Peter said was true.

They had no real reason to keep Peter and John in prison, so they had to let them go. But they warned them not to talk about Jesus anymore.

"We can do nothing else!" Peter and John replied. "Which would you do? Obey God or obey people?"

When Peter and John returned to their friends, they prayed together, asking for God's help so they would not be afraid to speak boldly about Jesus, no matter what happened to them. They were filled with the Holy Spirit and went out as God's messengers.

NOVEMBER 18—GAMALIEL'S ADVICE

Wherever the apostles went, people brought their friends and family to meet them. The streets were lined with those who were sick and lying on their mats or beds. The people in the nearby villages heard what was happening in Jerusalem, and crowds of people in need of help were brought to the apostles.

The high priest and his officials saw how many were being healed day after day. They saw how many new believers there were, and they were very angry. They arrested all the apostles and locked them up in the public jail.

During the night an angel came to the prison, opened the gates, and led the men out of jail.

"Go to the Temple," the angel said. "Tell everyone about the new life God has given you."

The next morning the high priest and the elders met to decide what to do with the prisoners. But when they sent for them, they were told the news of their disappearance.

"The prison doors are still locked and the guards are on duty, but the men we arrested are no longer in the prison!"

A man then came to them from the Temple.

"I have seen your prisoners," he said. "They are not hiding but in the Temple, teaching the people."

The captain of the Temple guard was sent to bring them back without causing a riot.

"We told you not to talk about Jesus anymore!" the high priest said to them. "You not only disobeyed us, you are also blaming us for his death!"

"We obeyed God," replied Peter. "Our sins have been forgiven—we must share this news with everyone."

The members of the high council were so angry that they wanted the apostles to be killed, but one man, Gamaliel, asked for the men to be taken out of the room so he could speak to the council privately.

"Leave these men alone," he said. "Every now and then someone rises up and tries to lead the people. After a while, people forget about him. His followers disappear. Perhaps this will be the same. But if it comes from God—if this is what they say it is—nothing we can do will stop it."

The council decided to listen to Gamaliel. They had the apostles beaten and set free, with an order to stop telling others about Jesus. But as soon as the apostles left, they continued to teach people that Jesus is the Messiah.

ACTS 5:12-42

Peter and the apostles replied, "We must obey God rather than any human authority."
Acts 5:29

NOVEMBER 19—STEPHEN IS KILLED

Now that there were so many believers, the apostles needed help to share all they had so that no one was in need. Seven wise men were chosen, and Stephen was among them.

Stephen had been blessed by God with some special gifts and had healed

many people. One day, some of Stephen's enemies, who were jealous of his wisdom and power, accused him of speaking against God because they wanted to get rid of him.

Stephen knew this was a serious crime, but he listened calmly to the lies spoken against him before the high council. His face shone like the face of an angel.

When it was his turn to speak in his defense, Stephen told them all about God's plan to save his people, from the time of Abraham. His closing words made them cover their ears in their anger:

"You are as stubborn as our ancestors! God tried to speak to you, but you rejected him. God sent Jesus to you, but you had him killed. Now you are rejecting the gift of the Holy Spirit!"

They marched Stephen outside the city and threw down their coats at the feet of a man named Saul. Then they threw stones at Stephen until he fell to his knees.

"Lord Jesus," said Stephen, "forgive them for this sin, and receive my spirit!" Then Stephen died.

Saul watched Stephen's death with interest. He was pleased that Stephen was no longer a threat.

ACTS 6:1–8:1

[Stephen] fell to his knees, shouting, "Lord, don't charge them with this sin!" And with that, he died.

Acts 7:60

NOVEMBER 20 — SAUL, THE ENEMY

ACTS 8:1-8

The believers who were scattered preached the Good News about Jesus wherever they went.
Acts 8:4

Stephen's friends went to get his body and bury him, and there was great sorrow at his death.

But there was not much time to think about it. That very day, Saul and the other authorities started trying to destroy the Christian church. Saul went from house to house, dragging believers out of their homes and locking them up in prison.

The Christians were scattered. Some hid from their enemies, and others moved away from Jerusalem. But wherever they went, they told people about the Good News of Jesus.

Philip, another of the seven men who had been chosen to help the apostles, went to Samaria. He shared all he knew about Jesus with the people there, and many came to hear him speak. People who were sick or paralyzed came and were healed by him. And many more were baptized in Jesus' name.

NOVEMBER 21 — AN ANGEL SENDS PHILIP

Philip was still in Samaria when an angel spoke to him.

"Get ready to travel south on the desert road to Gaza," the angel told him.

Philip went, and as he traveled along the road, he was passed by a man

seated in a carriage. The man was the treasurer for the queen of Ethiopia. He had been to Jerusalem to worship God and was now reading the words of the prophet Isaiah.

The Holy Spirit prompted Philip to go over to the man's carriage and walk along beside it. The Ethiopian looked confused.

"Can I help you?" offered Philip.

"I need someone to explain these words to me," the man replied. Then he invited Philip into the carriage to travel with him.

"'Like a sheep that goes to be killed, like a lamb that goes to have its wool cut off, he was silent and did not complain,'" he read aloud. "'He was treated unfairly; his life was ended before its time.' Who is the prophet speaking of?" the man asked.

So Philip told him. Philip explained that Isaiah knew about the Savior God would send to his people. He would be taken and killed and would die in the place of sinners.

ACTS 8:26-39

Beginning with this same Scripture, Philip told him the Good News about Jesus.
Acts 8:35

"He is talking about Jesus, who died so that all who believe can be made right with God!" said Philip.

The Ethiopian treasurer now understood and believed. He wanted to be baptized.

"Here is a river," the Ethiopian said. "Will you baptize me?"

Both men went into the water, and Philip baptized him. The man continued his journey happy, but he never saw Philip again.

NOVEMBER 22—SAUL, THE CHANGED MAN

Saul continued to look for all Christian believers, threatening to kill them for preaching about Jesus. He hated them and wanted to destroy them all.

"I want to go to Damascus," Saul told the high priest. "I need letters asking for help from the local places of worship so I can find and arrest any Christians who are there."

Saul set out along the road with some friends. When the city was finally in sight, a bright light from the sky suddenly shone down on him.

Saul fell to the ground and heard a voice coming from nowhere. "Saul, Saul, why are you hurting me?"

ACTS 9:1-9

[Saul] fell to the ground and heard a voice saying to him, "Saul! Saul! Why are you persecuting me?"
Acts 9:4

"Who are you?" asked Saul.

"I am Jesus, the one you are fighting against," said the voice. "Get up and go to Damascus, and you will be told what to do next."

Saul got to his feet but found that he could not see. His friends were as confused as he was—they had also heard the voice but had seen no one. They led him by the hand into the city of Damascus. Saul's sight did not return for three days. He ate nothing during that time but spent his time praying.

NOVEMBER 23—A NEW LIFE

Meanwhile, Jesus spoke to a Christian believer in Damascus named Ananias.

"Ananias, I want you to go to Straight Street to the house of Judas. There is a man there from Tarsus named Saul. He is blind and is praying right now. He has seen a vision of you touching him and restoring his sight."

"But, Lord, I know of this man! He hates all Christians and has come here to destroy us!" Ananias replied.

ACTS 9:10-19

The Lord said, "Go, for Saul is my chosen instrument to take my message to the Gentiles and to kings, as well as to the people of Israel."
Acts 9:15

"I know all this, and I have chosen him to suffer for my sake," said Jesus. "He will tell my people and foreigners and even kings about me."

So Ananias went to find Saul. He placed his hands on him.

"Brother," said Ananias, "Jesus himself has sent me here so that you will see again and be filled with the Holy Spirit."

Saul was able to see again! He was baptized and given something to eat. Then he stayed with the believers for a few days.

NOVEMBER 24—ESCAPE BY NIGHT

Saul went to the local places of worship and preached.

"Jesus is the Son of God," he said. "Jesus is the Messiah!"

The people who heard him were amazed.

"Isn't this the man who killed Christians in Jerusalem?" they asked. "We thought he had come here to do the same—yet now he speaks like one of them!"

Soon the Jews were making plans to kill Saul. They put guards at the city gates so he could not escape. But Saul had friends. One night they lowered

him in a basket down through a gap in the
city walls.

Saul went back to Jerusalem and tried to find the believers so he could join
them. But they were afraid—he had been arresting and killing their friends
only weeks before!

Then Barnabas spoke up for Saul. He went with him to the apostles and
explained what had happened to Saul on the road to Damascus. He told them
how Saul had preached the Good News about Jesus in the worship places
there.

"I have seen Jesus for myself," Saul told them, "and Jesus has spoken to me."

Saul then went into Jerusalem. Because he spoke Greek, he preached
to the Greek-speaking Jews there until they, too, wanted to kill him.

Then the apostles helped him escape to Caesarea and sent him back to
Tarsus, his hometown.

ACTS 9:20-30

*During the night,
some of the other
believers lowered
him in a large
basket through
an opening in the
city wall.*
Acts 9:25

NOVEMBER 25 – AENEAS AND TABITHA

Meanwhile, Peter traveled to many places, teaching and encouraging all the
Christian believers he met.

Once he went to Lydda, about 25 miles northwest of Jerusalem, where he
met a man named Aeneas, who had been paralyzed for eight years.

"You are healed in the name of Jesus Christ," Peter said to him. "You can get up and make your bed."

Aeneas was able to get up and walk from that moment. Many people in Lydda saw God's amazing healing power and put their trust in him.

The news of this healing reached Joppa, near the coast. The Christians in Joppa were very sad because their friend Tabitha had just died. Tabitha had been a good friend to everyone who was poor or in any kind of need. So the believers asked Peter to come and visit them.

Peter walked the 12 miles to Joppa and went to the place where Tabitha's body lay. All the friends were there, weeping and talking at once and showing him all the beautiful clothes Tabitha had made while she was alive. Peter sent everyone out of the room, then prayed for a while in the silence.

Then he turned to the body and spoke. "Tabitha, get up!"

She opened her eyes and sat up when she saw Peter there. Peter let the other women come back into the room. He saw how happy they all were that Tabitha was alive again.

Everyone soon heard what had happened, and many more people became Christians because of it. Peter then stayed in Joppa for a while at the house of a man named Simon.

ACTS 9:32-43

Turning to the body [Peter] said, "Get up, Tabitha." And she opened her eyes! When she saw Peter, she sat up!

Acts 9:40

NOVEMBER 26—AN ANGEL IN CAESAREA

The city of Caesarea, the headquarters for the Roman forces in Judea, was about 30 miles north of Joppa. Cornelius was a Roman officer in the Italian army stationed there.

Cornelius loved God and prayed to him regularly. He was also kind and generous to the poor, but he did not know about Jesus.

One afternoon, Cornelius was praying at the normal time of 3:00 in the afternoon when he saw an angel who called to him by name.

"What do you want from me?" Cornelius asked the angel.

"God has heard your prayers and seen how well you have treated those in need around you," the angel replied. "God wants you to invite a man named Peter here. You will need to send someone to Simon's home to find him. Simon works with animal skins, and his house is by the sea in Joppa."

When the angel had gone, Cornelius called two of his servants and one

ACTS 10:1-8

"Send some men to Joppa, and summon a man named Simon Peter. He is staying with Simon, a tanner who lives near the seashore."

Acts 10:5-6

of his soldiers who also believed in God. He told them what he had seen and then sent them to Joppa to find Peter.

NOVEMBER 27 — THE ROOFTOP VISION

While the men were traveling to Joppa, Peter was praying on the rooftop of Simon's house. He was hungry, and a meal was being prepared for him. Then Peter saw a vision of a large sheet being lowered down by its four corners in front of him. The sheet was full of animals that were good and acceptable to eat but also those that were not allowed according to Jewish law.

ACTS 10:9-23

"Do not call something unclean if God has made it clean."
Acts 10:15

"Here is food for you, Peter. Take what you need. Prepare it and eat," said God's voice.

"But I can't!" said Peter. "Some of these animals are unclean and not acceptable to eat."

"You don't need to call them unclean any longer. I have made them clean," said God. The sheet came and went three times in Peter's vision before the sheet disappeared.

Peter didn't have long to sit and think about what the vision might mean.

"Three men are at the gate looking for you," the Holy Spirit said to him. "I have sent them. Don't be afraid to go with them."

Peter went downstairs and met the three men who had just arrived and were asking for him.

"I am Peter," he greeted them. "Why are you here?"

When the men explained about the angel who had spoken to Cornelius, Peter invited them to stay until the next morning. He was beginning to understand the meaning of his vision.

NOVEMBER 28—GOD'S BLESSING FOR ALL PEOPLE

Peter traveled to Caesarea the next day with some of the other believers. When they arrived at Cornelius's house, they found that he had invited all his family and friends to hear what Peter had to say.

ACTS 10:24-48

"Can anyone object to their being baptized, now that they have received the Holy Spirit just as we did?"
Acts 10:47

"You know that Jewish law doesn't allow a Jew to come into the home of someone who is not a Jew. I am here because God has shown me that he does not have favorites. God accepts all who come to him and want to do what is right, no matter where they are from, no matter what their background is." Then Peter told them everything he knew about Jesus.

While Peter was speaking, the Holy Spirit blessed all the people there. Cornelius and all the people believed that Jesus had died and risen so that their sins could be forgiven. They praised God and spoke in different languages. So Peter arranged for all of them to be baptized.

The believers who were with Peter were amazed. They all saw that what Peter had said is true: God's invitation is to everyone.

NOVEMBER 29—DEATH AND IMPRISONMENT

King Herod started to hunt down the believers. First he arrested them. Then he arranged for the death of James, John's brother, who had been one of Jesus' first followers. Then he had Peter put in prison.

The night before Peter's trial, there were soldiers outside the prison cell and soldiers on each side of Peter as he sat in chains. All his friends in Jerusalem were praying for him.

Then while Peter was asleep, his prison cell was filled with bright light as an angel woke him. The chains fell from his wrists and the prison gates opened as the angel led Peter past the guards.

Once they were in the street, the angel disappeared. Peter, who had thought it was all a dream, went to the house where everyone was praying. Peter knocked at the door, and Rhoda, the servant girl, recognized his voice. She ran to the others and told them he was outside. At first no one believed her, but Peter kept on knocking. When they opened the door and found that he was there, they could hardly believe it! God had answered their prayers.

Peter told them to explain to the other believers what had happened, and then he went away so that Herod would not find him. Herod was furious when he found out Peter was gone, and he had the guards killed. But no one could tell him how it happened.

ACTS 12:1-19

While Peter was in prison, the church prayed very earnestly for him.
ACTS 12:5

NOVEMBER 30—THE MISSION TO CYPRUS

There were many Christians in Antioch in Syria. After Stephen's death, some of the believers had gone there to escape getting harassed by Herod. They had told people in Antioch about Jesus.

Barnabas was sent there to encourage them, and he brought Saul with him.

Then one day the believers heard the Holy Spirit telling them that Saul and Barnabas had been chosen to take the message about Jesus to the people on the island of Cyprus in the Mediterranean Sea. John Mark went with them.

They traveled across the island, teaching in the local worship places. When they reached Paphos, they met a man named Elymas, who communicated with evil spirits. He worked for the Roman governor, Sergius Paulus. The governor sent for Saul and Barnabas, because he wanted to hear about God. But Elymas did not want them to talk to his master.

"Don't listen to them!" he told the governor.

Saul, who was also known now as Paul, looked straight at Elymas.

"You are full of tricks and lies," Paul said. "You are an enemy of God and all his work. As your punishment, you will now lose your sight."

From that moment, Elymas went blind. He could do nothing without someone to lead him. Sergius Paulus saw what had happened and was amazed. He believed in the power of Jesus.

DECEMBER 1 — A BRUTAL ATTACK

John Mark went back to Jerusalem while Paul and Barnabas sailed to Galatia.

In Lystra, a man sat listening to Paul as he talked about Jesus. The man had never been able to walk but began to believe that Jesus could heal him. Paul saw that the man had faith.

"Stand up and walk!" said Paul, looking straight at him.

When the crowd saw the man get up and walk among them, they started talking excitedly.

ACTS 13:1-12

One day as these men were worshiping the Lord and fasting, the Holy Spirit said, "Dedicate Barnabas and Saul for the special work to which I have called them."
Acts 13:2

"These men must be Zeus and Hermes! The gods are here among us!" the crowd cried out. Then one of the Greek priests came with wreaths of flowers and tried to prepare sacrifices for Paul and Barnabas.

"Stop this!" Paul shouted. "We are here to tell you not to worship worthless things but the God who made heaven and earth! We are God's messengers. We are human, just as you are!"

Still the crowd would not listen. Then some Jews came among them, and they convinced the crowd that Paul and Barnabas had come to trick them. The mood of the crowd changed. Soon they were throwing stones at Paul in an angry attack until he fell down. Paul lay on the ground, not moving at all, until the men dragged his body outside the city.

Paul's friends came to help him. He returned to the city but left Lystra with Barnabas the next day.

ACTS 13:13; 14:8-20

When the crowd saw what Paul had done, they shouted in their local dialect, "These men are gods in human form!"
Acts 14:11

DECEMBER 2 — THE COUNCIL IN JERUSALEM

With so many people coming to believe in Jesus, disagreements began to arise about how best to follow him.

Paul and Barnabas argued with some in Antioch who said that the non-Jewish Christians had to go through the Jewish ceremonies as Moses had taught.

The issue was so important that Paul and Barnabas were sent to Jerusalem to discuss it with the leaders there.

"The Holy Spirit knows what goes on inside everyone," Paul said. "He came to those who aren't Jews and blessed them just as he came to us and to other Jewish believers. We are all saved because of God's grace alone, not because of any Jewish custom."

Eventually the leaders agreed on what should be taught to everyone. They gave a letter to Paul and Barnabas to take to the believers in Antioch.

"Paul and Barnabas come with our love and good advice. They have risked their lives already in teaching people about Jesus," the letter said. "Now we agree that there is no need for Jewish ceremonies when people become Christians. There are other rules we think are more important."

Paul and Barnabas took the letter and stayed for a while in Antioch, teaching the people there.

ACTS 15:1-41

"We believe that we are all saved the same way, by the undeserved grace of the Lord Jesus."
Acts 15:11

When the time came to move on, Barnabas wanted to take John Mark with them, but Paul did not. The two men agreed to work in different places. Barnabas went with John Mark to Cyprus, while Paul went with Silas to Syria and Cilicia.

DECEMBER 3 — FREE TO LOVE

Paul wrote to the Christians in Galatia about how they should worship God.

"You are children of God because of your faith. There is no difference between the Jewish believer and the non-Jewish believer, between the believer who is a servant and the believer who is free, between the male believer and the female believer.

GALATIANS 3:26-29; 5:13, 22-23

"Once you are Christians, you are all the same. You are all equally children of Abraham and will receive all the blessings that God promised him. God has given you the Holy Spirit as proof of that—the Spirit that cries out to God and knows that he is your loving Father.

There is no longer Jew or Gentile, slave or free, male and female. For you are all one in Christ Jesus.
Galatians 3:28

"So you are all free—free to love and serve God as equals. This freedom is not so that you can behave badly but so that you can love each other as Jesus showed us how to love.

"Don't let your human nature control you, but let your lives be controlled by the Holy Spirit. Then you will produce love, joy, peace, patience, kindness, goodness, faithfulness, gentleness, and self-control."

DECEMBER 4 — PAUL BAPTIZES LYDIA

Paul and Silas met Timothy, the son of a Jewish Christian mother and a Greek father, among the Christians in Lystra. Paul invited Timothy to join them.

Everywhere they went, they encouraged those who already believed. They told others about Jesus, so that more and more people became followers. Soon they were also joined by a doctor named Luke.

During this time, Paul had a vision in which he saw a man from Macedonia asking for help. The friends decided to go there on the next part of their journey.

They stayed in Philippi for several days. On the Sabbath they went outside

the city to the river where the Jews met to pray. Paul sat down and began to speak about Jesus to some women who had gathered there.

Lydia was a businesswoman, a trader in expensive purple cloth. She already worshipped God, but as she listened to Paul and heard what he said about Jesus, she understood and believed that Jesus is God's Son.

After she and her family had been baptized, she invited Paul and his friends to stay as guests in her home.

ACTS 16:1-15

That night Paul had a vision: A man from Macedonia in northern Greece was standing there, pleading with him, "Come over to Macedonia and help us!"
Acts 16:9

DECEMBER 5 — THE FORTUNE-TELLER

There was a slave girl in Philippi who earned money for her owners by telling fortunes.

Wherever Paul and his friends went, the girl followed them.

"These men are servants of the Most High God," she told anyone who would listen. "They can tell you how to be saved!"

Paul knew that the girl had an evil spirit in her, and he wanted to help her.

"In the name of Jesus, come out of her!" he ordered.

The girl was healed immediately—the demon left her. When her owners realized what had happened, they were very angry. Now that she could no longer tell fortunes, she was worth nothing to them!

ACTS 16:16-24

*[Paul and Silas]
were severely
beaten, and then
they were thrown
into prison. The
jailer was ordered
to make sure they
didn't escape.*
Acts 16:23

The girl's owners took Paul and Silas to the marketplace and reported them as troublemakers. The crowd supported the girl's owners, and the local leaders ordered that Paul and Silas be beaten and thrown in prison, to be guarded carefully.

The jailer put Paul and Silas in an inside cell and locked up their feet. There would be no escape for them.

DECEMBER 6—THE VIOLENT EARTHQUAKE

It was night. The prisoners were in darkness.

But Paul and Silas were not afraid, and they were not asleep. They prayed and sang songs to God as the other prisoners listened.

Suddenly, every door in the prison burst open, and the prisoners' chains came loose! A violent earthquake shook the foundations of the prison.

The jailer had been sleeping. When the earthquake woke him and he saw the prison doors open, his first thought was that the prisoners had escaped. In a panic, he drew his sword to kill himself.

"It's all right! We're all here!" shouted Paul. "No one has escaped!"

The jailer stopped and brought lights so he could see. Then he fell to the ground in front of Paul and Silas.

"Tell me how I can be saved," he asked.

"Believe in Jesus," said Paul, "and you and your family will be saved." Then Paul and Silas told the jailer all about Jesus' death and resurrection and how he could be forgiven for all his sins.

The jailer washed and treated the wounds the men had received from their beatings, and he asked to be baptized. Then he took Paul and Silas to his home and prepared a meal for them.

In the morning, the jailer received a message that the men could be set free, but Paul was angry. He told the officers who had come that he and Silas were Roman citizens and could not be treated so unfairly.

The officials had not realized they were Roman citizens, and they were concerned. They came nervously and led them out of the prison, hoping there would be no more trouble.

Then Paul and Silas went to Lydia's house for a while, where they met with their friends before leaving Philippi.

ACTS 16:25-40

[Paul and Silas] replied, "Believe in the Lord Jesus and you will be saved, along with everyone in your household."

Acts 16:31

DECEMBER 7 — THE UNKNOWN GOD

When Paul talked about Jesus in Thessalonica, he caused a riot among some of the Jews. His friends encouraged him to go on alone until they could join him.

While he waited for them, Paul walked the streets of Athens, which was full of beautiful buildings. But he was very troubled when he saw how many idols the Greeks there worshipped.

In the local worship place, Paul talked to the Jews, and in the marketplace he talked to other people. Soon he was taken to the high council of the city, where the Athenians discussed all the latest ideas.

"Tell us about your ideas," they said to him. "This is all new to us. We have never heard anything like this before."

Paul was glad to explain his message to them.

ACTS 17:1-9, 16-34

"As I was walking along I saw your many shrines. And one of your altars had this inscription on it: 'To an Unknown God.' This God, whom you worship without knowing, is the one I'm telling you about."
Acts 17:23

"People of Athens," he started, "I can see that you are very religious. As I walked around your city, I saw many objects of your worship. I even saw an altar to an unknown god.

"Now you worship him as unknown, but I can tell you all about this God, because I know who he is.

"The living God, who made the earth and everything in it, is so great he does not need to live in a temple made by the people he created, and he does not need anything from us. Rather, God himself gives us life and provides everything we need. God made us so that we would seek him and find him. And he gave us his Son, Jesus, who rose from the dead, so that our sins could be forgiven."

The people listened. Some wanted him to come back and tell them more, and others made fun of his message. But some—Dionysius and Damaris among them—believed him and became followers of Jesus.

DECEMBER 8 — TENTMAKERS IN CORINTH

ACTS 18:1-8, 18-26

After spending some time in Antioch, Paul went back through Galatia and Phrygia, visiting and strengthening all the believers.
Acts 18:23

Paul went from Athens to Corinth, where he met a tentmaker named Aquila and his wife, Priscilla. They were among the Jews who had been ordered by Emperor Claudius to leave Rome. Paul stayed and worked with them, helping them make tents.

Week after week, Paul went to the local place of worship to preach and explain that Jesus was the one they had been waiting for. But few would listen, and most were angry with Paul. So Paul spent most of his time in Corinth with people who weren't Jews. Many of them became believers and were baptized.

When Paul left Corinth for Ephesus, he took Priscilla and Aquila with him. He left them there while he sailed to Antioch.

Priscilla and Aquila then welcomed Apollos, a Jew from Egypt, into their home. Apollos was a believer and preached in the local worship place. Priscilla and Aquila were able to encourage him and teach him more because of the time they had spent with Paul.

DECEMBER 9—PAUL GOES TO EPHESUS

When Paul returned to Ephesus, he met 12 believers who had never heard of the Holy Spirit, even though they had been baptized. Paul explained to them about Jesus, and when he put his hands on them, they were filled with the Holy Spirit.

For the next two years, Paul preached in the local worship place, read the Scriptures, and talked in public places so that as many people as possible could hear about Jesus. God worked through Paul so that many sick people were healed just by touching cloths that Paul had touched. The believers also saw the power of God changing them and making them more like Jesus.

One day Demetrius, who made things from silver, called together all the other workers who also made items to help people worship the god Artemis.

"This man Paul could stop us from earning any money," Demetrius said. "He goes around telling people that there are no handmade gods, and lots of people—in Ephesus and beyond—believe him. We could lose our jobs, and the great goddess Artemis will be forgotten."

"Artemis is great!" the workers shouted, walking through the city. Soon there was a riot, and the crowd grabbed two of Paul's friends and dragged them to the city's big meeting place. Eventually an official stopped the riot.

ACTS 19:1–20:1

God gave Paul the power to perform unusual miracles.
Acts 19:11

"Ephesians!" he shouted. "Our city is well known as the home of the great goddess Artemis. But these men have done nothing wrong. Demetrius must go through the courts if he has a problem with them. You must let these men go before something happens that everyone will regret."

The crowd broke up, and Paul's friends were let go. But Paul decided it was time to move on.

DECEMBER 10—PARTS OF ONE BODY

1 CORINTHIANS
12:12-27

There are many parts, but only one body.
1 Corinthians 12:20

Paul wrote to the Christians in Corinth while he was in Ephesus.

He had heard that some of the new Christians were jealous of each other and were arguing among themselves. Paul wanted to show them how important it was for them to care about each other and to work together peacefully.

"Christ is like one body that is made of many different parts. We were all baptized so that we are part of that body, and we were all given the Holy Spirit.

"Each part of the body has its own special place—each part is important.

If each part works and does its job well, the whole body works well. But if any part fails to do its job, the whole body suffers.

"So it's no good if the foot decides it won't be a part of the body because it is not a hand. And it's no good if the ear decides it won't be a part of the body because it is not an eye. If the whole body were an eye, it could not hear. And if the whole body were an ear, it could not smell.

"In just the same way, one part of the body cannot decide that another part is not important or doesn't belong in the body. The eye cannot tell the hand that it is not needed. And the head cannot tell the feet that they are not needed. Every one of you is part of the body of Christ. God has given each person gifts to use for the good of everyone else. We all need each other. We suffer together, and we are happy together. God has given us each other so that his work can be done."

DECEMBER 11 — THE MEANING OF LOVE

Paul explained in the same letter to the Corinthian Christians how God wanted them to behave so that others would know they loved him.

1 CORINTHIANS 13:1-8

"I may be able to speak many languages —I may even be able to speak the language of angels. But if I cannot love, then all I do is make a loud and horrible noise!

Love will last forever!
1 Corinthians 13:8

"I may be able to predict the future and explain things that others find difficult. I may understand what others cannot know, and I may have enough faith to move mountains. But if I don't have love, I am nothing.

"Love is patient and kind. Love is not jealous or proud. Love is not rude or selfish or bad tempered. Love doesn't get angry easily, and it doesn't hold grudges. Love is kind and forgiving. Love is only happy with the truth. Love always protects, always hopes, and always keeps trying. Love never fails."

DECEMBER 12 — PAUL'S SUFFERINGS

While Paul was in Macedonia, he wrote again to the Christians in Corinth.

"Let me tell you about some of the things I have done. Let me brag a little about what has happened to me since I first heard Jesus call me to follow him.

"I have worked harder than anyone, been in prison more often, been beaten more severely, and been near death more times than I can count. Five times the Jews gave me 39 whippings, and three times the Romans beat me with rods. Once I had stones thrown at me, and three times I was shipwrecked. I have moved from place to place, unable to rest and live a normal life. I have been in danger from floods and from robbers. I have lived in fear of my fellow Jews and in fear of others too. I have known danger in cities, danger in the countryside, and danger at sea. I have sometimes not known whom I could trust. I have worked so hard I thought I could not survive it. I have often gone without sleep or food or water, and I have known what it is to be hungry and thirsty. I have suffered cold and been without shelter or enough clothing.

"To stop me from becoming proud, God also gave me a problem I have to keeping dealing with. When I asked God to take it away, he told me that his grace was enough for all my needs. When I am weak, I ask for his help and strength, and he gives it.

"So whatever hardships or difficulties I endure, however weak I feel, I can be happy in them, because I know that it is in those situations that God can make me strong."

2 CORINTHIANS 11:23–12:10

Each time [the Lord] said, "My grace is all you need. My power works best in weakness."
2 Corinthians 12:9

DECEMBER 13—GOD'S LOVE

Paul was in Corinth when he wrote a long letter to the new Christians in Rome.

"I believe that anything we suffer now will seem like nothing compared to all the good things that wait for us in the future. Everything in this world is waiting for the day when God will make all things perfect. We are looking forward to that day too, when we will be changed and made perfect.

"We know that in everything God works for the good of the people who love him. And if God is on our side, who can fight against us? What can separate us from God's love? Can trouble come between us and God? Can hard times or suffering, hunger or poverty, danger or death? No! Jesus loves us, and nothing can separate us from his love—not death or life, danger or trouble, angels or devils. Nothing that has ever been made can separate us from the love of God. It is ours because Jesus loves us."

ROMANS 8:18-39

Despite all these things, overwhelming victory is ours through Christ, who loved us.
Romans 8:37

December 14—A Miracle in Troas

Paul traveled for a while, sometimes changing his route when he was warned of plans against his life.

Then, staying briefly in Troas, Paul met one evening with some believers in an upstairs room. They ate together, and because Paul knew he would leave the next day, he talked long into the night. He felt there was so much to tell them.

A young man named Eutychus was sitting on the windowsill, listening to Paul. The room was lit by oil lamps, and Paul talked on and on. Around midnight, Eutychus became so sleepy that he fell out of the window. He died as he hit the ground.

Paul rushed downstairs and threw his arms around Eutychus.

"It's all right!" Paul said to the other believers. "He's alive!"

The young man's friends were very relieved that he had been brought back to life. Paul went back upstairs and had something to eat before continuing to talk about Jesus until dawn.

Acts 20:1-12

Paul went down, bent over him, and took him into his arms. "Don't worry," he said, "he's alive!"
Acts 20:10

December 15—Danger in Jerusalem

Paul knew that it was time to go back to Jerusalem. But he also knew that it would be dangerous. The Holy Spirit had warned him that prison and difficult situations awaited him there.

After some time at sea, Paul landed at Caesarea and stayed for a few days with Philip, an evangelist, and his family. While he was there, a Christian named Agabus came to see Paul. God had given Agabus the ability to tell what would happen in the future. He took Paul's belt and tied up his own hands and feet with it so that he could not move.

ACTS 21:1-15

"This is what the Holy Spirit says will happen to the owner of this belt when he goes to Jerusalem," said Agabus. "The Jews in Jerusalem will capture him and give him to the others who are against him."

He said, "Why all this weeping? You are breaking my heart! I am ready not only to be jailed at Jerusalem but even to die for the sake of the Lord Jesus."
Acts 21:13

All his friends were very worried about Paul's safety. They begged him not to go to Jerusalem when they heard this. But Paul would not listen.

"Don't cry for me," he said. "I am prepared to die in Jerusalem for Jesus, if that's what lies ahead."

The believers knew that they could not stop him. His mind was made up. "God's will be done," they said.

Then they prepared to let him leave for Jerusalem.

DECEMBER 16—PAUL CAUSES A RIOT

Paul met his friends in Jerusalem and told them about the thousands of people who had become believers in the places where he had traveled. At first they praised God and were happy with Paul. But then they warned him that this very good news would cause problems for him.

They were right. When Paul went to the Temple, he was recognized.

"Look!" a group of men shouted. "This is the man who tells people to ignore our Jewish customs!"

ACTS 21:17—22:23

"You are to be his witness, telling everyone what you have seen and heard."
Acts 22:15

People rushed into the Temple from all directions. They grabbed him and, dragging him outside the Temple area, started to beat him to death. There was such an uproar that Roman troops were sent to stop the riot. As soon as the soldiers rushed into the crowd, the men attacking him stood back.

"Arrest this man," the Roman commander ordered, "and lock him up." Then he asked the crowd what Paul had done.

Everyone in the crowd started shouting, but the commander could not understand what they were saying.

"Take him to the military station," the commander ordered. But the crowd became so noisy and violent at this that the soldiers had to carry Paul over the heads of the crowd.

Before he was taken to the military station, Paul asked the commander if he could speak to the crowd. He then turned to talk to them. He explained how God had changed him and given him the task of speaking to people who weren't Jewish. But this was too much for the crowd.

"Get rid of this man!" they shouted. "Put him to death!"

DECEMBER 17—PLANS TO TAKE PAUL'S LIFE

Paul was taken away. The orders were to beat him with a whip—a cruel type of torture. But as the soldiers were getting ready to beat him, Paul asked whether it was legal to whip a Roman citizen who had not been found guilty of any crime.

The officer stopped immediately and told his commander that Paul was a Roman citizen. The commander questioned Paul himself, and when he found that it was true, he released him.

ACTS 22:24-30;
23:12-30

The commander was frightened because he had ordered him bound and whipped.
Acts 22:29

A plan was then uncovered against Paul—40 Jewish men had met secretly and promised they would not eat or drink until Paul was dead.

"Prepare 200 soldiers, 70 horsemen, and 200 men armed with spears," the commander ordered. "Paul will be taken safely to Caesarea tonight!"

The commander sent a letter to Governor Felix explaining what had happened. He asked him to judge the case when Paul's accusers arrived there.

DECEMBER 18 — PAUL ON TRIAL

Five days later, Ananias, the high priest, plus some elders and a lawyer named Tertullus arrived in Caesarea.

"This man is a troublemaker," Tertullus said to Felix. "Talk to him yourself, and he will not deny what happens wherever he goes!"

Felix gestured to Paul to defend himself.

ACTS 24:1–25:12

Festus conferred with his advisers and then replied, "Very well! You have appealed to Caesar, and to Caesar you will go!"

Acts 25:12

"I had only been in Jerusalem for 12 days before I was taken prisoner," Paul said. "I am guilty of nothing. I caused no riot or disturbance. I did not go around with a crowd causing trouble. But I am a Christian, a follower of what is called the Way, and I know that I have made some people angry because I believe in life after death."

Felix had heard of the Way, and he put the case on hold. He kept Paul under guard but made sure his friends were allowed to see him and make him comfortable. Felix and his wife, Drusilla, even met Paul and listened to him as he talked about Jesus.

Felix waited. He hoped that Paul would offer him a bribe to release him, but after two years, Paul was still in prison.

Then a new governor took over. When Porcius Festus arrived, Paul's enemies tried to set a date for a new trial in Jerusalem so they could arrange to kill Paul on the journey there.

Festus refused. Instead, he went with the Jewish leaders to Caesarea, and the new trial began. Still nothing could be proved.

"I have broken no Jewish law, and I have not broken Caesar's law," insisted Paul. "I am a Roman citizen, and I have the right to take my case to Caesar."

Festus talked with his advisers.

"You have asked to go to Caesar," he said. "We have wasted enough time. Now Paul, you will go to Rome!"

DECEMBER 19 — THE SHIPWRECK

Paul was finally on his way to Rome.

An officer named Julius took charge of Paul and some other prisoners, and they set sail for Italy. They sailed from port to port, but the winds were against them, as it was nearly the time of the autumn storms.

When they reached the island of Crete, Paul tried to warn Julius that lives could be lost in such bad conditions, but Julius would not listen. They continued the journey.

Soon they were hit by a strong wind with the force of a hurricane. The sailors struggled to keep the ship under control. It suffered so much damage they had to throw some of the supplies overboard. Then thick clouds made it impossible to direct the ship, as the sailors could not see the planets and stars to guide them. The ship was tossed around by the wind and waves.

Day after day, the storm raged. No one ate. Everyone believed they would die—everyone except Paul.

An angel appeared to Paul one night and told him not to be afraid.

"You must go to Rome to stand trial," said the angel. "God will save the lives of all who sail with you."

Paul told the rest of the ship's passengers that the ship would be lost but they would be saved. He encouraged them to eat to save their strength.

There were 276 people on board the ship. When daylight came, they saw land, but the ship hit bottom and broke apart. The soldiers wanted to kill the prisoners so they wouldn't escape, but Julius stopped them. All the passengers made their way to land, either by swimming or by holding on to pieces of the wrecked ship.

They had landed on the island of Malta.

ACTS 27:1–28:1

"Don't be afraid, Paul. . . . God in his goodness has granted safety to everyone sailing with you."
Acts 27:24

DECEMBER 20—MIRACLES ON THE ISLAND OF MALTA

Rain was falling heavily, and it was cold. The people who lived on the island rushed to the beach and made a fire. They helped the shipwrecked men to safety.

As Paul gathered some wood to add to the fire, a snake slithered out and sank its fangs into his hand.

The islanders who saw the snake whispered among themselves. "This man has escaped from the sea only to be killed by a snake! He must be a murderer!"

But Paul shook off the snake and did not seem to be in pain. They watched and waited, but Paul did not become sick or die.

"This man cannot be a murderer," they said. "Perhaps he is a god!"

The chief official in Malta was a man named Publius. He invited everyone to his home and made them welcome for three days. During this time, Paul found that Publius's father was ill. He lay in bed, hot and feverish and in great pain. Paul prayed with him, and the man was healed. After that, many people on the island came to Paul with their illnesses, and Paul healed them all.

When it was safe to continue their journey by sea once more, the people on the island made sure that they had all the supplies they needed. They sailed on an Alexandrian ship to Rome.

ACTS 28:2-11

Once we were safe on shore, we learned that we were on the island of Malta.
Acts 28:1

DECEMBER 21 — A PRISONER IN ROME

Paul arrived safely in Italy. He was placed under house arrest in Rome but was otherwise allowed to live freely.

First he called together the leaders of the Jewish population there. He explained to them why he had been sent there and tried again to help them see that Jesus was the one they had been waiting for. Some of them believed him; others were not convinced.

Paul now knew that his job was to reach people who weren't Jewish with his message. For two years he welcomed people to his rented house and taught them all he knew about Jesus. Many believed what he had to say and were baptized. Paul also wrote many letters to the Christians he had met over the years, helping them in their Christian faith and teaching them when there were things they did not understand.

ACTS 28:16-31

For the next two years, Paul lived in Rome at his own expense. He welcomed all who visited him.
Acts 28:30

DECEMBER 22 — GOD'S ARMOR

While he was a prisoner in Rome, Paul wrote to the Christians in Ephesus.

"Since you are God's children, you must try to be like him. Live your lives ruled by love, not hate, just as Jesus gave up his life because he loved us.

"Don't be afraid to stand up against what is wrong. Be strong, and remember that he will look after you and give you power. Wear God's armor so that you will be safe. Wear truth like a belt around your waist. Cover your heart with the protection of doing what is right. Wear shoes that make you ready to tell other people about the Good News of Jesus. Carry faith as your shield against all attacks. Accept as a helmet the salvation that Jesus bought with his life. And use God's Word as a sword."

EPHESIANS 5:1-2;
6:10-17

Put on all of God's armor so that you will be able to stand firm against all strategies of the devil.
Ephesians 6:11

DECEMBER 23 — GOD'S FRIENDS

One day a slave named Onesimus visited Paul in his house in Rome. Onesimus had run away from his master, but when he listened to all that Paul told him about Jesus, he became a Christian and helped Paul in his work.

Onesimus went with Tychicus to take a letter from Paul and his friend Timothy to the Christians in Colosse.

"Jesus is the human likeness of the invisible God. He existed before all things were created and is now the head of the church. It was because of the sacrifice Jesus made when he died on the cross that God could forgive sins and make peace with his people.

"Once you were far away from God—you were his enemies because of the evil things you thought and said and did. Now, because Jesus died on the cross, God has made you his friends."

PHILEMON 1:10-12;
COLOSSIANS 1:15-23;
4:7-9

Christ . . . existed before anything was created and is supreme over all creation.
Colossians 1:15

DECEMBER 24—THE RUNAWAY SLAVE

Onesimus still belonged to his master, Philemon, who was a leader in the church at Colosse. Onesimus had become a good friend while Paul was a prisoner, but Paul knew he could not let him stay in Rome. So Paul wrote a letter for Onesimus to take back with him to Philemon.

"My dear friend Philemon, I have heard so much about your love for God and for other people. Now I need to ask you to do something for me— something I am sure you would want to do anyway. Onesimus was wrong to leave you, and I am sending him back. But while he was away, he became a Christian. So now he is not only your slave but also your brother. I would have loved for him to stay and work with me, but I wanted your agreement first.

"Please welcome him back as you would welcome me into your home. If he owes you anything, I will pay it back. I hope to be able to visit you soon. Please get the guest room ready for me!"

PHILEMON 1:1-22

I appeal to you to show kindness to my child, Onesimus. I became his father in the faith while here in prison.
Philemon 1:10

DECEMBER 25—LIVING LIKE JESUS

The Christians at Philippi also received a letter from Paul while he was in Rome.

"What is life? For me, it is to love and serve Jesus, to do what he wants me to do. But if I die, that is good too, because then I will be with Jesus always. I cannot choose which is better: life or death!

"Make sure you live in a way that pleases God and shows other people

that you belong to him. Don't be selfish or proud, but be humble and think of others as better than yourself. Put other people first. Think about how Jesus treated other people, and try to be like him.

"Jesus was the Son of God. He had the nature of God himself—yet he didn't act like he was above anyone else or more important than the people he had come to serve. Instead, he came to earth as a human and then acted as a servant. He allowed himself to be turned in and embarrassed, beaten and then unfairly killed as if he were a criminal. Jesus did this because he did not think about himself—he obeyed God and put others first. So God has rewarded him and has given him the highest position in heaven and earth. One day, when people hear the name of Jesus, the whole world will bow down and call him Lord.

"So there is nothing I want more than to know Jesus and share in his sufferings, even if I die, because then I will also know his power over death and his eternal life. This is my goal in life: to follow Jesus to the end."

PHILIPPIANS 1:21-27;
2:3-11; 3:10-14

*To me, living
means living for
Christ, and dying
is even better.*
Philippians 1:21

DECEMBER 26—THE END OF TIME

Paul was not the only apostle to write letters to encourage other Christians. Peter wrote two letters.

"Some of you are suffering and going through difficult times because you are Christians. Be happy that you are sharing in what Jesus suffered for you, but tell God all about your troubles, because he cares about you.

"The time will come when everyone will know that God is King. But remember that God is outside time. For him one day is like a thousand years.

1 PETER 4:12-16; 5:6-7;
2 PETER 3:8-14

*Give all your
worries and cares
to God, for he cares
about you.*
1 Peter 5:7

He may return tomorrow, or it may be after we have died. God is patient and he wants all people to turn away from their sins and know him. God doesn't want anyone to die without knowing about his love.

"When that day comes, it will sneak up on us. The earth as we know it will be destroyed. There will be no warning. So we must live our lives so that we will not be ashamed when it happens. We must be ready for God to come in glory, and we can look forward to a new heaven and a new earth."

DECEMBER 27—JESUS, THE HIGH PRIEST

Another long letter was written to help Jewish Christians.

"God's Word is alive and active, sharper than any sword, helping us to judge between right and wrong. We can hide nothing from God. But we do not need to be afraid, because we have a special High Priest, Jesus, God's Son. He understands our human nature and our weaknesses, though he did not sin. We can come to God with confidence and know that we will receive his mercy and that he will help us in our need.

"We are saved by God because we have faith. Faith is being sure of what we hope for and certain of what we do not see. We are part of a huge number of others who had faith before us—such as Abel, Enoch, and Noah; Abraham, Isaac, Jacob, and Joseph; Moses and the people with Joshua, including Rahab; and all the faithful prophets and kings of Israel. So, with them, we must set out on the race God has set before us. Let's throw off all the sins that get in our way and look at Jesus, who suffered so much for us. Be strong, and don't be discouraged."

HEBREWS 4:12-16; 11; 12:1-4

Faith is the confidence that what we hope for will actually happen; it gives us assurance about things we cannot see.
Hebrews 11:1

DECEMBER 28—LOVE ONE ANOTHER

John, one of Jesus' special friends, wrote at least three letters to the Christians in new churches.

"God is light, and in him there is no darkness. We must live in that light too, and to do this we must admit our sins and not try to hide them or pretend we haven't sinned at all. If we admit our sins and tell God we are sorry, then he will forgive us.

"Loving God means loving other people. It is wrong to hate someone else. If we hate someone, we sin and we need to admit that sin. God's love is so great that he calls us his children! Let's live as if we are his children and love the other members of his family.

"We know what real love is by looking at Jesus. He gave up his life for us. We should be prepared to do that for someone else. If we have enough to eat and drink and a home to live in—and we know people who are starving or in any kind of need and we ignore them—then how can we say God's love is in us? Don't just talk about God's love! Show what it means by sharing what you have with people in need.

"We love other people because God first loved us. God is love. Now we must show that love to the people of the world by loving them."

1 John 1:5-10; 2:9; 3:11-18; 4:19-21

If we claim we have no sin, we are only fooling ourselves and not living in the truth.
1 John 1:8

DECEMBER 29—JOHN'S VISION

When John was an old man, he was forced to leave his home and live on the island of Patmos. One day the Holy Spirit revealed strange things to John and told him to write them down in a book and send them to the Christians in Ephesus, Smyrna, Pergamum, Thyatira, Sardis, Philadelphia, and Laodicea.

John looked to see who was speaking to him and was amazed to see Jesus, not as he remembered him from when they worked together in Galilee, but

Revelation 1:9-18

"I am the living one. I died, but look—I am alive forever and ever!"
Revelation 1:18

shining like the sun—God in all his glory. The sight was so amazing that John fell at Jesus' feet. Then Jesus touched John's head gently and spoke.

"Do not be afraid, John," he said. "I am the First and the Last, the living one. I was dead, but look, I am alive now, and I will live forever and ever."

DECEMBER 30—THE REVELATION OF GOD

John wrote down all that Jesus told him to say to the people in the seven churches. Then he looked up and saw a door opening into heaven.

"Come here!" said the voice that John had first heard. "I will show you what will happen in the future."

John felt like he was leaving earth, but he saw everything clearly.

He saw a beautiful throne surrounded by a green rainbow. Someone who seemed to shine like colorful gems was sitting on it. There were 24 other thrones, and on each one sat someone dressed in white, wearing a crown.

REVELATION 4

The throne in the middle was God's throne, and it flashed with light. From the throne came a sound like thunder. In front of it was a sparkling crystal sea.

"Holy, holy, holy is the Lord God, the Almighty—the one who always was, who is, and who is still to come."
Revelation 4:8

Around the throne were four strange creatures, each covered with eyes. They were like a lion, an ox, a human, and an eagle, but each had six wings.

"Holy, holy, holy God, who was and is and is to come," they kept singing.

The 24 people fell down before God and worshipped him.

"You are worthy to receive glory and honor and power. You created everything, and everything lives and breathes because of you," they said.

DECEMBER 31—A NEW HEAVEN AND A NEW EARTH

John saw thousands and thousands of people from all over the world, all dressed in white and holding palm branches in their hands. They stood before God's throne, which was surrounded by angels and the four creatures. They were all worshipping him. Then a man came from one of the thrones.

"These people are those who have suffered," he told John. "They have been saved because of the blood shed by Jesus, the Lamb of God."

Later, John saw that the earth was gone and that there was a new heaven and a new earth. He saw a wonderful new city.

"Now God will live with his people. There will be no more pain or death, no more sadness or crying. God will wipe every tear from their eyes," God said. "From now on, everything will be made new! I am the First and the Last, the Beginning and the End. All who come to me will drink and never be thirsty again. I will be their God, and they will be my children."

Then an angel showed John the beautiful new city, with the water of life flowing in a sparkling river. On each side of the river grew a tree of life. Its fruit brought healing and freedom to people of every nation.

John could see that God's throne would remain in the city forever and that God's people would be with him always. There would be no more darkness or night, for God himself would be their light.

Then Jesus spoke. "I am coming soon! I am the First and the Last, the Beginning and the End. Anyone who comes to me will be forgiven, and those who are forgiven will be happy and will live in the city and enjoy life. Anyone who wants to can come and drink freely from the water of life.

"I am coming soon!"

REVELATION 7:9-17;
21; 22

I saw a new heaven and a new earth, for the old heaven and the old earth had disappeared.
Revelation 21:1

LIFE IN BIBLE TIMES

Contents

The people of the Bible lived in a different kind of world from most of us in the 21st century. This section of the book is here to help you put their customs, practices, and beliefs—the way they led their lives and what guided them—into context. It explains how and why they did what we find recorded in the pages of the Bible.

You can read this section straight through to get an idea of the background to the stories and events, or you can look up individual entries as they occur in the stories. The main entries explain general ideas, while specific examples can be found in the margins with Bible references.

FOOD

The Israelites came to like leeks, onions, garlic, cucumbers, and melons when they lived in Egypt.
Numbers 11:5

When three strangers came to visit Abraham, he cooked a fine meal for them.
Genesis 18:1-8

Jesus told a story about a son who returned home—his father organized a feast to celebrate.
Luke 15:11-24

BEANS
Beans, lentils, and chickpeas provided protein and were used to thicken stews and soups.

BREAD
This was the most important part of the people's diet. It was usually made from wheat. The poor ate barley loaves, and bread made from millet was eaten only in times when there was little food.

BREAKFAST
This was a simple meal of bread with olives, cheese, or fruit.

CHEESE
This was made from sheep's milk.

CUCUMBERS
The Israelites ate cucumbers when they were slaves in Egypt. When they were wandering in the desert, they missed this juicy Egyptian food.

FATTED CALVES
It was the custom to welcome strangers passing through the village and to offer them food and drink and somewhere to stay. Fatted calves were prepared for special guests.

FEASTS
Feasts were often given in thanksgiving for events such as weddings and new babies.

FIGS
Fig trees were often grown at the side of a house. Figs were either eaten fresh or dried in pressed cakes. Figs were also used as medicine.

FISH
Fishing was a big industry in Galilee but nowhere else in the region. There were said to be 24 different types of fish in Lake Galilee. Any fish that were not eaten fresh or traded were kept for later by salting or drying.

FRUIT AND NUTS
Figs, dates, pomegranates, mulberries, almonds, and pistachios were commonly eaten.

GRAPES
Most grapes were made into wine, but some were dried in the sun to make raisins. Some were boiled to make "grape honey," a thick substance used as a sweetener.

HONEY
Much honey was made by wild bees that nested in hollow trees and rocky holes. It was a welcome addition to the normal diet, as there was no sugar.

LENTIL STEW
After the day's work was finished, most families gathered together to eat a vegetable or lentil stew flavored with herbs and spices. This was eaten from one pot, using a piece of bread to scoop it out.

MEAT
Usually kept for feasts or other special occasions, this was not eaten every day. Sheep's meat and goat's meat were easily available, plus game birds and deer. Meat was usually boiled,

except the lamb for the Passover meal.

MILK
This was collected from both sheep and goats, but goat's milk was more commonly drunk and made into yogurt and cheese.

OLIVES
Some olives were eaten fresh or pickled, but most were made into olive oil.

PASSOVER MEAL
The Israelites ate unleavened bread (bread made without yeast), roast lamb, bitter herbs (to remind them of their suffering), and a special sauce each year at the Passover festival, with wine to drink.

SPICES
Groups of traders came with exotic goods, such as herbs and spices, that did not grow naturally in Bible lands. Cumin, dill, cinnamon, and mint were used as flavorings for food and wine. Cassia, spikenard,

and aloes were used as cosmetics. Frankincense was used in worship, and myrrh was a burial ointment.

VEGETABLES
Mallow, sorrel, and artichokes were grown so that their green leaves could be cooked and eaten. Others, such as onions, leeks, and cucumbers, were either eaten raw or cooked.

WATER
When collected from a well, water was safe for cooking but not for drinking.

WINE
Made from the grapes that grow so easily in hot climates, this was the most common drink, because it did not spoil in hot temperatures as milk did, and it was safer than water.

King Hezekiah had a medicine of pressed figs placed on a sore to heal it.
Isaiah 38:21

Jesus fed more than 5,000 people when a boy gave him his lunch of five bread rolls and two small fish to share.
John 6:1-13

John the Baptist ate locusts and wild honey.
Mark 1:4-6

Samson found bees making honey in the body of a dead lion.
Judges 14:8-9

Esau sold his rights as the first son for a bowl of lentil stew.
Genesis 25:27-34

Jesus met with his disciples for a Passover meal shortly before his death.
Matthew 26:17-29

Frankincense and myrrh were two of the gifts brought by the Magi after Jesus' birth.
Matthew 2:11

FARMING

Jesus turned water into wine when the wine had run out at a wedding feast.
John 2:1-11

Rahab hid the Israelite spies under flax drying on her roof.
Joshua 2:4-6

Ruth gleaned the leftover grain from Boaz's fields.
Ruth 2

Elisha was plowing a field with oxen when he was called to be a prophet.
1 Kings 19:19

Miriam's baby brother, Moses, was placed in a basket made of papyrus reeds from the banks of the Nile River.
Exodus 2:1-9

Jesus spoke about himself as being a shepherd for his followers.
John 10:14-16

BARLEY
Barley was grown in the central hilly region of Israel, where the soil is thin and stony. Flour made from barley was used to make barley loaves.

FISHING
This was done in the evening or early morning, when fish tend to be closer to the surface. Fishermen cast nets from boats or waded into the water with large nets to draw in the smaller fish that fed in the warmer water near the shore.

FLAX
The flax plant could grow to more than three feet tall, with beautiful blue flowers and shiny seeds. It was harvested in March or April by cutting at ground level. The fibers were then soaked in water. Flax was left to dry in the sun, often on flat roofs. The fibers were separated into threads so they could later be woven into linen for clothes.

Flax was also used to make string, nets, sails, and wicks for oil lamps.

GLEANING
By law, the Israelites had to leave part of their crops of grain, olives, and grapes for poor people to pick up, or glean, after the harvesters had done their work.

GOATS
Most families owned goats, which were kept for their milk and meat. Goat hair and goatskins were used for making tents and wine containers. In Old Testament times, a man's wealth was measured by the number of sheep or goats he had.

MILLET
Flour made from millet grain produced the lowest quality of bread.

OLIVE PRESSES
Olives were placed in olive presses and crushed by a round stone that rolled over them. The oil flowed out from an opening at the bottom, and the oil was used for cooking and lights.

OLIVE TREES
Olive trees were usually grown in groves or orchards. Olives were harvested in the autumn by shaking the tree branches or beating them with a long pole to make the olives fall to the ground.

OXEN
Oxen were working animals, used on the farm rather than as food. They pulled plows or other heavy loads.

PAPYRUS
Papyrus is a reed found in marshy areas, particularly beside the Nile River. It grew to about 10 feet tall, with heads of greenish fern-like flowers. Its three-cornered stem was cut into strips, and the two layers were beaten together to make paper.

PLOWING
The farmer plowed the fields to push the seeds

into the soil. Plows were made of wood, with metal cutting edges. They were pulled by either a single ox or two oxen hitched together.

SHEEP

Most families owned sheep, and wool would be spun into cloth. Sheep's fleece was worn for warmth, and sheep horns were used to store olive oil.

SHEPHERDS

These men led flocks from one grazing area to another. Shepherds gave names to their sheep and protected them from attack by wild animals. They carried staffs that were about six feet long with curved ends. They used them to guide the sheep or to pull them out of dangerous places.

SOWING

At the beginning of the farming year, farmers walked up and down the fields carrying bags of seed, which they scattered over the ground.

THORNS AND THISTLES

In dry areas, the only plants that could grow were thistles and thornbushes. There were more than a hundred kinds of thistle.

THRESHING

After grain was cut or threshed in the fields, it was tied in bundles and brought on carts to the threshing floor. The bundles were scattered over the ground and then beaten with sticks or trampled by oxen to separate the grain from the stalks.

TITHING

The Israelites tithed or gave a tenth of all the food they grew to God.

VINES

Vines were cut back in the spring to give a good crop of grapes. Harvesting—begun in late spring and lasting through the summer— had to be done quickly before the fruit rotted. Often the whole family helped in the work,

and sometimes they lived in small shelters in the vineyard during harvest.

WHEAT

Wheat was grown on the rich soil of the coastal plain and the Jordan Valley. Seeds were sown in late autumn after the October rain had softened the earth. The harvest was in the spring of the next year to make flour for bread. Bread made from wheat was offered to God by the priests.

WINNOWING

After threshing, the grain was tossed into the air using winnowing forks, which had long wooden handles with wooden forks at the end. The wind blew away the light seed coverings, while the heavier grain fell on the threshing floor to be gathered and stored.

Jesus used thornbushes and thistles to tell about people who took no notice of God.
Matthew 7:16-20

Noah was the first person to cultivate vines after the flood.
Genesis 9:20

Gideon threshed wheat in a winepress while hiding from his enemies.
Judges 6:11

The people of the Bible were totally dependent on God to give good harvests.
Psalm 67:5-7

PLANTS AND ANIMALS

The queen of Sheba visited King Solomon with a large group of camels that were carrying gifts for him.
1 Kings 10:1-13

Balaam's donkey kept him from disobeying God because it could see the angel that Balaam refused to see.
Numbers 22

Zacchaeus climbed a sycamore-fig tree so he could see Jesus.
Luke 19:1-10

God sent manna and quail for the Israelites to eat in the desert.
Exodus 16:1-18

BIRDS
Sparrows, swallows, and swifts were common kinds of smaller birds. Storks, cranes, and ostriches were among the larger birds.

BIRDS OF PREY
Shepherds protected their new lambs from being attacked by birds such as kites, eagles, hawks, falcons, harriers, and owls. All these were "unclean" and were not eaten by people. Ravens were also considered unclean.

CAMELS AND DONKEYS
Most people owned a donkey to help carry heavy loads or turn a stone wheel to grind corn. Donkeys were strong and cheap to feed. Sometimes people owned a mule, a cross between a horse and a donkey. Oxen were even stronger. Camels were useful for journeys across hot, dry lands.

CHICKENS
Certain birds raised for food, possibly geese, were known in Solomon's time. By the time of Jesus, people kept chickens for meat and eggs.

DEER AND GAZELLES
Fallow deer, roe deer, elks, gazelles, and oryx were hunted for food.

DOVES AND PIGEONS
Wild rock doves lived in holes and ledges in the desert, but in Bible times turtledoves was farmed. All doves were "clean" according to Jewish food laws, so they could be eaten and used as sacrifices. Even the poorest families could afford two doves for a sacrifice of thanksgiving at the Temple in Jerusalem.

EVERGREENS
Firs, pines, cedars, junipers, and cypresses were all used in building. Lebanon, in the north, was famous for cedars. Cypress wood was especially useful in ship building, and cedar was used in King Solomon's fancy building projects.

FLOWERS
The hills of Galilee were covered with wildflowers, including blue hyacinths, anemones, cyclamens, crocuses, yellow chrysanthemums, white daisies, poppies, and narcissi.

FRESHWATER FISH
Lake Galilee was famous for its fish, including tilapia, trout, and perch.

FRUIT TREES
Date palms, olive trees, pomegranate trees, fig trees, and sycamore trees all provided essential parts of the Israelite diet. Almonds were grown for their nuts and also to make oil.

GAME BIRDS
In addition to keeping doves and pigeons to eat, people hunted birds such as the rock partridge and the quail.

HERBS
Used as flavorings for food or in medicines, these included aloe, coriander, cumin, dill, garlic, hyssop, rue, mint, and mustard.

HORSES
Only kings and army commanders rode horses.

INSECTS
A swarm of locusts could strip an entire crop of wheat in seconds. Bees provided people with the only real sweetener. Moths and fleas were also common.

MIGRATORY BIRDS
Many birds passed over Israel in spring as they flew from Africa to their summer breeding grounds in Europe. In autumn they returned home. These included cranes, storks, swallows, and quail.

REPTILES
Harmless lizards and geckos were everywhere. Lizards helped keep houses free of insects by eating them. People had to watch out for snakes, scorpions, and flies.

RIVERSIDE TREES
A number of trees grew beside streams and rivers and at desert water holes, including willows and poplars. Tamarisks had distinctive feathery branches and tassels of pink and white flowers. Balsam poplars had a beautiful scent.

ROCK HYRAXES
Rock hyraxes were completely harmless wild animals about the size of rabbits, with small ears and no tails.

RODENTS
Rats, mice, gerbils, jerboas, and voles were common, as were blind mole rats.

SEA CREATURES
The Old Testament describes the great fish and sea monsters that swam in the "Great Sea" (the Mediterranean).

SHEEP AND GOATS
These were kept for meat and for sacrifice. They were also milked to produce cheese and yogurt. Fat-tailed sheep were most commonly found—they stored fat in their tails for when food was scarce. Ibex, or wild goats, lived on rocky hillsides.

VINES
These creeping plants were planted in rows on sunny hillsides and were among the most important fruit crops.

WILD ANIMALS
All shepherds had to keep their sheep and goats safe from dangerous predators, such as lions, leopards, bears, foxes, jackals, hyenas, wolves, and wild dogs.

Job owned 7,000 sheep and was thought to be a very wealthy man.
Job 1:1-3

David killed bears and lions to protect his sheep.
1 Samuel 17:34-35

FAMILIES

Mary wrapped baby Jesus in tight strips of cloth after he was born.
Luke 2:4-7

Jesus brought Lazarus back from the dead after four days in the tomb.
John 11:1-44

Jacob had 12 sons but made 11 of them jealous because Joseph was his favorite.
Genesis 37:1-4

Jesus healed the only daughter of Jairus, a local religious leader.
Luke 8:40-56

Parents brought their little children to Jesus so that he could place his hands on them and pray for them.
Matthew 19:13-14

Jesus was circumcised when he was eight days old, as were all Jewish baby boys.
Luke 2:21

In one of Jesus' stories, the younger son asked for his share of money before his father's death.
Luke 15:11-32

BABIES
The skin of new babies was usually rubbed with salt; then the babies were wrapped up in strips of cloth—like wide bandages. People believed that this would help children's legs and arms to grow straight.

BETROTHAL
Parents would arrange a marriage with a betrothal, or engagement, first. This was a legal contract in which the man or his family paid the bride's father some money and the bride's father gave his daughter or her new husband a present, or dowry.

BURIAL
Since the ground was rocky and hard, dead bodies were usually placed on ledges in caves, which would then be sealed. Later, when only the bones were left, they were put into a small stone box called an ossuary to clear space in the cave for more bodies. Burial caves usually belonged to families.

These burial places were considered unclean to strict Jews. Tombs were painted white so that they could be avoided.

CHILDBIRTH
Midwives were often there to help pregnant women with difficult births, but even so, sometimes women died in childbirth.

CHILDREN
It was important for couples to have children to pass on the family job and to support them in their old age. Many children died before they reached their fifth birthday, so parents had lots of children. People considered children to be a blessing from God. Having no children was viewed as a source of shame and unhappiness.

CIRCUMCISION
Boys were circumcised on the eighth day after birth as a sign that they belonged to the people of God. This involved removing a small part of the baby's skin.

CONCUBINES
In Old Testament times, having a family was so important that it was common practice for a man to take a second wife or concubine if the first was unable to give him children. The wife might also give her servant girl to her husband so that any child born would be part of his family.

DIVORCE
A man could divorce his wife, but a woman could not divorce her husband. Men were only supposed to ask for a divorce rarely, usually only if the woman had gone off with another man. But by the time of Jesus, the law had been twisted so that a man could divorce his wife if she burned his meal.

EDUCATION
There were no schools in Old Testament times. A boy would learn his father's work at home, and a girl would learn from her mother. Later, it was common for boys to go to school in the

synagogue (the local place of worship).

FAITH
Over meals and at religious festivals, families shared the stories of their faith. Wisdom—living God's way—was considered more important than knowledge of facts.

GROWING UP
At about the age of 13, a boy had his bar mitzvah, or coming-of-age ceremony. He became a "son of the law" and would be treated as an adult.

HEALTH
Keeping God's laws was a large part of staying healthy. The Israelites had to rest one day a week, and daily cleanliness was very important. There were foods that were not safe to eat in a hot climate, such as pork, and water had to be free of germs. Men were circumcised, which prevented infection.

LAND
Each family was supposed to have a piece of land or property. When the father died, the oldest son became the head of the family. This meant that the family always had somewhere to live and work.

MARRIAGE
Although in Old Testament times men were allowed more than one wife, by New Testament times Jews and Christians usually had only one spouse. It was unusual for people not to get married.

MEN
The father of the family was in charge. Laws were taught and enforced in the home even more than by the local or national government.

WEDDINGS
The whole community was invited to wedding feasts. They were great opportunities for singing, dancing, eating, and drinking.

WIDOWS AND ORPHANS
Each family was supposed to look after members who were ill or whose spouses had died. Widows and disabled people had to rely on their families to feed and house them, or they had to go out and beg.

WOMEN
Women were owned by their husbands. Women walked behind, not beside, men. Women were not allowed to teach in local places of worship. Their work was hard and in the home, caring for the family.

When Ruth and Naomi were both widows, Ruth married Naomi's relative Boaz. This helped to provide for their family. Ruth 4:9-10

Jesus raised to life the son of a widow at Nain. Luke 7:11-17

When he was on the cross, Jesus placed his mother into the care of his disciple John and told his mother to consider John her son. John 19:25-27

Jesus was unique for his time because he allowed women, such as Mary and Martha, to be his followers and friends. Luke 10:38-42

CLOTHING

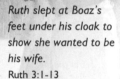

Ruth slept at Boaz's feet under his cloak to show she wanted to be his wife.
Ruth 3:1-13

Samuel's mother made a new coat for him each year while he was a boy helping in the Temple.
1 Samuel 2:18-19

Joseph was Jacob's favorite son, and Jacob gave him a special robe with long sleeves.
Genesis 37:3

Tabitha helped the poor and made clothes for widows.
Acts 9:36-39

When Abraham's servant met Rebekah, he gave her a nose ring and gold bracelets.
Genesis 24:22-31

CLOAKS
Warm woolen cloaks were essential on cold days and were also used as bed coverings at night. They were either blanket-shaped wraparound coats with holes cut for arms or coats like bathrobes with wide sleeves.

CLOTHES
Everyone except the very poor had everyday clothes and another set of clothes for the Sabbath. The style of both sets of clothes might be the same, but the materials would be different. The Sabbath day clothes were made of more expensive material and were usually white.

COSMETICS
Some women wore dark eye shadow around their eyes made from colored powder mixed with water, oil, or gum. Wealthy women might have used lipstick made from crushed insects. Some used face powder and painted their fingernails and toenails.

DYES
The main dyes were red, blue, and purple and came from plants or shellfish. Dyeing was done in big stone jars.

HEAD COVERINGS
Simple pieces of cloth that covered the head and the neck, kept in place by bands of cloth, were important protection from the intense sun. Men sometimes wore coverings similar to turbans. Women always wore head coverings in public as symbols of modesty.

JEWELRY
Many women wore earrings, nose rings, and necklaces, as well as bracelets on their wrists and ankles, and fancy tiaras or headbands. Hair combs and other accessories were often made from ivory. Jewelry was made from gold, silver, or other metals or from polished stones.

LINEN
Richer people wore soft clothes made of linen.

The stems of flax plants were cut, dried, washed, and dried again before the fibers were spun into off-white thread.

LOOMS
Most people made their own clothes at home by weaving them on a simple loom. The different sections of clothes were usually sewn together by hand, although some were woven whole and had no seams.

MATERIALS
Cloth made from camel hair was rough but lightweight. Cloth made of goat hair was brown or black and heavier weight—ideal for shepherds' cloaks. Woolen clothes were woven from sheep's wool, which was washed several times to get rid of the grease before being spun into creamy white, dark, or speckled thread. The cloth sometimes had simple patterns or stripes woven into it. Linen made from flax was used for priests' clothes, for rich people's

clothes, or on special occasions. Leather was used for sandals and some clothing.

MOURNING CLOTHES
When someone died, people would tear their clothes or wear a simple mourning tunic made from camel or goat hair, which was very itchy and rough.

NIGHTCLOTHES
When people went to sleep, they took off their outer clothing and belts and slept in their tunics, using their cloaks as blankets.

PERFUMES
Israelite women probably used perfumes made from spices mixed with olive oil or sap from trees.

SANDALS
Poor people wore no shoes. Others wore simple open sandals made of leather, tied on with a strap. Sandals were always removed before entering someone's home or a place of worship.

SHAWLS
Women wore embroidered or tasseled shawls over their long tunics and wrapped them over their heads.

TUNICS
Both men and women wore simple, loose tunics—pieces of cloth with holes in the middle for the head. Men's tunics were knee-length and made of colored material. Women's tunics were ankle-length and often blue. The hems of women's tunics were sometimes embroidered.

WEDDING CLOTHES
Everyone was expected to dress up for weddings, and rich families might even provide wedding clothes for the poorer guests. Brides wore veils over their faces, had their hair braided with precious stones, and wore long wedding dresses in bright colors.

Samson offered 30 plain linen robes and 30 fancy robes to his 30 companions if they could solve his riddle.
Judges 14:1-13

Lydia, one of Paul's followers, was a trader in purple cloth.
Acts 16:14

John the Baptist wore clothes made from camel hair.
Matthew 3:4

The tunic that Jesus was wearing when he was taken to be crucified was seamless.
John 19:23

DAILY LIFE

Joseph and Mary realized that 12-year-old Jesus was missing on the way back from the Passover festival in Jerusalem.
Luke 2:41-52

Martha was busy doing housework when Jesus came to spend time at the home of Mary, Martha, and Lazarus.
Luke 10:38-42

God gave the Israelites the Ten Commandments as their rules for life.
Exodus 20:1-17

BAKING
Women had to bake bread every day. First the grain had to be ground into rough flour. Then it was kneaded into dough before being baked.

CHILDCARE
Women cared for babies and very young children while working in or around the home. Babies were strapped to their backs so they could work while holding them.

COOKING
Women cooked over open fires or in small ovens that had fires in or under them. Most meat and vegetables were cooked in water; some were cooked in oil. For special occasions, meat was roasted on a spit, a wooden frame over an open fire.

ENTERTAINMENT
A number of musical instruments were used to entertain people for special occasions, such as weddings and celebrations. People played pipes, small harps, and tambourines while others sang and danced. Storytelling was also good entertainment.

FUEL COLLECTING
Younger children helped their mothers by collecting sticks and manure, which would be burned as fuel for the oven or open fire.

GAMES
When children weren't working at home, they played games together outdoors. Researchers have found remains of children's toys—clay animals, hoops, rattles, spinning tops, and board games like chess or checkers.

HOLIDAYS
There were three festivals a year when people had to visit Jerusalem: Passover, the Festival of Weeks (Pentecost), and the Festival of Tabernacles (harvest). Whole villages would travel to Jerusalem, camping each night on the way.

HOUSEWORK
Women would sweep the floors and keep the house neat, though people didn't own much.

LAUNDRY
Women washed clothes at the local streams or rivers by pounding them on rocks and scrubbing them with soap made of olive oil and ashes. Then the clothes would be left to dry on rocks in the sun.

MEN'S WORK
Families started work soon after sunrise. Many men were involved in food production. Later, craftsmen worked from home in different trades. Boys worked with their fathers, often looking after the animals or tending the vines.

PETS
The only pets owned by Israelites mentioned in the Bible are lambs. A

lamb might have been raised in the home if its mother had died. It would sleep with the children and even eat from the same dishes.

RELIGION

Home was the first and most important place where children were taught. They were taught the Jewish Scriptures and God's laws. The Ten Commandments formed the basis of daily life for everyone.

SABBATH

Everyone kept God's law: to rest on the seventh day (Saturday). No one worked on the Sabbath, and even household chores were kept to a minimum.

SCHOOLS

Many of the first Gentile (non-Jewish) Christians came from a Greek background, where the education system was quite different from a Jewish education.

Strongly influenced by Greek culture, boys were taught science, philosophy, and sports, as well as math and literature.

SHOPPING

Booths were set up in the gateways to the towns or villages, with people who sold the same kinds of products beside each other. Before coins became common, items were paid for by barter, exchanging one kind of item for another.

SLEEP

At the end of the day, everyone met together to eat and then went to sleep with the house lit by a small oil lamp.

SYNAGOGUE SCHOOL

These schools, for boys only, probably began in the period between the Old and New Testaments (from about 400 BC to the time of Jesus) and were held in the synagogue (the Jewish place of worship).

Rabbis, the local religious leaders, taught reading, writing, basic math, and religious law.

WATER CARRYING

Women or girls got water from wells or local springs early every morning. They poured the water into large pots which they carried on their heads or shoulders.

WOMEN'S WORK

Women prepared food and made clothing. They milked the goats and turned the milk into yogurt or cheese. They spun, wove, and dyed wool to make cloth at home. Girls helped their mothers.

The early Christians shared their possessions, and some sold land or houses so that the apostles could use the money for those in need. Acts 4:32-37

Rebekah was collecting water when Abraham's servant saw her and knew that God had chosen her to be Isaac's wife. Genesis 24:15-21

HOMES AND HOUSES

Before the first Passover, the Israelites had to put blood from a lamb on the sides and tops of the door frames of their houses.
Exodus 12:1-13

Jesus told a story about two men who built houses, one on solid rock and one on sand.
Matthew 7:24-27

Rahab hid the Israelite spies under piles of flax on her rooftop.
Joshua 2:4-6

A wealthy couple in Shunem had a room built on their roof so that Elisha had somewhere to stay whenever he visited.
2 Kings 4:8-10

ANIMALS
Animals such as goats were kept in the yard outside but brought inside at night.

BATHS
Large shallow bowls were used for washing. Since there was no running water, taking a bath was not easy for people in Bible times.

BEDS
Mats made from sheep's fleece were used for sleeping on the floor, with outer cloaks used as coverings. Mats were rolled up during the day when not in use. Sometimes mattresses took the place of mats for sleeping, and they were rolled up and stored in spaces in the wall during the day. Richer people had couches covered with cotton, wool, or silk, which became beds at night.

BUILDING MATERIALS
Early houses were built of bricks made out of mud. By New Testament times, those who had more money built houses made of stone. The rich had bigger houses with rooms around a central courtyard, where shrubs and flowers were sometimes grown.

CHAIRS AND TABLES
In early times, people sat on mats on the floor rather than on chairs, and when they lived in tents they used circles of leather for tables. These "tables" had rings around the edges so they could be drawn up with cords and used as carrying bags. In New Testament times, tables were usually low, and people sat around them on cushions to eat during the day. They sometimes slept on them at night.

DOORS
The doors of houses were usually left open during the day as a symbol of hospitality.

FLOORS
The floors inside simple houses were just the ground, made smooth and beaten hard so they could be swept. Later, the floors in rich houses were made of large pieces of stone. Some Jews even copied the style of the Romans and made mosaic floors of colorful tiles. Some people also painted scenes on the walls of their houses.

HEATING
Sticks, dried grass, thornbushes, and animal manure were burned to make fires for warmth and cooking. Fires were made outside in the open or inside in hollowed-out spaces by rubbing sticks together or making sparks with flint.

HOUSES
In Bible times, the home was where people were born, got married, and died. Several generations lived together, and there was very little privacy. When the Israelites settled in the land of Canaan, they took over the towns that the Canaanites had built. Here the houses were small and packed tightly together. After a time, the Israelites began to build slightly larger houses for themselves.

LIGHTING
Light was supplied by clay lamps, set in spaces in the wall. Lamps were filled with olive oil and lit by wicks made of flax. Sometimes they were set on bronze lamp stands.

ROOFS
Roofs were flat and made of large logs laid across from wall to wall, with smaller beams crossing the longer ones. Above these logs was a layer of twigs, grass, or reeds. Next was a thick layer of wet mud, packed down tightly with a large stone roller. Though they were firm enough to walk on, the roofs could be broken open.

ROOMS
Most homes in Old Testament times had just one room where the family cooked, ate, and slept. There were few windows, which kept houses dark but cool.

STAIRS
Outside staircases led to the roofs of houses, which were used for washing and drying.

STORAGE
Baskets and goatskin bags were used as containers. Pottery bowls and dishes were used in food preparation. There were often shelves in homes for cooking pots, but in tents or simple houses, most items were hung from the roof.

TENTS
In early times, the people of Israel lived in tents made of black or dark brown goat hair, woven into strips on the family loom. These strips were sewn together, and leather loops were added so they could be attached to the guide ropes. The average tent was about 16 feet long and 10 feet wide. Inside the tent there was usually one room for women and one for men, separated by a curtain.

WATER SUPPLY
Rainwater was collected and stored in cisterns, underground storage tanks for holding water. These were cut out of rock and made waterproof with plaster. The women had to collect water from the cisterns daily using buckets to draw up the water.

While Peter was in Joppa, he went up onto the flat roof of the house to pray.
Acts 10:9

Four men broke open a roof so that Jesus could heal their paralyzed friend.
Mark 2:1-12

Eutychus was listening to Paul when he fell asleep and fell from a windowsill three stories up.
Acts 20:9

Joseph was thrown into a cistern by his jealous brothers.
Genesis 37:23-24

TOWNS AND CITIES

King Hezekiah built a long tunnel from a stream outside Jerusalem to carry water into the city.
2 Chronicles 32:30

Rahab could help the spies escape because her house was built into the city walls.
Joshua 2:15

To escape from the Jews who were plotting against him, Saul was lowered in a large basket through an opening in the city wall.
Acts 9:23-25

Nehemiah made sure that the damaged walls and gates of Jerusalem were rebuilt.
Nehemiah 2:11–3:32

AQUEDUCTS
By New Testament times, the Romans had built huge aqueducts, tunnels for carrying water across the country. There was one near Caesarea, a city rebuilt by Herod the Great in the first century. The aqueduct was almost six miles long and brought water to the city from Mount Carmel.

BUILDINGS
Babylon had massive palaces and government buildings. Nineveh in Babylon had one of the biggest libraries of the ancient world.

CITIES
If the protective barrier around a city was a solid wall, it was considered a fortified, or protected, city.

CITY WALLS
Walls were made of stone at first, then later of brick. Some city walls were made of two walls over three feet thick. They were built with a ditch about 10 feet wide in between them. Sometimes they were joined by cross walls, and houses were built into the gaps.

DRAINS AND SEWERS
A few places in Canaan, such as Beersheba, had drainage tunnels, which took wastewater and sewage out of the city. Water was often thrown into pits outside the city or village. The Dung Gate in Jerusalem led to the Valley of Ben-Hinnom, the city garbage dump, which was always burning slowly.

FORTS
Sometimes there were strong forts, or citadels, in the middle of cities. These were towers where people could hide if attackers broke in to the city.

GATES
Thick wooden doors or gates were placed in the big stone gateways of cities to keep enemies out. Sometimes the doors were covered with metal so they could not be set on fire. Doors were wide enough for carts to get through. The doors were locked at night—or when attackers came—by sliding heavy wooden beams across the two doors from the inside.

GRAIN STOREHOUSES
In villages and small towns, people shared grain storehouses, threshing areas for cutting the corn from the straw.

MARKETS

Most towns and cities had a marketplace, where people bought and sold things. There were probably different areas where people with various jobs worked or sold their items. Jerusalem had several gates: the Fish Gate, the Sheep Gate, and the Tower of the Ovens, which was probably the bread-making area.

ROMAN CITIES

The Romans built cities with large stadiums, public meeting places, apartment blocks, and large country homes for rich people.

STREETS

The streets were the spaces between houses and were usually very narrow. They were made of packed-down mud and led into even narrower alleyways to give access to the areas behind the houses. In the time of the Greeks and Romans, the streets were paved.

TOWERS

Fortified cities had big half-circle or rectangular shaped towers built at certain points, making the walls stronger. These overlooked the city gate, and soldiers could fire arrows from the towers if the city was attacked. In peacetime, the shade provided by the towers and high walls made the gate a good place for meetings or public speaking.

TOWNS

If there was a defensive wall around a village, it was considered a town. Towns had irregular shapes but were designed so that anyone approaching had to come uphill.

TUNNELS

Cities needed good water supplies that attackers could not cut off. In Jerusalem, water entered the pool of Siloam from a stream outside the city walls.

VILLAGES

Villages were clusters of houses, often built with the blank walls forming a defense. People could enter through one gap or gate. If an area was attacked, villagers would go to the nearest town or city for safety.

WELLS

Cities, towns, and villages were always built near a water supply. Women went to the well every morning to fetch water for their families. They carried it home in jars on their heads or in sewn-up animal skins placed on the backs of donkeys.

WINEPRESSES

Winepresses were holes dug out of the rocky ground with stone walls around them. People squashed the grapes with their feet there, singing and shouting as they did so. Juice ran out through holes at the bottom of the press, where it was collected in vats and then poured into jars, where it turned into wine.

Joseph kept grain in storehouses so that it could be sold to those in need when there was no food.
Genesis 41:56-57

Saul was taken to a house on Straight Street in Damascus after he heard Jesus speaking to him on the road.
Acts 9:1-11

King Zedekiah's officials threw Jeremiah into the bottom of a dry well.
Jeremiah 38:6

Jesus talked to a woman drawing water at a well about the water of eternal life that he could offer her.
John 4:4-15

Gideon separated grain in a winepress to hide it from the Midianites.
Judges 6:11

RELIGION

After the flood, Noah built an altar to the Lord.
Genesis 8:20-22

Paul sent greetings to Priscilla and Aquila and to the church that met at their house.
Romans 16:3-5

Jesus' friends were preparing the Passover meal before Jesus was betrayed and arrested.
Luke 22:7-23

The Holy Spirit came to many believers at Pentecost.
Acts 2:1-12

ALTARS
Old Testament altars were made of stones and had four corners, the high points of which were called horns. The blood of sacrificed animals was sprinkled on them.

ARK OF THE COVENANT
This box contained the stone tablets on which the Ten Commandments were written, a jar of manna, and Aaron's walking stick. It had two figures of angels on top and rings at the four corners so that it could be carried on poles without being touched.

COVENANTS
God made a covenant, or agreement, first with Abraham, then with Jacob, then with Moses. Unlike the nations around them that worshipped false gods, the Israelites had a close relationship with God.

DAY OF ATONEMENT
The priests usually offered sacrifices to God on behalf of the people, but at this festival, the high priest performed special ceremonies to take away the sins of the people and to cleanse the Temple.

EARLY CHURCH
The first followers of Jesus met in the Temple in Jerusalem to pray and worship God, but as the Good News about Jesus spread from town to town and region to region, people began meeting in homes. The word *church* does not mean a building but a group of believers.

FEAST OF DEDICATION
This feast was also known as Hanukkah or the Festival of Lights. Every household lit a candle for eight days to remember the time when the Greeks were thrown out of the Temple and it was rededicated to God. The feast was a reminder of when the Jews had found a small container with only enough oil to light the candle holder for one day. Miraculously, the oil lasted for eight days.

HEROD'S TEMPLE
King Herod complained that the Temple of Zerubbabel was built like a fortress and was shorter than Solomon's Temple by about 90 feet because of an order made by Darius, the Persian king. Herod began rebuilding the Temple in white stone so it towered above all the other buildings in Jerusalem. Jesus himself worshipped at the Temple but predicted that it would be destroyed, as it was in AD 70. A wall surrounded the whole area, and a small part of it remains to this day. It is known as the Wailing Wall.

HIGH PRIESTS
Aaron was the first high priest, or chief priest. He wore special clothes, including a vest decorated with 12 different precious stones. He was the only one allowed to enter the Most Holy Place on the Day of Atonement.

INCENSE

This was made from frankincense, the sap of a Persian plant, and two other ingredients that gave it its scent. It was holy and used only for burning on the altar in worship.

LAW

It was important for people to know God's law so that they could live in a way that pleased him. The word *law* applies both to stories about God and his people in the Old Testament and to actual laws, such as the Ten Commandments.

LEVITES

Levites, who came from the tribe of Levi, helped the priests. They worked as ushers and musicians.

MUSIC

In the early days, women were the musicians. They sang, chanted, and danced at victories in battle. Miriam played the tambourine and led the Israelites in dancing and singing when God helped them cross the Red Sea. Before he became king, David played the harp for King Saul.

PASSOVER

This was one of the three main Jewish festivals. It was the celebration of how God brought his people out of slavery in Egypt. The Israelites acted out the events of that first night all over again and ate the feast dressed as though they were going on a journey. By the time of Jesus, most Jews went to the Temple in Jerusalem at Passover.

PENTECOST

Also known as the Festival of Weeks, this was a thanksgiving festival for the beginning of the harvest, 50 days after Passover. The Israelites offered the first of their crops to God. In New Testament times, Pentecost was the day the believers in the early church received the Holy Spirit.

PHARISEES

A group who opposed Jesus and eventually arranged for his death, the Pharisees were religious men who studied God's law and followed complicated rules of living. They were strict about praying, fasting, and giving, and they criticized those who did not meet their high standards. They thought Jesus was wrong and wanted to get rid of him.

PRIESTS

Descended from Aaron, priests offered sacrifices and prayers on behalf of the people. They wore special clothes and carried out the Temple rituals. They had to teach the people about God and live good lives.

PROPHETS

Prophets were good and holy people, chosen by God. Their messages were often reminders to turn away from idols and back to God, or to stop cheating and lying and to treat other people fairly. The Old Testament prophets were often unpopular and faced danger and criticism.

PSALMS

When David became king, he wrote many of the psalms and organized a Temple choir and orchestra.

PURIM

At this festival, the Jews remembered the time when Esther saved the Jewish people from being killed by the Persian king Xerxes.

SABBATH

In the account of creation, God rested on the seventh day. The fourth commandment told the people that they and their whole household should rest from their work that day. By the time of Jesus, the Sabbath was the day when people wore their best clothes, went to the synagogue, and returned to a good family meal. But other rules had grown up around the keeping of the Sabbath that prevented it from being a joyful day and turned it into a day of difficult rules.

SACRIFICES

Animal sacrifices were an important part of the Israelites' religion. The best of their goats, oxen, and sheep, as well as doves and pigeons, were presented to God in special ceremonies in the Temple as a way of giving thanks to God or saying they were sorry and receiving God's forgiveness for sins.

SADDUCEES

The Sadducees, who came from rich families with power and influence in Jerusalem, were friends with the Romans. They disliked Jesus, whom they saw as a troublemaker. They did not believe in the resurrection or the afterlife.

SCRIBES

By the time of Jesus, scribes not only copied or wrote books and letters, but they also taught people the laws. By that time, there were many complicated Jewish laws that were not found in the Old Testament.

SHOFARS

Made of rams' horns that turn up at the ends, these instruments played only two notes.

SIN

God is perfect and holy. He created a world that has laws, and he made people to live within those laws so that they could be safe in his world. When people chose to disobey and break those laws, they sinned and ruined the relationship they had with God. The results of that sin are chaos and death.

SOLOMON'S TEMPLE

Solomon's Temple was built according to the plan of the Tabernacle, except that it was built out of stone, and a number of courts were added. It was a magnificent building where people could worship God. The walls were paneled with carved cedar wood and lined with gold. People came into the courtyard to worship God and make sacrifices. This Temple was destroyed by the armies of Nebuchadnezzar at the fall of Jerusalem in 586 BC.

SYNAGOGUES

When God's people were captured and forced to live away from Jerusalem, they were not able to worship at the Temple. So they began to meet together to hear God's law and to pray in a simple building known as a synagogue. After the Israelites returned home, every town and village had a synagogue, which became the center of village life. Rabbis or teachers taught all the men and boys the Jewish laws, and the Scriptures were read aloud. Boys were educated there during the week.

TABERNACLE

During the time of Moses, worship was conducted in a tent called the Tabernacle. The tent had curtains in purple, red, and blue and an animal-skin covering for a roof. It reminded the people that God was always with them. People gathered in the courtyard to hear God's law, offer sacrifices, say prayers, and praise God with words and music. Inside the tent, where only the priests could go, were these special items: an altar where incense was burned, a golden lamp stand, and a table with special bread. Only the high priest could enter the inner tent, the Most Holy Place, once a year. This is where the Ark of the Covenant was kept.

TABERNACLES FESTIVAL

At this autumn festival, the Israelites thanked God for the harvest. People often made shelters out of palm leaves and slept outside under them as a reminder of how God's people had slept in tents in the desert.

TITHING

The Pharisees were very strict about giving God a tenth of all they had, even down to the herbs in their gardens. This giving was called tithing.

ZERUBBABEL'S TEMPLE

Solomon's Temple was rebuilt under the leadership of Ezra and Zerubbabel when the Israelites returned from captivity. After some centuries, it was seized by Antiochus Epiphanes and was later looted by the Romans and left in ruins.

God set apart the Sabbath as a day of rest and a time to worship.
Exodus 20:8-11

Cain brought some of his crops to God as a sacrifice, while Abel brought some of his sheep.
Genesis 4:3-4

The prophet Micah said that what God wanted more than any other sacrifice was for people to act justly, love mercy, and walk humbly with God.
Micah 6:6-8

WORK

CARPENTERS

Ordinary houses were built from sun-baked mud bricks and wood. Many people built their own homes, but the village carpenter would have helped. Carpenters made the roof beams, doors, door frames, and shutters for village houses, as well as simple furniture. They also made tools and plows for farmers, hitches for oxen, and carts.

CLOTH WORKERS

Most families spun and wove wool to make clothes. By the time of the late Old Testament, there were also people who wove cloth or made clothes to sell at the local markets.

DYERS

Many clothes were cream, beige, brown, gray, or black, depending on the sheep the wool came from. Coloring the wool meant soaking it in vats with dyes. Red coloring came from small red insects; yellow came from almonds; blue came from the outside of pomegranates; and purple, the most expensive dye, was made from the shells of certain shellfish in the Mediterranean Sea. Only very rich people could afford purple clothing.

FARMERS

The Israelites were a people of the land. Nearly everyone was involved with farming in some way. They sowed seed and plowed and harvested crops. Harvests could be ruined by lack of rain or by pests, so people trusted God to provide them with all they needed.

FISHERMEN

Lake Galilee was the center of the fishing industry. Fish were caught with fishing poles, with spears, or with nets. The nets, which were weighted at the edges, were dropped over schools of fish that were then trapped underneath and pulled to the shore or onto the boat.

LEATHER WORKERS

Making leather from the hides of camels, goats, sheep, and cattle was messy and smelly. The hair and fat had to be removed from the skins; then the skins were soaked in water with leaves, oil, and bark. Leather workers had to work on the edge of the town so the wind could carry the smell away. Tents, sandals, belts, wine containers, buckets, and animal harnesses were all made out of leather.

METAL WORKERS

Gold and silver were mined in nearby countries and shaped or beaten into thin sheets and used to decorate the Ark of the Covenant and the Temple. The high priest wore chains of pure gold and engraved precious stones set in gold. Bronze was made by adding tin to copper and heating it in a furnace and then pouring it into molds. Bronze was used for tools, weapons, lamps, pots, pans, and even mirrors. Iron was dug out of the ground, melted in a furnace, and beaten into shape while hot. Iron was stronger than bronze and was good for making swords, knives, plows, and other tools.

POTTERS

The local potter shaped clay on a wheel and baked it in a kiln, a hot oven with a fire inside it or underneath it. Pots for everyday use were plain, but special pots were made of decorated colored clay or with patterns etched into the clay with shaped tools or woven ropes. Everyday plates, dishes, cups, and containers were made from clay in this way.

SHEPHERDS

Shepherds had a lonely job, out on the hills, watching over sheep and goats and leading them to new pasture. Shepherds protected their flocks from wild animals with their rods and rescued them from dangerous places with their walking sticks. They wore camel-hair cloaks and carried horns of oil for any wounds the sheep might get. They also used slings against any predators that threatened their animals.

SLAVES

The Israelites had been slaves in Egypt until God freed them. King Solomon treated his own people as slaves, making them work long hours on his building projects. Later the Romans had a complex system of slavery. Some slaves had very hard lives, but others were servants of rich people and were teachers or civil servants, helping to manage the Roman Empire. Slaves belonged to their masters by law. Paul told Christian slaves to work hard as if they were serving God—but he also told Christian slave owners to be fair and kind.

STONE LAYERS

Skillful stone layers shaped stone blocks with their tools. The Temple in Jerusalem was a large undertaking, with intricate carvings on the stonework, such as pomegranates and vines. Other big buildings stone layers worked on included important homes and a large Roman building called the Antonia Fortress.

Paul stayed with Priscilla and Aquila, who were tentmakers.
Acts 18:1-3

Bezalel and Oholiab were skilled metalworkers who helped make the Tabernacle.
Exodus 31:1-6

Jeremiah watched a potter working at his wheel, shaping and remolding the clay into pots.
Jeremiah 18:1-11

Paul told slaves to work hard for their masters, as if they were working for God.
Colossians 3:22–4:1

Paul asked Philemon to forgive Onesimus after he ran away from his master.
Philemon 1:10-19

TRADE AND TRAVEL

The Queen of Sheba traveled to Jerusalem with a train of camels carrying gold, jewels, and spices.
1 Kings 10:1-13

Solomon gave a gift of wheat and olive oil to King Hiram.
1 Kings 5:11

King Solomon imported many products from foreign lands.
1 Kings 10:14-29

Jesus told a story about a traveler who was attacked by robbers along the road.
Luke 10:25-37

BOATS
Although travel by boat was common on Lake Galilee (a huge lake also called the Sea of Galilee), the Israelites had no natural harbors on the Mediterranean coast and disliked traveling on the open sea.

CAMELS
Camels could travel long distances and did not need water for several days. Camel trains could be hundreds of animals long. Supplies were carried in large bags on the camels' backs.

DONKEYS
Donkeys and mules carried supplies, while their owners walked beside them.

EXPORTED ITEMS
In the time of the kings, Israel traded mostly crops: wheat, olive oil, fruit, nuts, honey, spices, wool, and woolen cloth. Israel and Judah were never among the great trading nations.

HORSES
Horses could cover about 25 miles in a day, but they were rare and used only by messengers or kings. Chariots pulled by horses were used by kings and leaders of the army.

IMPORTED ITEMS
Solomon brought in many items from other countries: cedar wood to build the Temple, horses, chariots, tin, lead, gold, silver, copper, ivory, precious stones, myrrh, frankincense, monkeys, and peacocks. By the time of the Romans, the Israelites were also buying cotton, silk, Greek wine, apples, cheese, glass items, baskets, and slaves.

LOCAL TRADERS
Everyday foods from farms, such as wheat, wine, grapes, and figs, plus pottery and cloth, were sold in local marketplaces.

MESSENGERS
Messengers walked, ran, or rode from place to place carrying information from rulers to their assistants. In the days of the early church, Paul used messengers to take his letters to churches in many different places.

OVERNIGHT STOPS
In New Testament times, there were only a few inns, and they were often unpleasant places. Travelers usually camped in their own tents and carried all the food they needed for the journey. The Romans introduced stopping points for travelers, where horses could be switched and food could be bought.

OXEN
Carts were pulled by oxen for local journeys. Oxen were like cows, only larger and stronger.

ROADS
First the Persians began a road-building program, and then the Romans built a network of paved roads across their empire. This made travel easier and quicker. Even so, Paul and his friends

covered huge distances on foot across the Roman Empire to tell people the Good News of Jesus. People usually traveled in large groups to guard against being attacked and robbed.

ROUTES

In early times, travelers followed the tracks made when farmers moved their flocks from one grazing place to another. Other routes were made by merchants or invading or ruling armies as they made their way across the country.

SHIPS

The largest Roman supply ships were about 200 feet long and were powered by sails and oars. There were no instruments to help sailors find their way across the sea, so most ships sailed close to the shore and were brought in every night. Sailors guided their ships by the stars—when they could see them. There were many storms on the Mediterranean Sea,

particularly between November and March. Paul was shipwrecked off the coast of Malta in the autumn storms on his journey to Rome.

TRADING NATIONS

The great traders in Old Testament times were Babylon to the east and Tyre on the Mediterranean coast. In New Testament times, the Roman Empire transformed trading opportunities with its excellent network of roads and sea routes.

WALKING

Those who did not own donkeys carried their goods to and from the market and made their local journeys on foot.

King Solomon had a fleet of merchant ships built along the shores of the Red Sea.
1 Kings 9:26-28

Paul was shipwrecked on the island of Malta while traveling to Rome.
Acts 27:27–28:1

God warned traders against using false scales to weigh their products.
Micah 6:9-12

CIVILIZATIONS

Zelek, an Ammonite, was named as one of David's 30 mighty men.
2 Samuel 23:37

Jonah was sent to warn the Assyrians in Nineveh about God's judgment for their wickedness.
Jonah 1:1-2

Shadrach, Meshach, and Abednego survived being thrown into a fiery furnace by the Babylonians.
Daniel 3

AMALEKITES

The Amalekites were descendants of Esau. This tribe moved from place to place and fought against God's people from the time of Moses until the time of King David. By the reign of King Hezekiah, there were very few of them left.

AMMONITES

The Ammonites were descended from one of Lot's sons. They lived to the east of the Jabbok River and surrounded their territory with small fortresses. Under King David, their capital, Rabbath, was captured by the Israelites, but some of the Ammonites became David's friends.

AMORITES

The Amorites were descended from Canaan, Noah's grandson, and were enemies of Israel. They lived throughout the hill country on both sides of the Jordan River. The defeat of two Amorite kings, Sihon and Og, was the beginning of the Israelites' entry into the Promised Land.

ASSYRIANS

The Assyrians had a huge, wealthy empire with rich land. Assyria's main cities were Ashur and Nineveh. It had an aggressive army that burned whole cities and was known for its violence. In 722 BC, the northern kingdom of Samaria fell to the Assyrians, and as many as 27,000 people were taken away as prisoners of war. Nineveh was captured by the Babylonians in 612 BC.

BABYLONIANS

The Babylonians came to power by overcoming the Assyrians. They destroyed Jerusalem in 586 BC, and all God's people were taken into exile in Babylon. The Babylonians made weapons and statues from copper and bronze, as well as jewelry from silver, gold, and precious stones. The Babylonians were best known for their writing system, which spread throughout the Near East.

CANAANITES

The Canaanites invented the alphabet between 2000 and 1600 BC. They traded cedar wood, olive oil, and wine with Egypt, Crete, and Greece in return for writing paper, pottery, and metals. They worshipped gods made of wood, metal, and stone and practiced witchcraft. Sometimes they sacrificed children in an attempt to please their gods. The main gods were Baal, the storm god, and Astarte, a fertility god.

EDOMITES

The Edomites lived in the south between the Dead Sea and the Gulf of Aqaba. They were copper miners, farmers, and traders but treated the Israelites as enemies.

EGYPTIANS

Egypt became a great civilization that grew up in the Nile valley more than 5,000 years ago. For 3,000 years it was ruled by kings called pharaohs who were buried in painted stone tombs called pyramids. The Egyptians had a strong belief in the afterlife and preserved the bodies of the kings with spices. They also buried with them all the things they thought they would need. Egyptians worshipped a variety of gods and goddesses, including Re, the sun god, and built temples where priests served these gods.

GIBEONITES

Gibeon was an important city when the Israelites invaded Canaan. After Jericho and Ai were defeated, the Gibeonites tricked Joshua into making a treaty with them.

GREEKS

Greece was rich and powerful in the fifth century BC and was the home of many great thinkers, such as Plato and Socrates. The Greeks built many beautiful temples and were very religious.

They loved art, beauty, sports, and literature. They enjoyed discussing ideas, and their freedom was very important to them. They lost this freedom to the Romans, who destroyed Corinth and later Athens in the century before Jesus was born. Before the time of Jesus, the land that the Israelites knew as their home had been ruled by the Greeks.

HITTITES

The Hittites were descended from Canaan, Noah's grandson. The Hittite nation came to an end in about 1200 BC, but the people in a number of areas were known as Hittites for some time after that. Abraham lived among the Hittites and bought a field from them as his family burial ground. After King Solomon's reign, the Hittites are not mentioned again in the Bible.

HIVITES

The Hivites lived in Syria and Palestine. They made their homes in the hills of Lebanon until at least the time of King David. They worked in Jerusalem on some of King Solomon's buildings.

JEBUSITES

The Jebusites were descended from Canaan, Noah's grandson. They lived in the hills around Jerusalem. Jebus was the name they gave to Jerusalem, the main city in their land. They lost control of the city when the Israelites captured it and burned it.

The Babylonians threw Daniel into the lions' den because he would not worship anyone except the true God.
Daniel 6

The Canaanites were defeated when Deborah and Barak led the Israelites into battle.
Judges 4

Moses was born in Egypt and was saved from death by an Egyptian princess.
Exodus 2:1-10

God sent 10 plagues on Egypt because Pharaoh would not free the Israelites from slavery.
Exodus 7:14-11:10

There were Gibeonites who helped Nehemiah rebuild Jerusalem's walls.
Nehemiah 3:7

Paul told the Greeks in Athens that their "unknown God" was the God who made heaven and earth.
Acts 17:16-34

MIDIANITES

The Midianites lived in desert lands south and east of Palestine. They were descended from Midian, one of Abraham's sons. Moses married a Midianite woman.

MOABITES

The Moabites, like the Ammonites, were descended from a son of Lot. They lived in the hilly lands east of the Dead Sea and the Jordan River. The Moabites worshipped many false gods, and human sacrifices were part of their worship.

PERIZZITES

The Perizzites were one of the groups of people that the Israelites defeated so they could enter the Promised Land. Like the Jebusites, they lived in the hills.

PHILISTINES

Known as the "Sea People," the Philistines had come from across the Mediterranean Sea to settle in Canaan. They were a fierce warlike group that waged war against the Israelites over hundreds of years. The Philistines were skilled in working with iron and metal, so they had superior weapons.

PHOENICIANS

The Phoenicians lived near Tyre and Sidon in the north. They were good sailors. King Solomon hired Phoenician sailors and boats when he needed them.

ROMANS

The Roman Empire was very large, with Rome at its center. The Romans were organized and hardworking. They built roads, stadiums, aqueducts, large houses, and buildings all over the empire. Romans worshipped a number of false gods and idols, some of them taken from other cultures. Temples were built in different parts of the empire, and some were dedicated to Roman emperors, who were also worshipped as gods.

Joseph was sold by his brothers to a group of Midianite traders who were on their way to Egypt.
Genesis 37:12-28

Gideon defeated the Midianites with just 300 men.
Judges 7

The Philistines wouldn't allow the Israelites to have blacksmiths, because they didn't want them to make weapons.
1 Samuel 13:19

David, a shepherd boy, fought the Philistine champion Goliath.
1 Samuel 17

Jesus was born in Bethlehem because of the Roman census being taken at that time.
Luke 2

Zacchaeus was a tax collector for the Romans.
Luke 19:1-10

A Roman officer believed that Jesus was the Son of God after he had witnessed the crucifixion.
Matthew 27:54

WEAPONS AND WARRIORS

ARROWHEADS

Bronze arrowheads were widely used until iron weapons replaced them. The Philistines likely brought iron into Canaan around 1200 BC. But around 1040 BC, the Philistines were guarding the secrets of ironwork closely, as they were at war with the Israelites.

AXES

Around 2000 BC, long, thin axes were used as weapons.

CATAPULTS

Large stones, weighing between 20 and 70 pounds, were fired over long distances from catapults and other war machines. They were effective and frightening weapons. They were often used in attacks of protected towns and were part of the Assyrians' weapons when they invaded Israel and Judah in the eighth century BC.

ROMAN ARMOR

Roman soldiers wore metal jackets for body armor. They also carried wooden shields with metal covers over the handles.

ROMAN SOLDIERS

The main armed forces of the Roman Empire were the foot soldiers. Marching up to 20 miles a day, each soldier carried a pack weighing about 80 pounds, which included a woolen cloak, a leather water bottle, food for three days, and tools for building protective barriers and digging ditches.

ROMAN WEAPONS

Roman soldiers fought with heavy spears and short, two-edged swords.

SICKLE SWORDS

Sickle swords were widely used throughout Egypt and Canaan, and they were designed to cut through body armor. Joshua and the Israelites probably used this kind of sword in their battles.

SLINGS AND STONES

An ancient and simple weapon, the sling could be accurate and deadly. A small pouch made of leather or cloth was whirled around, and the slingshot—a smooth, round pebble or specially shaped piece of clay—was fired by releasing one end.

SPEARS

Armed with bows, arrows, and long spears, the royal archers, or "Immortals," helped King Darius I (521–485 BC) expand his empire.

Pharaoh's chariots, horses, and chariot drivers were lost when the sea swept over them.
Exodus 14:26-28

Deborah and Barak led Israel to victory over the army of Sisera when the Lord threw all Sisera's warriors and chariot drivers into a panic.
Judges 4:14-16

The Babylonians built ramps against the walls of Jerusalem, and when they had defeated the people inside, the Babylonian army tore down the city walls.
2 Kings 25:1-21

David brought down the Philistine hero Goliath with a stone in a sling.
1 Samuel 17

Isaiah prophesied that all nations would turn their swords and spears into farming equipment.
Isaiah 2:3-4

INDEX

BIBLE PEOPLE

JESUS' MIRACLES

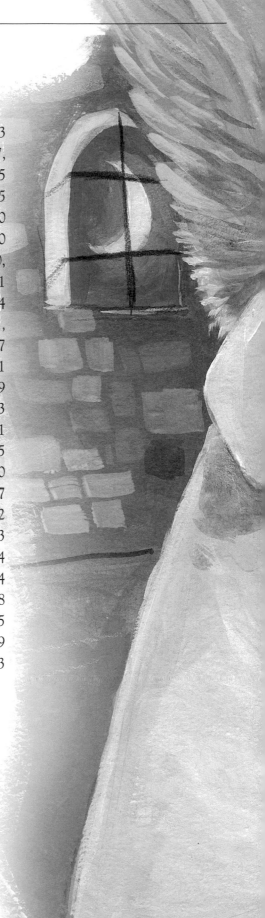